EXPL(

KIRYU ASHiu AND NIKKO

EXPLORING
KIRYU ASHIO AND NIKKO

MOUNTAIN WALKS IN THE LAND OF SHODO SHONIN

MICHAEL PLASTOW

NEW YORK • **WEATHERHILL** • TOKYO

First edition, 1992

Published by Weatherhill, Inc.
420 Madison Avenue, 15th Floor
New York, N.Y. 10017-1107

Library of Congress Cataloging in Publication Data

Plastow, Michael, 1959–

    Exploring Kiryu, Ashio, and Nikko : mountain walks in the land of
  Shodo Shonin / by Michael Plastow. — 1st ed.

        p.   cm.
  Includes bibliographical references and index.
  ISBN 0-8348-0242-2 : $15.95

  1. Kantō Region (Japan) — Description and travel — Guide-books.
2. Mountains — Japan — Kantō Region.   3. Walking — Japan — Kantō Region —
Guide-books.   4. Mountain worship — Japan — Kantō Region.   I. Title.
DS894.42.P57   1991
915.2'130.449 — dc20   91-18786
                                            CIP

ISBN 0-8348-0242-2

CONTENTS

ACKNOWLEDGMENTS

So many people, many of whom were met on mountain paths and whose names I never knew, have helped me in the writing of this book that it is impossible now to give thanks everywhere they are due. Special mention should be made, however, of the great assistance and encouragement given me by the Kiryu International Exchange Association, the *Kiryu Times* newspaper, the Kiryu Nature Sanctuary, the Tobu Railway Company, Motokawa Takaharu, Oshimi Masashi, Takahashi Hironao, Miyazawa Kohei, Ozawa Masakichi, Fujii Tatsuto, Asakura Yoichi, Ishijima Etsuko, Mr. Fujikura of the Nemoto Shrine, and, for many of the photographs, to Adachi Hirobumi, Azuma Village Hall, Kanuma City Hall, the Tochigi Tourist Office in Tokyo, and Ishijima Michiyasu of Pride One.

This book would also have been impossible to write without recourse to the excellent local histories of the region, among which I found the three-volume *Kiryu-shi Shi* (History of Kiryu), *Seta-gun Azuma-mura no Minzoku* (Folk Traditions of Azuma), *Akagi Fumoto Seishin Fudoki* (Sexual Faiths in the Foothills of Akagi), *Ashio Tokorodokoro* (Around Ashio) and Iida Michio's *Koshin Shinko* (The Koshin Faith) particularly helpful. Thanks are especially due to the editorial, production, and design staff of Weatherhill, Incorporated.

INTRODUCTION

THE REGION   Of the many problems confronting the foreign resident or tourist in Japan, two of the most common are not knowing where to go and not understanding what one sees when one arrives. There are, of course, some excellent guidebooks to the famous places of Tokyo, Kamakura, Nikko, Kyoto, and Nara. These cities, though, are so crowded, expensive, and geared to the tourist that many foreigners, after seeing the main sights, just want to get away from it all and go somewhere quieter and a little more representative of Japan as a whole.

In rural Japan, however, all of the signs, maps, and guidebooks are written in Japanese. The temples and shrines seem somehow faceless, the gods indistinguishable, the wayside statues and stones incomprehensible, and the paths very difficult to find. In addition, very few of the people one meets speak English, and residents often know little about the best walks and sights in their own areas.

The reason for this last difficulty, of course, is quite simple: most Japanese would never consider going on holiday to such places. What is mundane for a Japanese, however, is almost sure to be new and exciting to a foreigner. This book is therefore written with the aim of providing foreigners in the Kanto area with a comprehensive guide to one of the more fascinating of these ordinary regions of Japan. In addition to giving precise instructions about how to get there and where to go, this guide also fills the walker in on details of the local culture, religious faiths, history, and wildlife.

The chosen region is a mountainous area bounded by the two great volcanoes of Mount Akagi and Mount Nantai. Traditionally, this region has long been divided by state and, later, prefectural boundaries. Akagi lies in Kozuke, present-day Gunma Prefecture, while Nantai is the best-known mountain of Shimotsuke, which has now become Tochigi Prefecture. Akagi faces down toward Maebashi and Takasaki; Nantai toward Nikko and Utsunomiya. In terms of cultural geography, they belong to quite disparate parts of Japan. One of the great pleasures of mountains, however, is precisely the joy of crossing such boundaries on foot and descending to a different world on the other side.

The walks in this book begin not on Akagi itself but in the old textile city of Kiryu.

The central part of this city lies at an altitude of scarcely one hundred meters, and even Kiryu's highest mountains barely top a thousand. The lowness of these walks is more than compensated for, however, by the gentleness of the scenery and, in the remoter parts, the richness of the wildlife. Whereas the first walks from Kiryu reveal a culture only a hairsbreadth removed from that of Tokyo, the trails from Nemoto on belong to a different world entirely. It is unlikely that the hiker will meet a soul on some of these courses.

Crossing through the forests of Nemoto and Himuro, the route descends to the little-known village of Awano, in Tochigi Prefecture. Awano lies more than an hour's ride by bus from Kanuma, the nearest city. There is a camping ground and a holiday village, with excellent fishing in the river. Climbing the other side, the trail then reaches the beautiful upland marsh of Ido, the dairy farm at Yokone, and the Furumine Shrine, an ancient foundation with the largest landscaped garden in Japan and accommodation for eight hundred pilgrims. Finally, the path follows an ancient pilgrimage route to emerge at Chanokidaira and the Kegon Falls, two of the renowned beauty spots of Nikko.

Having reached Lake Chuzenji by one route, we then approach it by another, along the opposite side of the deep valley of the Watarase River. There are hikes on the slopes of Akagi, the second broadest volcano in Japan; and also around its huge caldera, which contains a marsh and two great crater lakes. Next comes the quiet rural scenery of the Watarase Valley itself and the long but tremendously rewarding walk up the slopes of Kesamaru.

The last main group of hikes deals with Ashio and the routes from there to Nikko. Ashio was once known as the biggest copper mine in Asia, but its fortunes started running down in the middle years of the twentieth century. Operations finally came to a stop with the closure of the mine in 1973. The result is a magnificent fossil, revealing at once the horrendous aftereffects of one of Japan's most famous cases of industrial pollution and an incomparable glimpse of how life in much of Japan used to be. Ashio's relics include a mine that is open to the public; the oldest iron road bridge in Japan, still in use today; and the remains of Japan's first hydroelectric power station. Yet, just beyond the devastation, there are also sacred mountains of surpassing interest and beauty, notably the two volcanoes of Koshin and Sukai.

At the finish, for those who truly wish to get away from it all and to know what it once was like to travel Japan on foot or by horse, there is the difficult, but utterly unique hike on the disused track across the Hangetsu Pass to Lake Chuzenji. The final walks then take in some of the fascinating, but quiet and little-known sights of Nikko itself.

The result, it is hoped, is a happy combination of the totally fresh and the extremely famous, giving the tourist with a week or two to spend exploring a single region an unparalleled introduction to the variety of life and nature in Japan. In addition to the near certainty of seeing deer, serows, and monkeys, and the very slight danger of meeting bears, there is also the warmth of the people — a friendliness that can hardly be expected in the established resorts. You are sure to be offered lifts frequently, and almost everyone you meet in the mountains will want to strike up a conversation.

Although this guide is written with the assumption that the reader knows no Japanese, the hikes and walks do require that some turns be made at posted signs. To assist those who do not read Japanese characters, directions for all turns are given, as well as any indicated distances (which are posted in Arabic numerals). In addition, to help users decipher signs, each hike concludes with a list, in English and Japanese, of all important place names, destinations, and inscriptions mentioned. These will also prove helpful for hikers who speak no Japanese and manage to get lost (although I hope they are only infrequently put to this use!).

Another basic assumption is that the reader will not have a car available. In some cases, a car would obviously be useful. For most of these hikes, however, it would actually be an inconvenience, because the need to return to a parked vehicle makes it impractical to descend on the far sides of the mountains or passes.

Almost every course starts and ends at a station, bus stop, or place to stay. The one exception is Kiryu, where taxis are readily available. If one is planning to use the bus, however, it is always a good idea to check in advance that the route is still in operation. Although all of the short walks and a few of the hikes can be completed on day trips from Tokyo, most of the hikes require at least one night's accommodation. A list of hotels, Japanese inns, and hot springs is provided under PRACTICAL INFORMATION. Additional advantages of exploring undeveloped areas are, of course, the lack of other tourists and the cheapness of accommodation.

Since this is not a well-traveled region, in most places one can simply pitch a tent for free.

The majority of the sights to be seen in the region are explained in the text along the way. It is, however, advisable first to get acquainted with the general historical and cultural background of the area. For this reason, several additional accounts are included here, introducing: the many ancient legends that connect Mounts Akagi and Nantai; the ancient ascetic pilgrimage routes, known as the *shugendo*; a little-known, but intriguing, religious cult called Koshin; the history of the Ashio copper mines; the history of Kiryu; and the flora and fauna of the region.

AKAGI AND NANTAI   Although Mount Akagi and Mount Nantai appear quite separate in the world of man, in legend they have always been paired. There are many stories that tell of the ancient rivalry between these two mountains, and of how they fought each other to settle their present boundaries. One story, for example, recounts how the god of Akagi and the god of Nantai agreed to leave their homes simultaneously and fix their border at the place where they might meet. Akagi, however, rode a horse, while Nantai mounted a bull, with the result that Akagi traveled faster and farther. Consequently, even today the border of Gunma and Tochigi Prefectures lies closer to Nantai than Akagi.

Another story recounts the jealousy of Akagi for the abundance of Nantai's water, which was stored in Lake Chuzenji (Hikes 5, 11, 12, 13). One night, the god of Akagi slipped over to Chuzenji to steal some of it. Just as he was about to lean out over the lake, however, the furious god of Nantai caught him in the act and seized hold of his left arm. The god of Akagi, thinking quickly, cupped his right hand and used it to throw as much water as he could possibly grasp back toward his own mountain. That was the origin of Onuma, the larger of Akagi's two crater lakes. Appalled, Nantai let go of Akagi's left arm and caught hold of his right instead. The god of Akagi then used his left hand to scoop up some more water and throw it back home. And that is said to have been the origin of Konuma, the smaller of Akagi's two main lakes (Hike 6).

By far the most famous legend, however, recounts how Akagi and Nantai squabbled over who was the taller. They agreed to settle the issue by force of arms, commencing battle at cockcrow. Akagi prepared a giant army of centipedes;

Nantai, of snakes. On the big day, however, Nantai's cock failed to crow. Taken by surprise by the centipedes of Akagi, Nantai was utterly routed at the marsh of Senjogahara (Battlefield Plain, Hike 13), just north of Chuzenji.

Nantai, however, was not going to accept defeat so easily and enlisted the help of a magnificent archer called Otaro. A second fierce battle was then fought at Senjogahara, culminating at Shobugahama (Victory Beach) on the shores of Lake Chuzenji itself. There, Otaro shot out the eye of the biggest centipede, and the forces of Akagi fled. And so it is that today Nantai rises to a maximum height of 2,484 meters, while Kurobi, the tallest peak of Akagi, these days is a mere 1,828 meters high.

SHODO SHONIN AND THE MOUNTAIN PRIESTS   The historical figure who still seems to hold sway over this region, even after twelve hundred years, is a mountain priest called Shodo Shonin. This name might be rendered in English as Saint Shodo. Shodo is known as the man who opened Nikko to the light of Nara civilization, founding the first temples and shrines there, discovering Lake Chuzenji, and scaling Mount Nantai. He is also credited with establishing the first temples and shrines of Ashio and having built the shrine at Daido, on the top of Akagi. The son of the lord of Shimotsuke, he became the religious leader of Kozuke. Above all, he is remembered as the father of the ascetic pilgrimage courses in the mountains of Nikko.

These pilgrims' courses, the *shugendo,* were derived from an intriguing combination of ancient faiths, in which gods and dead spirits were thought to dwell in the mountains, and of the newly introduced religion of Buddhism, with its own tradition of mountain hermits. It is perhaps impossible now to judge exactly what Shodo and his followers believed. These ascetics appear to have been paying their respects to the old gods and sacred mountains, but at the same time they reinterpreted these spirits according to the newly imported Buddhist pantheon. Peaks that from ages past had been perceived as the repose of the dead became associated with the various Buddhist heavens and hells. Just as the old religions had perceived the mountains as a gateway to another world, so, too, the ascetics revered the towering peaks as an almost animate ally in their bid to push back the confines of this world.

These ascetics trained themselves by ritual fasts, ablutions in cold water (preferably under waterfalls), fire ceremonies, the chanting of sacred words, and, of course, the physical rigor of crossing the mountains, especially in the deep of winter. Their activities were also closely associated with mysticism, natural magic, exorcism, and service to the community as mediums for guardian or ancestral spirits. Their beliefs thus encompassed both shrines and temples, ancient folk religions and sophisticated Buddhist thought, and veneration for a broad range of gods, as well as a mission to convert or expel evil spirits. Any perceived inconsistency in all this is probably really of our own making. In India, even the Buddha himself had recognized the popular gods, the Devas, as beings more powerful than ordinary men. The ascetics lived their religion to the full amid the many gods whom they encountered.

Shodo Shonin was born on April 21, 735, in what is present-day Moka City, Tochigi Prefecture. Buddhism was then already more than a thousand years old, and had a history of nearly two hundred years in Japan. Ever since the time of Shotoku Taishi, who had ruled Japan for thirty years from 593, Buddhism had been closely linked to the Japanese state. Now, however, the religion was flourishing as never before. The emperor in Nara was Shomu, the man who had constructed the great Buddha of Todaiji. The Brahman Bodhisena arrived in Japan the year after Shodo's birth and stayed for twenty-four years. He was followed in 754 by a Chinese monk, Jianzhen. Then, in 764, Japan almost became a truly Buddhist state. The Empress Shotoku, despite having taken Buddhist vows as a nun, returned to the throne and tried to abdicate in favor of the leader of the Hosso sect.

There were six main schools of Buddhism in Japan when Shodo was young. Of these, the most important were the Sanron sect, which taught a philosophy of negation; the Hosso sect, which focused on enlightenment by meditation and intense intellectual effort; and the Kegon sect, which propounded the metaphysics of a harmonious cosmos. What they all had in common was the creed that man has to free himself from externalities in order to open the path to the ultimate reality. Beliefs such as these must clearly have influenced Shodo in his own search for enlightenment through ascetic practices in the mountains. Although Shodo's precise position with regard to these sects is unclear, there is some circumstantial evidence to suggest that he may have subscribed to the Kegon faith.

Shodo's father was the lord of Shimotsuke, the northernmost province of Japan. In a sense, this was something of a wild, frontier province far removed from the center of Japanese culture. It was, however, also the location of the Yakushiji, at Minami Kawauchi. This temple is regarded by some as one of the three most important in Japan at the time, the two others being Todaiji, in Nara, and Chikushi Kanzeonji, in Kyushu. Unfortunately, almost no trace of Yakushiji survives today.

Todaiji was consecrated in a fabulous ceremony at Nara in 752, with dignitaries from as far away as India attending. Two years later, at the age of twenty, Shodo began three years of ascetic practices at Izuru. As related in Short Walk 2, this was the place where his mother had prayed for his birth. After his practice in Izuru, he crossed the mountains to Yokone, on the border of Ashio and Awano, and spent another three years in ascetic training there.

Returning home in 760, Shodo entered Yakushiji the following year, at the age of twenty-seven. He spent five years in that temple, then returned to Yokone in 765 and established his hermitage at Kobugahara (Hikes 4 and 5). Shodo finally set out for Nikko in 766, making his way via Mount Jizo and Mount Yakushi (Hike 6) and descending from there to the Daiya River. His target was the conical volcano of Mount Nantai, a mountain that had been sacred since ancient times, but which Shodo seems especially to have associated with Kannon, the Buddhist bodhisattva of mercy.

This figure was clearly very important to Shodo. Kannon was the bodhisattva to whom his mother had prayed at Izuru. Likewise, the first temple founded by Shodo at Nikko, Shihonryuji (on Short Walk 3), was dedicated to Kannon; and his most famous sculpture was the Tachiki Kannon, which still survives at Chuzenji today (Hike 11). The old name of Mount Nantai, Futarasan (Fudarakusan), is thought to be a Japanese rendering of Potalaka, the name of the mythical paradise of Kannon in India.

Unfortunately, Shodo's first attempt to climb Nantai ended in failure in 767. Shodo's party had set out from Shihonryuji on the extraordinarily difficult route via Mounts Nyoho, Komanago, Omanago, and Taro. They reached as far as the present location of the Shizu Lodge (Hike 13) on the northern foot of Nantai, but then had to abandon their attempt in heavy snow. Rounding the mountain by the same route as at the end of Hike 13 to Senjogahara, they did, however, discover Lake

Chuzenji on the southern side of Mount Nantai. Accordingly, Shodo named this body of water "South Lake." This same year, 767, is thought to have been when he founded the temple Renkeiji in Ashio and climbed Mount Koshin (Hike 10).

Nothing is known about Shodo's activities in the 770s, but in 781, he led another expedition to Mount Nantai, which again ended in failure. He finally reached the top in 782, at the age of forty-eight. Two years later, Shodo built Chuzenji temple on the north bank of the lake. He was to stay there for four years before becoming the religious leader of Kozuke in 789. This was a decidedly political job, a direct appointment from the emperor, which carried with it the responsibility of spreading Buddhism in order to promote the peace and stability of the nation. This post came only five years before the capital was moved from Nara to Kyoto. Shodo scaled Mount Nantai once again, in his declining years, in April of 816, at the age of eighty-two. Shodo Shonin died on March 1 of the following year, after fifty-six years of practice in the mountains.

Shodo's fame and influence throughout the area will quickly become apparent simply by how often his name crops up while using this book. He is also credited with founding several other temples and shrines, including the Sarutahiko shrine on Mount Koshin, and many curious legends are attached to his name. Like almost all mountain ascetics, he was said to possess remarkable visionary and magical powers. He is thought to have had his first Buddhist vision at the age of seven. He is even said, at the most extreme, to have caused the Kegon Falls to appear in 807 by praying for rain in a time of drought. The various legends are noted as the walks proceed. At this point, however, it is worth emphasizing that ascetics like Shodo were not regarded as mere recluses, either by the emperors or by the population at large. On the contrary, they were thought to be laboring actively for the benefit of both society and mankind as a whole.

Statues of Shodo Shonin can be seen at Rinnoji in Nikko; close to Chuzenji (Hike 11); Kaizando (Short Walk 3); and Kongosanji (Hike 5). His graves (his body was divided) are to be found in Hike 11 and Short Walk 3. In addition, the treasure house at Rinnoji in Nikko displays an iron staff (*shakujo*) that is said to have been used by Shodo himself. Various other relics are preserved at Chuzenji.

Shodo was one of the early famous mountain ascetics in Japan, his most notable predecessors being En no Gyoja and Taicho. Two of Shodo's junior contemporaries, however, were truly to change the face of Japanese Buddhism. Their sects also became closely associated with the routes of the mountain priests described in this book. The two were Kukai (also known as Kobo Daishi) and Saicho (Dengyo Daishi) who respectively introduced the Shingon and Tendai sects to Japan.

Kukai (744–835) was a most colorful character who is still remembered in countless legends. Several of these relate to places in this region, too, most notably in Hike 8. The genius of Kukai's writings is undoubted, and it is to him that we owe our earliest descriptions of the life of Shodo Shonin.

Kukai crossed to China in 804 and remarkably, once there, was chosen by the Chinese master of the esoteric Shingon sect to be his heir. Shingon Buddhism teaches the supremacy of Dainichi, the Great Sun Buddha, Vairochana in Sanskrit. Whereas exoteric Buddhists study the teachings of the historical Buddha, the esoteric Buddhists seek those hidden truths that have yet to be revealed. Shingon is based on mysteries of the mind, body, and speech that are passed on secretly from master to pupil. There is a great web of mystical practices using mantras and mandalas to express this universal harmony.

In particular, in the Tibetan tradition, the cosmos is represented by two mandalas, the Kongo kai (Diamond World) and the Taizo kai (Womb World). The Kongo kai represents all that is ideal, unchanging, indestructible, and male; while the Taizo kai is the world of change. The Kongo kai is regarded as the wisdom of Vairochana. This may sound a little abstruse but it is important because the ascetics closely associated their practices in the mountains with these two mandalas, hence, for example, the name of the Kongosanji Temple. Kongo Doji, the Diamond Child(ren), was one of their main gods, and Shomen Kongo (Blue-faced Diamond, the bodhisattva Vajrapani) was the Buddhist god of the Koshin faith described below. The collection known as the *Kongo Sutra* ranks alongside the *Dainichi Sutra* as one of the two main texts of the Shingon faith. The many Shingon temples in this region include not only Kongosanji but also Manganji, at Izuru.

In addition to his many other achievements, which are said to have included the invention of the *hiragana* syllabary, Kukai is credited with naming Nikko when he visited Shodo's temples in 820. Nikko means "sunlight," although perhaps those who visit the city in the summer will suspect that "cloud" or "fog" would have been more appropriate. The association, however, is not with the weather but with

Vairochana, the Great Sun Buddha. Much later, Shogun Tokugawa Ieyasu was given
the posthumous name of Tosho Gongen — Buddha Incarnate as the Sun God in
the East — when he was enshrined at Toshogu. Even Basho, the great haiku poet,
chose sunlight as the theme for his poem on Nikko in his *Narrow Road to the Deep
North,* despite the fact that it rained on one of the two days he visited.

The god Shomen Kongo revered by the Koshin faith is actually more generally
associated with the other great esoteric sect in Japan, Tendai. Saicho (767–822),
who introduced Tendai to Japan, had sailed on the same mission to China as Kukai.
Tendai Buddhism takes the *Lotus Sutra* as its main text, a sutra that tells how the
life of Buddha unfolded for universal salvation. Since Tendai Buddhist teachings
emphasize the importance of the things of this world as well as of the transcenden-
tal world, it is not in fact an exclusively esoteric sect. Indeed, Saicho himself,
although interested in esoteric ideas, had placed his main emphasis on the need to
lead a life of moral purity and contemplation. Later in the ninth century, however,
Ennin (Jikaku Daishi), the third leader of the sect, introduced the esoteric strain of
Tendai from China.

Ennin was a native of Shimotsuke, and Tendai was soon to become not only the
dominant sect of the Nikko *shugendo* but also that of the most famous shrines and
temples in the city. Shihonryuji, Rinnoji, and Chuzenji were all to join the Tendai
sect. The chief abbot of Rinnoji also controlled the Futarasan Shrine and, later,
Toshogu, right up until the separation of Shinto and Buddhism in 1877. It was the
Tendai abbot Tenkai (Jigen Daishi) who arranged for Ieyasu's remains to be brought
to Nikko and placed in the great Toshogu. Tenkai was later buried beside Shodo
Shonin on Kozuke Island (Hike 11).

The Nikko *shugendo* appear to have been born during the lifetime of Shodo
himself, as his disciples were encouraged to enter the mountains and experience
the same hardships as their master. The practices flourished in the Middle Ages and
continued energetically through to the Meiji Restoration. The *shugendo* faiths were
then proscribed in 1873 by the new government as part of its policy to suppress
Buddhism and purify Shinto. The Nikko *shugendo* are said to have survived until
1878. In the twentieth century, there has again been something of a revival, and
pilgrims still enter the mountains from the Furumine Shrine (Hike 4) and
Kongosanji.

Traditionally, there were four main courses. The spring *shugendo,* known as Hanaku, was associated with the Taizo kai. It began with eleven days' preparation in Nikko before leaving for Kobugahara, the Jinzentomoe Hermitage, the Hosoo Pass, and Utagahama. (The course from Kobugahara to Utagahama is that of Hike 5.) Participants would then spend twenty days reading sutras by the lake. An alternate route led down from the Jinzentomoe Hermitage to Ryuzoji, in Ashio (Hikes 4 and 12).

Summer training started at the Shinkyo, or "Sacred Bridge" (Short Walk 3), and led via Mount Yakushi and the Hosoo Pass to Chanokidaira, Utagahama, Senjugahama, Mount Shirane, and around the top to Taro and Nyoho before descending back to the Sacred Bridge. This extremely arduous route is thought to have taken about one hundred days, including all the retreats, and seems to have been discontinued in the late sixteenth century.

The autumn practices started at the main Futarasan Shrine, near the Sacred Bridge, and followed the course of Short Walk 3 up to Gyojado, then continued to Nyoho and Nantai by the route used by Shodo, as related above.

Winter training was especially associated with Kongo Doji and the Kongo kai. The route originally commenced from Shodo's first retreat at Izuru, leading from there to the Jinzentomoe and Ryu no Yado hermitages, Mount Jizo, and Mount Yakushi, as in Hike 5, but then descending to Mount Narimushi and the Hoshi Hermitage at the Sacred Bridge. From the Middle Ages, however, the ascetics stopped going as far as Izuru and went directly to the hermitages instead.

In addition to these four main courses, there were many other retreats in the mountains of Nikko and Ashio whose names are recorded but whose locations are no longer known. Likewise, Tendai and Shingon hermits and other ascetics were unusually active in the mountains of Kiryu at least from the Warring States period (1482–1558).

THE KOSHIN FAITH   What one notices traveling on foot is often quite different from what is seen going from place to place by car. The driving tourist in Japan is likely to see mainly the big temples and shrines, plus a few famous viewpoints for admiring the scenery. The walker, by contrast, soon starts responding to an entirely different set of landmarks, the most ubiquitous of which are wayside stones.

Whereas the *shugendo* embodied the extremes of religious practice, the wayside stones of Japan are perhaps the most intimate representations of the faith of the ordinary people. Wayside stones come in a wide variety of shapes, with quite diverse meanings. In this book, most stones are described when they are first encountered. These include the Kannons and Jizos (Short Walk 1), the statues of Fudo Myoo (Hike 2), phallic stones (Hike 7), plus others celebrating the full pantheon of Buddhist and Shinto gods.

One type of stone in particular seems to appear more often than the others; these are the Koshin stones. To my mind, they encapsulate the very essence of popular religion in Japan, yet few foreigners have ever even heard of them and they do not lend themselves to easy explanation. Koshin rites are held even today throughout this region, especially in the Watarase Valley. Mount Koshin, in Ashio (Hike 10), has long attracted pilgrims as one of the focal points of the Koshin faith. It is recorded, for example, that as recently as 1865, more than three thousand pilgrims made the journey to the mountain from Edo (present-day Tokyo). Some account of the Koshin faith is thus helpful here.

First, the meaning of Koshin: unlike Kannon or Jizo, Koshin was not originally the name of a bodhisattva. Rather, Koshin is a time on the old sexagenary cycle of Chinese astrology. This sixty-day or sixty-year cycle is based on ten stems and twelve branches. The ten stems correspond to ten days, three groups of which make up one month. The *ko* of Koshin is the seventh of these. The twelve branches correspond to the number of months in the year and are probably familiar to everyone as the twelve creatures of the Chinese calendar: the mouse, ox, tiger, rabbit, dragon, snake, horse, sheep, monkey, cock, dog, and boar. The *shin* of Koshin is the ninth of these, the monkey.

These ten stems and twelve branches combine in a sexagenary (rather than a hundred-twenty-day or -year) cycle by linking only odd stems with odd branches and even stems with even branches. Even today, all over East Asia, a sixtieth birthday is considered very special because of this system, for it represents the completion of a great cycle. The Koshin combination occurs on the fifty-seventh day or year of the cycle.

The stems and branches of the Chinese calendar are also paired with the five Chinese "elements" (wood, fire, earth, metal, and water), and the stems further categorized according to their yin and yang aspects. In Chinese belief, yin represents the moon and all that is cold, while yang corresponds to warmth and the sun. These various associations are used to determine lucky and unlucky days and years. As it happens, both *ko* and *shin* are associated with the element metal, making Koshin a powerful metal-metal combination. This fifty-seventh day or year is therefore believed to be particularly awful because the coolness of metal freezes everything in both heaven and earth, including the hearts of men.

If this weren't bad enough, worse is to come. *Ko,* at least, despite being metal, is nonetheless yang. The fifty-eighth day or year, Shinyu, is a metal-metal combination where the stem is yin! Shinyu years were thought to be so catastrophic that Japanese era names were changed sixteen times out of nineteen Shinyu years between 781 and 1861. It should come as no surprise, therefore, that special rites were required on the night of Koshin.

In order to understand these rites, however, one further aspect of Taoist belief has to be introduced. The early Taoists had supposed that life moves in cycles between the material and the spiritual phases. The main goal of later Taoists, though, became that of achieving immortality in the material phase of the cycle. That is the root of Chinese alchemy, including the notion of an elixir of life.

Specifically, these Taoist thinkers believed that three parasitic worms or corpses inhabit the body and that they are the direct cause of mortality. Accordingly, the Taoist techniques to attain immortality were primarily aimed at the expulsion of the worms from the body. The regimen included special breathing exercises, exposure to the sun for men or to the moon for women, Kung Fu, sexual practices (together with various rules proscribing them at particular times), and selective fasting. This latter, in fact, reemerges in the practices of the mountain ascetics of the *shugendo*. The Taoists believed that the five grains — wheat, rice, millet, barley, and beans — were the favorite food of the three worms and hence abstained from these as a sure way to starve them out. It is interesting to note that the mountain ascetics fasted in exactly the same way.

Returning to the night of Koshin, however, we now require something of a mental leap. The object of the rites of that night was not to *expel* the worms, but to keep them inside! On the night of Koshin, the worms were thought to leave the body of their own free will through the nails, ascend to heaven, and inform the celestial god of all the bad things that their host had been doing during the previous cycle. The celestial god would note these down in his book of life and shorten the host's lifetime accordingly. The belief developed, therefore, that one should stay awake all night on Koshin in order to prevent the worms from leaving the body.

The Koshin rituals are thought to have been introduced to Japan during the early part of the Heian period (794–1185). Legend has it that the Koshin faith arrived in 701, just a little over thirty years before the birth of Shodo Shonin. This was a time of great epidemic. When the priests of Shitennoji, in Osaka, prayed for assistance, a supernatural fourteen- or fifteen-year-old boy appeared before them. This child proceeded to explain for them the precepts of Koshin and, once finished, was magically transformed into Shomen Kongo, the Blue-faced Diamond, Vajrapani, mentioned earlier.

Records suggest that in the Heian period, Koshin nights were mainly observed by the court. This was known as "Playing Koshin" (Koshin *asobi*), which suggests, quite probably misleadingly, that the event was not taken very seriously. The government, however, certainly did have very ambivalent feelings about Taoism in general; in the normal course of events this would indeed have severely handi-capped the spread of the Koshin faith. Koshin nonetheless took hold, however, because it was absorbed by the Tendai Buddhism of Saicho and also by Japanese Shinto.

For the Tendai priests, the key element in the Koshin faith appears not to have been so much its Taoist roots but the association with the Buddhist god Shomen Kongo. Exactly where this association came from is hard to say, but it is clearly related to the tradition that Shomen Kongo is a fierce, indomitable enemy of all demons, including, one may suppose, the worms of mortality.

In Japan, it is often explained that Shomen Kongo was originally a devil who ate the spirits and bodies of men, but that he was later converted by the Buddha Amida and turned his sword instead against the demons of sickness. In the Tibetan tradition, however, a rather different story is told about why Vajrapani particularly loathes the demons. In that account, Vajrapani was once given charge of the Water of Life, but then had it stolen from him by a monster, Rahu. After a great struggle, Vajrapani managed to win it back, but by that time it was thoroughly polluted. The

Buddhas punished Vajrapani by making him drink the water, with the unfortunate result that he turned blue!

In Tibetan art, Vajrapani is depicted with a variety of ferocious forms. One, however, is particularly worth noting, for reasons that will become apparent below. In this form, known as Mahachakra Vajrapani, he has three heads, six arms, two legs, and is painted blue. He is shown with a thunderbolt, a serpent, a skullcap, and a chopper. Beneath his feet, he treads on Brahma and Shiva. He also often appears with a rope and a mythical bird, the *garuda*.

Besides the veneration of Shomen Kongo, there are many other points which also link Tendai, Koshin, and by association, the mountain priests as well. It is noticeable, for example, that the three main Koshin halls of worship in Japan during the Edo period (at Iriya in Tokyo, Shitennoji in Osaka, and Yasaka in Kyoto) were all attached to Tendai temples. Likewise, a Tendai priest appears to have written the earliest surviving account of the Koshin faith in Japan. The faith is also especially strong in an area of Kyushu where Saicho once spent a whole year. These and other important points are related in a fascinating book by Iida Michio, *Koshin Shinko* (The Koshin Faith; Kyoto: Jinbun Shoin, 1989). In view of the power of Tendai Buddhism at Nikko, the strength of the Koshin faith both in this region and in the Mount Koshin area in Ashio then comes as no surprise. Ashio had been under the religious jurisdiction of Chuzenji from as early as 790.

Before we can comprehend the Shinto as well as the Buddhist connections, however, a few words should be said about monkeys. As almost every foreign tourist knows, one of the most famous sights at Toshogu, in Nikko, is a carving of three monkeys who see, hear, and speak no evil. These too are Koshin symbols, and many Koshin stones portray them, though sometimes with only two, or even a single monkey. As it happens, the monkey is also the sacred intermediary of the temple on Mount Hiei, in Kyoto, the center of the Tendai sect. Tradition has it that Saicho himself created the symbol of the three monkeys as a didactic tool. Toshogu was built by the Tendai priest Tenkai and controlled by the Tendai Rinnoji. And the monkey, as noted already, is also the creature that corresponds to the *shin* branch of Koshin in the Chinese calendar.

Where is all this leading? First, this monkey (*saru*) connection may partly account for the absorption of Koshin by Shinto, for the Shinto god who is now always associated with Koshin rites is the monkey god Sarutahiko. This is the god who is enshrined on Mount Koshin, in Ashio (Hike 10). Sarutahiko also appears in the Japanese creation myth of the *Kojiki,* an ancient chronicle, as the one who escorts the divine party from heaven to earth. He is a god of borders and a god who wards off demons. For the Tendai sect, so is Shomen Kongo.

Now, it appears that we are reaching the heart of the matter. In his book, Iida Michio presents the case like this: Sarutahiko was originally perceived as the god who keeps out both invasion and epidemics. Similarly, Saicho's Tendai sect was widely regarded as the sect that protected the country. One of the main reasons the capital was moved from Nara to Kyoto in 794 was to shut the other sects out from politics. Tendai, based as it was on Mount Hiei, was the only sect to be established on the inside. Accordingly, Tendai and imperial rule became mutually supporting. Since this was an era of many epidemics, one of the most important requirements placed by the emperor on the monks of Hiei was to pray for relief from disease. Sarutahiko was the border god of the capital and the imperial palace; Shomen Kongo, the Tendai god who defended the country and protected it from disease. Quite naturally, the two became combined.

Here, we can at last begin to see fairly clearly why there are so many Koshin stones on the roadside. Originally, they must have been erected to protect the villages from disease at the most unlucky point of the calendrical cycle. The practice would have spread under the influence of the esoteric, magical strain of the Tendai sect. Historically, the erection of these Koshin stones seems to have risen with the reviving strength of Tendai Buddhism under Tenkai at the start of the Edo period (1615–1868), although the oldest surviving Koshin stones are more ancient than that. The oldest in Japan, at Kawaguchi, in Saitama Prefecture, dates from 1471, while the oldest in Gunma is the one at Kiryu that we see on Short Walk 1, which was placed there in 1548. Edo, however, was the great period for putting up these stones. Well over one thousand, for example, were erected in Gunma alone in each of the Koshin years of 1800 and 1860.

These stones come in all shapes, sizes, and guises. There are carefully carved stupas and natural stones; images of Sarutahiko, Shomen Kongo, Jizo, Amida, Dainichi, Yakushi, Kannon, Dosojin, the Mountain God, the God of the Fields, and so on; stones with just the characters for Koshin, Shomen Kongo, or Sarutahiko;

and also many put up for a new god who has now grown up in the popular mind, Koshin-sama! It would be fascinating to know whether there has ever been any other case of a calendrical date being transformed into a god, though the reverse, of course, has happened in the West.

Shomen Kongo and Koshin-sama are typically represented with one or three fierce faces, bulbous lips, and six arms, though sometimes they have as few as two or as many as eight. The hands hold such devices as ropes, clubs, swords, and dolls of half-naked women. The yang and yin symbols of the sun and the moon are carved above, and a devil or two (*amanojaku* or *amanojagume*) are portrayed being trampled underfoot. Such stones almost always display the motifs of monkeys and hens. Some believe that this last may be related to the fact that the day or year of the monkey is followed by that of the hen in the Chinese calendar. Others note that in both China and Japan, the hen, the messenger of Ise Shrine, is believed to ward off disease. I cannot help suspecting, however, that the hens could simply be Japanese versions of the *garuda*. Either way, the similarities with Mahachakra Vajrapani are extremely obvious.

How, then, is Koshin night actually observed in the villages? Some fascinating descriptions for this observance can be found in the local history of Azuma Village in the Watarase Valley (Hikes 2, 7, and 8), as written in *Seta-gun Azuma-mura no Minzoku*. A typical account is something like this: after supper, men, women, and children gather for what seems best described as an all-night feast. The foods include rice balls, red bean (*azuki*) gruel, and a vegetable chowder (*kenchinjiru*). The idea is to eat as much as you like. The house where the party is held is decided by lottery, but there is also a rotation system. The typical size of a Koshin group is about four to ten households, corresponding to the size of the smallest administrative units in Edo-period Japan.

Certain ceremonies open the feast. An offering of water, sweet potatoes, fried tofu, giant radishes, or petals, for example, may be placed before a scroll picture of Koshin-sama. Incense sticks are lit and a garbled, apparently meaningless, Sanskrit-like prayer is offered. One of the examples given is: *Namu Koshin sonsee sou maitari maisowaka*.

As for who Koshin-sama actually is, some describe him as a friend of the peasantry and the god of frugality. He has six hands, so he can work very well.

Others say that he is tremendously rich and that is why a fantastic banquet must be prepared. He is also variously described as the god of silkworms or the harvest!

Several important prohibitions apply on the night of Koshin, which seem to echo some of the Taoist roots of the faith. Sex is banned, for it is believed that children conceived on the night of Koshin will become robbers; fish is taboo, and so is sake; one must not talk about hunting; and the meeting must be rescheduled, or special rites performed, if there is an earthquake on that particular day.

The association with sex seems especially strong, for the three monkeys are often depicted as male, female, and neuter. One local historian of this village has suggested that the most common combination is for the male not to see, the female not to hear, and the neuter not to speak. Somehow, this does indeed sound appropriate for a night on which sex is banned.

These days, Koshin rites are rarely held on the exact days prescribed by the Chinese calendar; nor are they held six times a year, as would seem to be required. Rather, everything is arranged according to convenience. The most common day is October 16, for a tradition has developed that this is the day when Koshin-sama descends into the bowels of the earth. Consequently, the villagers are thought to be free to hold Koshin meetings on that day, whether it is the right one or not. The Koshin Festival at the Koshin Lodge (Hike 10) is held at approximately this time of year. Clearly, the faith has evolved (or degenerated) a long way. But it is still maintained, at least in the Umeda district of Kiryu, Azuma Village, and Ashio.

As were other non-Shinto faiths, Koshin was proscribed at the beginning of the Meiji era (1868–1912). The collapse of the Koshin pilgrimages to Ashio was really quite dramatic. The priest in charge at Ashio, a man named Daininbo, was executed in connection with a plot to overthrow the new government (see Hike 12). The leader of the conspiracy was Kumoi Tatsuo, a retainer of the Yonezawa fief. The Koshin pilgrimages from Tokyo consequently came to an abrupt halt. People really started returning to Mount Koshin only in the middle years of this century, when Mount Koshin became a part of the Nikko National Park. Yet the Koshin faith lives on, apparently quite separate from its Taoist, Buddhist, and Shinto roots. To me, it thus now seems to represent the purest type of religious faith, untrammeled by all the complexities of theology. The villagers are simply saying, "please look after us," and they expect that this god of their own making will do so.

THE ASHIO MINES   While few Japanese know about the connection between Ashio and Koshin, everyone has heard of the mines. Actually, the earliest-known settlements in Ashio date from around B.C. 5500. Domestic items from that period have been discovered on the opposite bank of the Watarase River from Haramuko Station. Despite, however, being placed under the direct jurisdiction of Nikko after the arrival of Shodo, Ashio remained a quiet backwater until the early modern period. As late as 1502, it was still a village of just two hundred fifty households.

The great change came in 1610 with the discovery of copper on Mount Bizendate (Hike 9) by two peasants named Jifu and Kura. It has been suggested that the local warlords had been mining copper here even before that time, and that the supposed discovery was simply rigged in order to strengthen the shogunate's rights to the claim. At any rate, the two peasants duly reported their find to the authorities in Nikko, and the mines were placed under the direct jurisdiction of the new Tokugawa shogunate in Edo. The shogunate's administrative office for the mines stood on a large plot where the Izumiya Ryokan and the Ashio Town Hall stand today. Here, merchants, contractors, and carriers used to gather.

Ashio was soon to become one of the great mines of Japan. It produced some twenty million copper roof tiles during the Edo period for use in such famous structures as Toshogu, at Nikko; Edo castle; Zojoji, in Shiba; and Kaneiji, at Ueno. From 1741, Ashio also started producing coins to supplement its income during a period of low production. These coins stayed in circulation until the end of the Edo period and can now be seen in the museum at the Tsudo mine. The development of the Ashio mines brought new life to, but was ultimately to cast a dark shadow over, all the settlements in the Watarase Valley.

In the Edo period, improved communications due to the construction of the Akagane Kaido, the Copper Road, brought major changes. This remote valley at the northern tip of the Kanto Plain was suddenly opened to the culture of the capital and transformed, at least by the standards of the times, into something of a thoroughfare for the transport of copper.

The Akagane Kaido was built in the middle years of the seventeenth century when the mines were returned to the shogunate after a brief period under the control of Toshogu. This was just about the time that the shogunate started selling copper to the Dutch at Dejima. The road wound up and down the steep sides of the valley and gorges. (This route is extremely hard to trace on foot today on account of the later construction of straighter and more modern roads.) The loads were carried on horses, taking two or three days to reach the banks of the Tone River for shipment to Asakusa, in Tokyo. At especially busy times, such as during reconstruction work on Edo Castle, loads were also taken across the Tone to the Nakasendo, one of the two main highways linking Tokyo and Kyoto, which ran just a few kilometers away from the other side of the river.

There were five hostels and forwarding agents along the road. The warehouses for overnight storage of copper were controlled by the village heads. When word of shipment came, these administators would appoint porters from their own or nearby villages to help. Although there were only five warehouses, a total of fifty-nine villages were included in this system. Wages were settled by the warehouse chief according to the weight of the copper, the distance to be traveled, and so on. In return, the chiefs were permitted to have surnames and carry swords (privileges usually reserved for samurai). The warehouse at Hanawa can be seen in Hike 7, and another stands quite close to Omama Station.

By the early nineteenth century, however, it seemed that the great days of the Ashio mines were already a thing of the past. Known veins were close to exhaustion and increasingly uneconomical to work. In 1817, the mines were even closed down for a while, and the shogunate's office was removed in 1866. That was still the situation in 1877 when the Ashio mines were suddenly bought up by a consortium led by a remarkable entrepreneur, Furukawa Ichibei.

Ichibei was born in Kyoto in 1832, the second son of a tofu (bean curd) maker. Business was not good, and Ichibei appears to have had a very hard childhood. First, he was apprenticed as a shop boy at the age of nine. Returning home two years later, he next sold tofu from house to house. Then, while still in his early teens, he went to Morioka to assist an uncle selling raw thread. All of this seems to have developed his money-earning instincts to the full. By the 1870s he had made such a reputation for himself in textiles and other business ventures that he was able to buy the Ashio mines (and another as well) with money borrowed from the financier Shibusawa Eiichi (1840–1931). The price was 48,380 yen. Ichibei vowed not to cut his hair until he earned ten thousand *ryo* a day (a *ryo* is an old unit of Japanese currency). Accordingly, very untypically of a man in his position in Meiji Japan, he kept his *chonmage* hair style until 1900, just three years before his death.

The investment paid off handsomely, for a major new find was made in 1884. Soon, with the introduction of advanced mining equipment from the West, Ashio was producing fully forty percent of Japanese copper, some six thousand tons per year. In 1889, that proportion was about half. This was the origin of the Furukawa Zaibatsu, a conglomerate that by the end of the Second World War had amassed some eighty-four affiliates and was capitalized at the equivalent of US $2.67 million. By that time, the group included, in addition to the Furukawa Company (mining), Furukawa Electric, Fuji Electric, Nippon Light Metal, and Yokohama Rubber. Furukawa Electric, incidentally, was the parent company of the computer maker Fujitsu.

Ashio, too, was to grow. By 1916, the population of Ashio had risen to 38,428, the second largest in Tochigi Prefecture after Utsunomiya. There was even talk of its becoming a city. As things turned out, however, the town was once again rapidly left behind in postwar Japan. The mining became uneconomical, and production was steadily slowed down. The final closure came in 1973, bringing an end to three hundred sixty years of mining history. During that time, Ashio had produced more than seven hundred thousand tons of copper. Today, the population of the town is less than five thousand, and with no new industries entering, the drift out continues. Although the mines have closed, however, the copper works are still producing at some minimal level, using ores imported from Southeast Asia.

To most Japanese today, however, the name Ashio means only one thing: pollution. The walker in this area will have no difficulty understanding why. The area around the copper mine, laid bare by terrible sulfur and heavy metal pollution from the copper works, remains a desolate wasteland. The river below the Ashio Dam is now basically clean. The fish have returned, and the vegetation is slowly recovering; but still, virtually nothing seems to grow on the slopes between the copper works and the dam itself (Hike 12). The overall effect is that of a kind of lunar landscape, depressing, yet somehow rugged and grand. The destruction has been so total that it almost forces respect. The tourist gasps as when standing before a magnificent waterfall or mountain peak. The fact that there are magnificent waterfalls, virgin forests, and stunning peaks close by hardly seems possible at the moment one confronts the damage.

The mine pollution has become such a byword and symbol in Japan that one finds it cropping up almost everywhere. Here, for example, is Enchi Fumiko (1905–   ) in her novel *The Waiting Years* (Tokyo: Kodansha International, 1971):

"Shirakawa could not avoid a sense of disheartenment at the crack he saw appearing in the disposition of this obdurate man who had once so blithely seized people's homes in what amounted to daylight robbery, and pulled them down to make way for a prefectural road — the man who had happily tolerated the poisoning by mineral wastes of a whole area along the banks of the Watarase River so that the copper mine at Ashio might prosper — all this done in the name of loyalty to the state."

In the world of film, Ashio was chosen as a location for Kobayashi Masaki's great three-part pacifist epic, *Ningen no Joken* (The Human Condition, 1959–61), based on the six-volume novel by Gomikawa Junpei. These films depicted the terrible conditions of the native slaves in the Japanese-controlled mines of wartime Manchukuo; the vicious treatment of Japanese military recruits; and the equally appalling prison camps for Japanese prisoners in post-war Siberia. At the end of that final film, the hero escapes only to die a pitiful death in the snow.

Waste from the Ashio mine was first reported to be polluting the Watarase in Tochigi and Gunma in 1885, and crop yields began to fall from around 1887. By the 1890s, pollution from floods was said to be affecting some five hundred thousand people in the northern Kanto area. There were serious cases of diarrhea, with quite a few deaths among the old and the very young, and large-scale protests and petitions by farmers and fishermen. The several thousand professional fishermen along the Watarase River were very soon completely out of work.

The great champion of the movement to halt the pollution from the Ashio mine was Tanaka Shozo, a moral giant whose entire life stands as an important reminder that not all of the saints belong to ancient history. Shozo was born in 1841, the son of the head of a small village in Shimotsuke called Konaka, which now lies in Sano City. His early life was little different from that of an ordinary peasant, and he continued to identify strongly with the peasantry right to the end of his days.

Shozo became head of the village himself at the very young age of seventeen. He was soon to be embroiled in a conflict with the local lord over a plan to exploit the peasantry and was thrown into prison in Tokyo. Confined in a cell half the size

Above The Watarase Keikoku Tetsudo runs up the valley of the Watarase River from Kiryu to Ashio.

Below Glimpse of Mount Nantai through the trees (Hike 12).

Left Shodo Shonin is said to have caused the Kegon Falls to flow when he prayed for rain (Hike 5).
Below Lake Chuzenji (Hikes 5 and 11).

Above Wetland in the Kanuma Nature and Bonsai Park (Hike 5).

Below left Memorial to the more than one hundred Chinese slave laborers who died in the Ashio mines during the war (Hike 9).

Below right Statue of Shodo Shonin outside Rinnoji, Nikko (Short Walk 3).

Left Memorial erected the day after the death in battle of Nitta Yoshisada, Tozenji (Short Walk 1).

Above Sleeping Buddha, on the path up Kesamaru (Hike 8).

Below The view of Mount Nantai from Yokone (Hike 4).

Above The plain of Senjogahara, site of the mythical battle between the snakes of Nantai and the centipedes of Akagi (Hike 13).
Below Inari Shrine and Koshin stone, Azuma (Hike 7).

Above Chuzenji, Nikko (Hike 11).

Below Mount Nantai, Lake Chuzenji, and Hatcho Dejima peninsula from Hangetsu. The small island on the left, Kozuke, is the site of one of Shodo Shonin's graves (Hike 11).

Early morning practice by the priests of Nikko (Short Walk 3).

Top left Fudo Myoo stands in the center of the deities at Buddha Rock (Short Walk 3).

Center left Roadside shrine by the entrance to the old Kodaki mine (Hike 9).

Below left Greeting the dawn on Nantai. Celebrants of Shodo's achievement climb the mountain en masse during the first week of August each year (Hike 13).

Above right Giant Tengu masks at Furumine Shrine (Hikes 4 and 5).

Below right Phallic stone at Toyosato Shrine, Azuma (Hike 7).

Below far right A Koshin stone at Senjuji, Kiryu. Erected in 1548, this is the oldest known Koshin stone in Gunma Prefecture (Short Walk 1).

Above left Quiet rural scenery of the Watarase Valley (Hike 7).

Below left *Nihonzaru* on Hangetsu, Ashio. These macaque monkeys are especially common in Nikko, Ashio, and Azuma (Hike 11).

Above The "Husband-and-Wife Frogs" on the path to Koshin Lodge (Hike 10).

Left Steps leading to Seisuiji, Godo (Hike 7).

Above right Koshin Lodge, below the cliffs of Mount Koshin, Ashio (Hike 10).

Center right Furumine Shrine, Kanuma, a base for mountain priests (Hikes 4 and 5).

Below right Priests of the Futarasan Shrine, Nantai, fire an arrow in the direction of Akagi, a ritual message that old scores have not been settled.

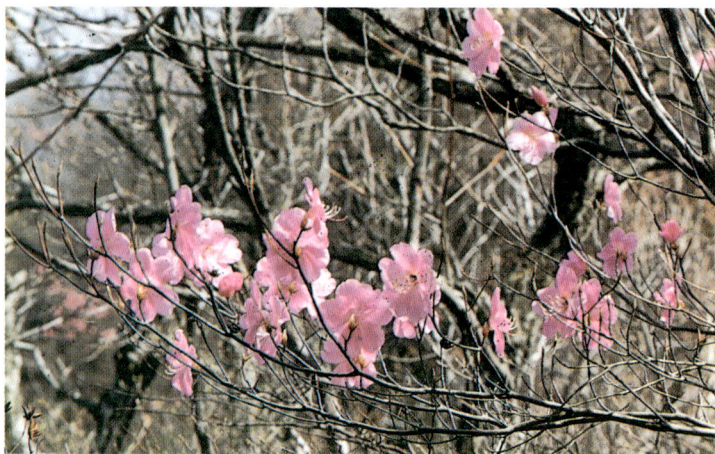

Above left *Nikko kisuge*, a mountain lily that takes its name from the region.

Above right *Kakkoso*, one of the representative flowers of Narukami, Kiryu, blooms in mid-May.

Below *Aka yashio*, one of the many species of azalea that brighten the mountains in May and June.

Above *Natsu tsubaki*, a camellia found on Nemoto, Kiryu, and elsewhere.

Below *Koajisai*, a ubiquitous hydrangea.

The Tachiki Kannon at Chuzenji, Nikko, said to have been carved by Shodo Shonin from a standing tree (Hike 11). .

of a tatami mat and with insufficient height to stand, he refused to eat for fear of being poisoned. He managed to survive on a little dried fish given him by a friendly samurai. A month later, The Meiji Restoration came. Accordingly, against all expectations, he actually managed to win his trial, though at the cost of expulsion from his village. A short while later he was again wrongfully imprisoned, this time for more than three years. Once released, he emerged as a staunch fighter for the rights of the oppressed.

Shozo took up the cause of the Watarase peasants suffering from pollution by the mines in 1890, the year he became a representative for Tochigi in the new national diet. In answer to his questions, however, the government responded only with tricks and stalling. The output of the Ashio mines was, after all, vital for the modernization of Japan. The minimal steps taken to control the pollution were of little or no avail, and then terrible losses were suffered in a major flood of 1899. Ten thousand peasants marched on Tokyo in the wake of this disaster. Shozo stopped that march outside Tokyo and led a delegation to the capital. Again, however, there were no significant results. A second big march was broken up violently the following year by saber-wielding policemen at Kawamata, on the Tone River, and a great trial was held in Maebashi. Shozo himself was indicted while trying to support those who had been arrested.

Judging that nothing but the sacrifice of his own life could draw sufficient public attention to the plight of the peasants, Shozo resigned his seat in 1901 to make a direct appeal to the emperor. He took the bold step of approaching the emperor's carriage on its return from the opening of the new diet, fully expecting to be killed by the guards. His life was only saved because he was caught before he got too close. Although he had failed to achieve his objective, the newspapers all now took note. This was the first attempt ever to make a direct appeal to the emperor during the Meiji period. Students' and women's groups were formed to pressure the government into taking effective action.

The result: a specially appointed committee concluded that the pollution was not due to the mines! Simultaneously, to contain the pollution, the government proposed to purchase three villages close to the confluence of the Watarase and Tone rivers in order to make a great sink to hold the polluted water. With Shozo's assistance, two of the villages successfully resisted the government plan. A third,

Yanaka, was already too bankrupt to put up an effective resistance. Shozo spent the rest of his life fighting for the right of the farmers of Yanaka to keep their ancestral land.

At the very end of his life, Shozo, having given away all of his possessions, was still on the road with a young helper from the village of Yanaka, surveying the pollution of the rivers of Tochigi. When he died of cancer in 1913, he owned only as much as he could could carry. Yet, tens of thousands of peasants from Tochigi, Gunma, and Saitama came to light incense sticks at his funeral. It is, sadly, hard in a brief account like this to find words to express what this man meant to the poor people of those places and times.

The level of the pollution was substantially lowered in the 1950s, but it continued at least until the mines finally closed. The following year, 1974, a group of Watarase farmers received the equivalent of seven million U.S. dollars as a result of the first major case under the government's new Environmental Disputes Coordination Commission, nearly one hundred years after the pollution had first come to light.

In addition to its history of pollution, Ashio also figures rather prominently in the story of labor in Japan. Troubles blew up in 1906, when the miners' union formed a branch of the Dai Nihon Rodo Shiseikai, a national confederation of unionists. They protested for better working conditions, higher wages, and an end to the labor-boss system under which they were contracted. They had even recently lost their two days' holiday a month. The Furukawa Company refused to budge, and the dispute flared into violence on February 4, 1907. The miners cut the telephone cables and stormed the guard towers and other company buildings.

These first demonstrations were broken up by the police. Two days later the protesting workers blew up the main guard tower with dynamite and set fire to no fewer than one hundred thirty mine buildings. The government declared martial law at the mine and sent in three militia units on February seventh. Eighty-two miners were jailed in the wake of these disorders. Subsequently, there were further disorders in 1919 and 1921, the year that the miners won their battle to put an end to the labor-boss system.

After all these momentous and tragic events, Ashio today is once again a quiet backwater. The combination, however, of a dramatic history and a peaceful present should be sufficiently attractive to visitors. The big souvenir in Ashio today is Ashioyaki pottery, seen in many shops along the main street and also at the mine (now open to the public) and the museum in Tsudo. This pottery has a history of only about twenty years. In the beginning, it was made using slime from the copper works, but this did not turn out to be all that suitable. Accordingly, the pottery is now produced from more conventional materials. The standard motif of the Ashio wares is the *koshinso,* a faint pink flower that blooms around the end of June and early July on the cliffs near the top of Mount Koshin. The *koshinso* is a designated national natural treasure and extremely rare except on Mount Koshin itself. I find a certain charm and justice in the thought that this flower should now be the chosen symbol of Ashio.

KIRYU, THE TEXTILE CITY   Kiryu, the start of these walks, is a city of around 130,000 people, located at a confluence of rivers where the mountains meet the plains. Mention its name to many Japanese and they will probably say something about high school baseball. Historically, however, Kiryu is famous as a city of textiles. Many high-quality textile products are still made here; and not so many years ago, the rivers would gleam with the brilliant colors of silk cloths laid out in the water for the final stage of the Yuzen dyeing process.

Tradition has it that the Kiryu silk industry began twelve hundred years ago, brought here by Shirataki Hime (the White Waterfall Princess), just at the time of Shodo Shonin (a legend related at the end of Hike 1). Since Kiryu is set wedged against the mountains, it is clearly short of agricultural land. Textile production probably emerged as a valuable supplement to the livelihood of the peasants. It would then gradually have grown first into a domestic, and then a workshop, industry. The original small-scale nature of the Kiryu silk industry is still very much in evidence. While walking around the area today, one hears the constant clatter of machines from countless tiny workshops beside the houses.

Kiryu textiles began making their mark from around the Middle Ages. There is a tradition that the banners for Nitta Yoshisada's armies (see page 64) in 1333 were made here in Kiryu. The techniques of the famous Kyoto silk industry were introduced some time during the Warring States period, and an order for a silk pongee from a lady attendant of the thirteenth Ashikaga shogun, who lived in the

27

mid-sixteenth century, is a designated cultural treasure of the city (the "Hikobeke Nitayama Tsumugi Chumonsho"). Kiryu was also ordered to provide the banners for the armies of Tokugawa Ieyasu that were used at the great battle of Sekigahara in 1600. Records indicate that each weaving shop produced one fabric, and a total of 2,110 cloths were presented to Ieyasu. Apparently Kiryu already had more than two thousand weaving shops even then.

Kiryu was also directly caught up in the long, big-fish-eats-little-fish process of the civil war period. The Kiryu family built a castle on Mount Hishaku in the foothills of Joyama (Hike 1) in 1350. Over the years, the Kiryu warlords expanded their domains to include a maximum of fifty-four villages, absorbing the territories of such clans as the Yamada, Hosokawa, and Matsushima. The Kiryu family itself was overthrown in 1573, however, by the Yura family of Kanayama Castle, in Ota, after a battle for control over irrigation water from the rivers. That same year Nobunaga destroyed the Ashikaga shogunate. The Yuras, meanwhile, were themselves subordinate to the Hojos of Odawara. Consequently, although at first the Yuras set up a new base in Kiryu, the castle fell into disuse after 1590, when Hideyoshi defeated Hojo in the siege of Odawara, thereby more or less completing the military unification of Japan. Kiryu then came under the direct administration of Tokugawa Ieyasu; hence, the order for banners for use at Sekigahara.

From the time of Ieyasu right through to the Meiji Restoration, Kiryu was obliged to pay unusually heavy duties of silk to the government in Edo. This, however, was also the period in which the Kiryu silk industry took off. The Kiryu Silk Market opened in 1646. Direct silk trading commenced with Edo in 1684, and with Kyoto from around 1692. New loom technologies were introduced in 1738. Not long after, a native of Kiryu, Iwase Kichibei, invented a new thread-plying machine that made it easier to mass produce twisted yarn. Kiryu became known as the Kyoto of eastern Japan.

The Kiryu silk industry was to be further stimulated by the opening of the country to trade with Europe and America. The city began exporting silk handkerchiefs in 1864, and wares from Kiryu appeared at the great exhibition in Vienna in 1873. In the Meiji era, Kiryu manufactured a wide range of high-quality products, from figured cloth and gossamer to crepe, satin, and gauze. Although small workshops continued to flourish, huge factories were also built from the late

1870s. These plants were equipped with the latest devices, such as jacquards, power looms, and piano machines, some of which were introduced directly from France and the United States. Although exports accounted for a large proportion of sales, in most years the domestic market remained supreme.

By 1904, there were over twenty-two thousand looms in Kiryu, including nearly forty-five hundred Western-style machines and one hundred fifty power looms. A textile school was opened in 1896. Although this closed in 1913, a new one was started only three years later. This was the forerunner of the Engineering Faculty of Gunma University, which is still located in the city today.

At its zenith, the Kiryu textile industry employed eighty percent of the working population, a very large portion of whom were women. The dark, satanic mills were no stranger to this city, for the working hours were long, and the conditions often appalling. Girls from the age of twelve were made to work from predawn to late at night, with only a short break early in the afternoon. Typical contracts were for three years, but younger workers had to sign on for five, seven, or even eight years. They also had to work the first three years without pay, until they had mastered the necessary skills. This tradition of working women is still a feature of the city today. Even now women are often engaged in poorly paid domestic or workshop assignments.

Kiryu was to resume its rapid growth in the boom years of the 1960s. In addition to textiles, its new industries include auto parts, car fittings, and engine and vehicle assembly. The textile industry, however, has struggled since the oil crisis and lost out considerably to competition from other Asian countries. Accordingly, it now employs only about twenty percent of the working population and has moved decidedly up-market to concentrate on wares like traditional Japanese kimonos.

The city's greatest claim to fame today is not one that is likely to invoke the empathy of foreigners: it has the largest pachinko (a game comparable to Western pinball) industry in Japan. Indeed, the three biggest pachinko machine manufacturers in the country are located here, and these also employ hundreds of subcontractors. Heiwa, the number one maker, has a direct workforce of only five hundred, but in 1988 recorded sales of over fifty billion yen and a profit of nearly fifteen billion. This company is capitalized at the equivalent of about US $3.4 billion which, according to *Fortune* magazine, ranks it twenty-seventh in the world.

Facts and figures like these, however, seem a million miles away when you are strolling on the modest high street or struggling along silent and beautiful paths deep in the mountains. Kiryu is the kind of city that can be all things to all people. Its natural heritage, as evidenced by the walks described in this book, is fully as rich as its industrial past.

FLORA AND FAUNA   When viewed from the perspective of the Kanto area, the most distinctive feature of this region is surely the magnificent abundance of its wildlife. I know of nowhere else in Kanto where one is as certain to come across deer, serows, and monkeys in the same natural habitat. There are also stretches of beautiful virgin forest and a tremendous range of habitats for wild birds and insects. Nikko, for example, is said to have no fewer than forty thousand species of insect (almost half of all the known species in Japan), and Akagi over a hundred different kinds of butterflies. Even Kiryu, in addition to its bears and deer, has one hundred fifty-three genera and over thirteen hundred species of plant. The rivers throughout this area are immensely popular with fishermen, and the mountains attract many nature photographers.

Almost all of the walks in the land of Shodo Shonin now lie within the boundaries of designated prefectural or national parks. Starting with the walks in Kiryu, there is the Gunma Prefectural Nemoto-Narukami Park. Beyond Nemoto, Hikes 4 and 5, via the Ido Marsh and Mount Yokone to Kobugahara and on toward Mount Yakushi, lie in the Tochigi Prefectural Zen Nikko Kogen Park. Finally, the mountains of Nikko and also Sukai, Nokogiri, and Koshin, in Ashio, all fall within the bounds of the Nikko National Park. Nikko is one of the four largest national parks in Japan and the place where the Japanese national park movement began. Across the Watarase, meanwhile, is the Gunma Prefectural Akagi Park.

The huge range of fauna in these mountains includes bears, deer, serows, monkeys, squirrels, various types of ermine, flying squirrels, *tanuki* (raccoonlike dogs), weasels, otters, rabbits, bats, foxes, badgers, moles, wild boar, and mice. Some of these, of course, are nocturnal, but the hiker is almost certain to see at least deer and serow, with also a very high chance of spotting monkeys, squirrels, and *tanuki*. Although you are not likely to meet any bears, you may come across their traces.

Regarding their distribution, deer and bears are found throughout the region beyond Narukami. Deer and serows are most concentrated in and around Ashio, while bears appear to be more plentiful around the northern borders of Kiryu. Smaller animals and wild boar do come down as far as Mount Azuma. While stray monkeys occasionally appear in Kiryu, the main groups live on the slopes of Mounts Akagi and Kesamaru, in Ashio, and in the mountains of Nikko. There are said to be seven groups of monkeys in Ashio, including three on the Koshin River (Hikes 9 and 10), one around Uchi no Komori (Hike 4), and one along the course of Hike 12. Another two groups inhabit the southern flanks of Mount Himuro (Hike 3).

Probably the first animals that you see will be deer, *nihonjika,* which are found in forested mountains and plains all over Japan. They are active mainly in the morning and evening, sheltering under trees in the daytime and at night. They eat grass, young shoots, and leaves. During the rutting season, between October and December, the mountains are filled with their cries throughout the day, and one often sees stags chasing their females across the slopes. The stags and does seldom mix at other times of the year. The stags shed their antlers in the spring, and the young are born soon after. The fawns stay with their mothers until they are old enough to look after themselves.

The serows, *kamoshika,* look rather like shaggy deer and here share the same habitats as the deer, which is unusual. Serows used to be very shy, but now that they are a protected species, they stand their ground until one approaches quite close. The serows can be seen everywhere around Ashio, especially on cliffs and rocky outcrops. In fact, I saw my first serow in this region from the platform of Mato Station! These animals eat bamboo grass and pine sprouts and are almost always alone. Although they so closely resemble deer, they actually belong to an entirely different genus. The serow is a very primitive kind of cow. One could even call it a living fossil. Serows are found in the mountains throughout Honshu, Shikoku, and Kyushu.

The monkeys, *nihonzaru,* are a kind of macaque. Also known as snow monkeys, these are the northernmost-dwelling monkeys in the world. They are very similar to the rock monkeys of India and Malaysia, with their red faces and bottoms, long hair, and very short tails. They typically live in groups of twenty to thirty, eating wild (and domestic) fruits, young shoots and roots, insects, small fish, and river crabs. I saw my first monkey in this area from the window of a train on the Watarase Keikoku Tetsudo (Watarese Gorge Railway), not far from Sori Station.

The bears, *tsukinowaguma,* are Asian black bears, just like those of Iran, the Himalayas, Indochina, Manchuria, Tibet, and China. They are still found in many parts of Honshu and Shikoku and have only recently become extinct in Kyushu. These bears are also known as "moon bears," because of the white crescent moon on their chests. Although omnivorous, a study of their droppings has revealed that almost ninety-nine percent of their diet is vegetarian. The rest is accounted for mainly by insects, but they have been known to attack and eat farm animals. Their typical foods are mushrooms, oak sprouts, and other fresh shoots in the spring; ants, honey, wild cherries, bamboo sprouts, and dogwoods in the summer; and acorns or other nuts in the autumn. They also rip the bark off trees in the early summer to gnaw at the sap. The bears hibernate lightly in the winter, typically in areas of deep snow, but can be active in the lower mountains throughout the year. The cubs are born in winter or early spring and stay with their mothers for one or two years.

Sadly, both bear and deer are widely considered to be pests by the local people because of the damage they cause to forestry. Accordingly, their numbers have been tragically depleted by hunting, and it is not too early to fear for their survival. The situation is especially critical for the bears, of which two to three thousand are killed annually in Japan. There are, in fact, no reserves for bears, for hunting is permitted even in the national parks. Although people are at long last slowly waking up to the danger of their extinction, as usual, the economic interests of man seem likely to have the final say. Some basic advice about safety in bear country is given under Tips for Hikers.

As noted above, the rivers throughout this region are very popular with fishermen. This includes the Watarase, which has now virtually recovered from its terrible bout with pollution from the Ashio mines. The sweetfish *(ayu)* season provides one of the remarkable sights of the locality, when thousands of fishermen in broad straw hats play their lines standing in the middle of the currents. The higher mountain streams have char *(iwana)* and *yamame,* a kind of salmon; with rainbow trout *(niji masu)* and pond smelt *(wakasagi)* at lower reaches, where the flow is less strong. Licenses are required, but cheap. In Kiryu, for example, a one-year permit to fish all the streams and rivers of Kiryu costs only about five thousand yen, and children can generally fish for free. Ask at your hotel or the offices of the local government concerned for details. Several campsites and bungalow villages specialize in fishing holidays, notably the Yama no Kami Bungalow Village, on the Omoi River (Hikes 3 and 4).

There is, of course, a huge variety of birds in these mountains. Typical residents range from Eurasian kestrels, sparrow hawks, and buzzards to the Japanese bush warbler (often erroneously called a nightingale), common and copper pheasants, bamboo partridges, azure-winged magpies, and woodpeckers. There are also robins, finches, flycatchers, buntings, tits, wagtails, grosbeaks, chats, shrikes, wrens, jays, crows, ducks, white-eyes, martins, swallows, owls, and eagles. Ashio alone is said to have eighty species of bird, and the total for the whole region is obviously far larger. The interested walker is advised to take along the excellent *Field Guide to the Birds of Japan* (Tokyo: Kodansha International, 1982), by the Wild Bird Society of Japan.

The trees of the region are described mainly as the walks proceed. In general, however, the representative pattern is bamboo at the foot of the mountains, changing to oaks, pines, cedars, hemlocks, and birches higher up. The silver birches, which appear at an altitude of around fifteen hundred meters, and the red pines, lower down, are often exquisitely beautiful, especially in the fall. Every hiker should make a special point of seeing the vivid autumn colors of Kesamaru, Koshin, and the Rokurinpan Pass.

One worrying trend that should be noted is the worsening problem of acid rain caused by pollutants carried on the wind from Tokyo. An Environment Agency study on the southern side of Mount Akagi, which has recently attained some notoriety nationwide, reports that some cedars already are wilting on that mountain. The relatively mild consequences of the pollution so far are probably due in part to the alkaline soils. It is only to be expected, however, that the situation will continue to deteriorate.

The representative flowers of these paths are undoubtedly the azaleas, the lilies, and the violets. Any general account, however, of the vast variety of flowers to be found in this region would require several volumes. As with the trees, some attempt will made to introduce the main plants as the walks proceed.

PRACTICAL INFORMATION

MAIN ROUTES FROM TOKYO

① Tokyo to Kiryu
Tobu express from Asakusa to
Shin Kiryu (bound for Akagi)

② Tokyo to Nikko
Tobu express from Asakusa to Nikko

③ Tokyo to Maebashi
JR Takasaki Line from Ueno to Maebashi or
Joetsu Shinkansen, changing at Takasaki

④ Kiryu to Nikko
JR Ryomo Line to Tochigi, then Tobu Nikko Line

⑤ Tokyo to Ashio
Tobu express from Asakusa to Aioi (bound for
Akagi),then change to Watarase Keikoku
Tetsudo

⑥ Nikko to Ashio
Bus from Nikko or Chuzenji to Kiyotaki,
then change for bus to Ashio

TIPS FOR HIKERS   In this region, of course, all of the usual advice about hiking applies. Many of the paths are quite rough, so you should have well-soled and water-resistant footwear. Also be sure to take along enough food and water for emergencies, as well as for your expected needs; tell people where you are going; remember that the mountains can be much colder than the plains; take a flashlight and also a compass for the remoter hikes; remember that signs and paths do change, and especially beware of being confused by new forestry paths; turn back if you get lost; give up if the path is too dangerous; start early and finish early to make sure that you do not run out of time; and be sure to obtain good maps for the remoter hikes (Hikes 2, 3, 8, 10, and 12). Early starts are especially a good idea in summer, so the main climb can be finished before it gets too hot. Then you can enjoy a lovely cool stroll in the uplands, while everyone else is sweltering on the plains.

The maps printed in this book should generally be sufficient, but it is always wise to obtain more detailed ones as well. The 1:25,000- and 1:50,000-scale maps listed at the head of each hike are single-sheet maps published by Kokudo Chiri In (the Japanese Ordnance Survey) and are available at major bookshops. All can be bought in the basement of the Yaesu Book Center, near Tokyo Station. There is, however, no need to buy every map that is listed. In fact, most hikes in this book (and all of those for which extra maps are necessary) are contained in just three 1:50,000- scale maps: those of Kiryu-Ashikaga, Ashio, and Mount Nantai.

Several of the hikes in this book coincide with the route of the Kanto Fureai no Michi, the round-Kanto hiking road, which is sponsored by the Environment Agency. These sections are generally very well signposted and maintained. They include parts of Short Walk 1 and Hikes 1, 6, 7, 8, 9, and 10 and the entire route of Hike 4.

In terms of climate, there is both good news and bad. On the bright side, Gunma Prefecture has 2,209 hours of sunshine a year, second only to Kochi Prefecture in all of Japan. It has even been suggested that Kiryu might have the most clear days of any place in Japan, for the Gunma figures are actually for Maebashi. The bad news is that Ashio and Nikko are the wettest places in the Kanto area!

In Kiryu, the highest recorded temperature is 38.4° C (101° F), which was measured in 1965; the coldest is −9.5° C (15° F), in 1963. Daytime maximum temperatures generally hover around 30° C (86° F) in July and August, falling only to around 3° C (38° F) in January and February. These figures are for an altitude of a little over one hundred meters. The general rule of thumb is to subtract 0.6° C for every additional hundred meters, making the top of Nemoto, for example, about 6° C cooler than the center of the city. The center of the city has snow only about ten days a year, but the figure is, of course, considerably higher in the mountains. The mountains of Ashio and Nikko, by contrast, have quite heavy snow in winter, well over a meter deep in places.

The three short walks and Hikes 1 and 7 are easy to do year-round. The hikes on Kesamaru, Koshin, and across to Nikko and Nantai are no-go areas for the inexperienced between mid-November and at least the end of April. The remaining walks fall somewhere in between. For some routes, such as Hike 4, which is extremely safe and well marked, the snow just adds to the fun on a clear day. Obviously, you must judge by the conditions that you find, but all courses have to be treated with special respect in winter. The very best seasons for climbing are late May and October, not only due to the temperature but also because of the blueness of the skies, the clarity of the views, and the May flowers or the autumn leaves. If you are walking in the rainy season of June and July, be especially wary of landslides. Also watch out for thunderstorms on summer afternoons. It is not without reason that Raiden, the god of thunder, was one of the most popular gods of Kiryu.

The walking times given in this book are my first times on each course. I usually find that my pace is faster by about twenty percent on subsequent visits, when I know where I am going. Since everyone has different ideas about rests, however, it should be noted that only a bare minimum of time is allowed for short breathers. Accordingly, a three-hour walk, for example, is quite likely to take four and a half hours. Depending on the person, a five-hour walk is liable to require most of the day. Be sure to give yourself plenty of time for the first walks, and then see how your pace compares with mine.

Lastly, a few words have to be written about snakes and bears, though it cannot be emphasized enough that trouble with these is extremely unlikely. There are poisonous vipers *(mamushi)* in both the mountains and the fields. Not all of the snakes that you will see are poisonous, but unless you are sure that you can distinguish between them, it is best to assume that they are. In all Japan, there are in fact some two thousand reported cases of snakebite each year, though happily, fatalities are very rare. If you do see a snake, don't aggravate it. Let it slip away. Medical advice differs about primary care if you do happen to be bitten. Japanese texts recommend that you suck the wound and cut it (just open it, don't cut out the flesh!) for aspiration. This is thought to be somewhat effective if the cut is performed within thirty minutes of the bite. American texts, by contrast, say that the cutting is likely to cause more problems than it cures. They recommend compression. Either way, it is probably a good idea at least to squeeze out some blood first and tie a light tourniquet. Then, get down to a doctor as quickly as possible to receive some serum. This should be done with as little effort as possible. Ideally, you ought to be carried. In mountains, however, this last piece of advice is not likely to be of much help.

Although you probably will see snakes, you are unlikely to meet with any problems. You are not likely to see any bears, but precautions ought to be taken, at least on the remoter walks. It would, even so, be nonsense to worry. Tokyo traffic is much more dangerous. In fact, only two or three people die each year from black bear attacks in the whole of Japan. I have met bears in these mountains myself (without incident), and so have most of the other people I know who enter these mountains regularly.

Opinions vary widely about just how one ought to avoid bears, but the general consensus is to make as much noise as possible. If walking in a largish group, you will be making so much noise anyway that the chances of even glimpsing, let alone surprising, a bear are negligible. Most lone walkers use radios or bells, though these have to be pretty loud to have any chance of being heard near some of the noisy mountain streams. If you are traveling deep in bear country, dogs should be kept on a lead. If you are a woman, you would be best advised not to use cosmetics or perfumes. Also, menstruating women would do well to wear pads, get back to civilization, and await a more propitious time for hiking. If you are camping, keep your food a long way from the tent, and avoid pitching the tent beside streams and other places where bears are likely to be active.

If you do happen to meet a bear, the most important thing is not to run away, because that could trigger its chasing instinct. Of course, don't be so idiotic as to scream or wave your arms. Climbing a tree is not likely to help much either, because these bears are better climbers than you. Even playing dead is discouraged, as that can just make a bear curious. One other important rule is not to scatter food to cover an escape unless you are absolutely desperate. A bear that learns to associate people with food will approach other hikers. Someone is likely to be hurt, and the bear will eventually be shot.

Instead, the advice is to back away quietly if you can, giving the bear all of the respect and space it seems to need. Do not threaten it by sudden movements or staring. If you see the bear first, once you are well out of sight and a good distance away, you might consider making some noise to encourage it to slip away. Bears almost always will avoid you when they don't know that they have been seen.

It must be stressed that bears will rarely cause any trouble unless surprised at close range. They are also likely to sense you before you notice them. The most anyone normally sees is a furry rump walking away. Gratis of hunters, man is the top bear around here, and those bears that have survived this long know it. So don't go looking for bears unless you are an expert, but don't be anxious about them, either. You will be very lucky if you see one at all.

TRANSPORTATION   Both Nikko and Kiryu are easy to reach from Tokyo using the Tobu Line from Asakusa. For Kiryu, take the express train to Akagi, and alight at either Shin Kiryu or Aioi. Aioi, the next station after Shin Kiryu, is the place for direct connections to the Watarase Keikoku Tetsudo (Watarase Gorge Railway) up the valley of the Watarase River to Ashio. Either way, the journey takes a little under two hours and costs around two thousand yen. In the mornings, Nikko is the terminus of the other express line. Later in the day, you'll have to take the express train bound for Kinugawa Onsen and change at Imaichi for the final ten minutes to Nikko. The cost and journey time are almost the same as to Kiryu. Express tickets should be bought at the ticket window, not from the machines. Of course, if you are traveling on a tight budget, there are also slower trains on the same routes for which the express supplements are unnecessary. The Tobu Railway Company also sells a four-day Nikko-Kinugawa Free Pass ticket for unlimited rides on Tobu trains and buses in the Nikko (but not Kiryu or Ashio) area.

If alighting at Shin Kiryu Station, you'll have to walk or take a bus into the city center. It takes only about twenty-five minutes to walk down to the main street. Just go downhill, cross the river, and follow straight up the main road on the other side. Turn left at the Daiichi Kangyo Bank for Kiryu Station, the terminus of the Watarase Keikoku Tetsudo. This station also lies on the JR Ryomo Line, serving Takasaki, Maebashi, Isesaki, Kiryu, Ashikaga, Sano, Tochigi, and Oyama.

The Watarase Keikoku Tetsudo, the single-track line that winds up the lovely river gorge, is the trunk line for most of the walks described in this book. A substantial tourist attraction in its own right, the Watarase Keikoku Tetsudo is beloved of railway buffs all over Japan. Tickets can be bought at several stations. Otherwise, you can pay on the train. Get on at the back, taking a numbered ticket from the machine, and pay the driver when you get off. The same system also applies for all of the bus routes used in this book though for buses you usually get on at the front. For transportation information, the following telephone numbers may be useful:

RAILROADS

TOBU RAILWAY COMPANY   **03-3623-1171**

WATARASE KEIKOKU TETSUDO   **0277-73-2110**

KIRYU

TOBU SHIN KIRYU STATION   **0277-54-1715**

TOBU BUS COMPANY   **0277-22-0111**

JR KIRYU STATION   **0277-22-2312**

  KIRYU TAXIS

ASAHI TAXI   **0277-45-2420**

KIRYU GODO TAXI   **0277-44-8001**

KIRYU HIRE CENTER   **0277-22-0175**

NUMATAYA TAXI   **0277-44-5242**

OMAMA

NUMATAYA TAXI   **0277-72-2219**

ASHIO

ASHIO TAXI   **0288-93-2346**

KANUMA

TOBU SHIN KANUMA STATION   **0289-64-2247**

JR KANUMA STATION   **0289-64-3223**

KANTO BUS COMPANY   **0289-64-3161**

KANUMA TAXIS

HEIWA TAXI   **0289-62-3135**

KANUMA GODO TAXI   **0289-62-3188**

MIYAKO TAXI   **0289-62-2920**

NIKKO

TOBU NIKKO STATION   **0288-54-0137**

TOBU BUS COMPANY   **0288-54-0122**

CHUZENJIKO KISEN (LAKE BOATING)   **0288-55-0360**

NIKKO TAXIS

NIKKO KOTSU   **0288-54-1188**

NIKKO KANKO HIRE   **0288-54-1155**

CHUO KOTSU   **0288-54-2138**

DAIWA KOTSU   **0288-54-1515**

SANEI JIDOSHA   **0288-54-1130**

TOURIST INFORMATION OFFICES   Those coming from Tokyo should prepare for their trip by visiting the Gunma and Tochigi tourist information offices in the Kokusai Kanko Kaikan building, just outside the Yaesu entrance to Tokyo Station. The Tochigi office is on the second floor, and the Gunma office on the fourth. Both have a great variety of maps and other tourist literature. The Yaesu Book Center nearby is a good place to buy the detailed Kokudo Chiri In maps recommended at the start of each hike.

The Nikko Tourist Information office lies on the course of Short Walk 3 (see page 232), and the Ashio office is just opposite the Izumiya Ryokan outside Tsudo Station. The following telephone numbers may also be useful (you may have to ask for the *kankoka,* the tourism department):

GUNMA PREFECTURE TOURIST INFORMATION

RECORDED MESSAGE IN JAPANESE **0272-52-3300**

MAEBASHI OFFICE **0272-21-1525**

TOKYO OFFICE **03-3231-4836**

UENO STATION OFFICE **03-3842-5013/4**

SHINJUKU OFFICE **03-3354-1899**

OSAKA OFFICE **06-341-5303**

NAGOYA OFFICE **052-262-3018**

TOCHIGI PREFECTURE TOURIST INFORMATION

TOKYO OFFICE **03-3215-4050**

OSAKA OFFICE **06-341-1925**

TOCHIGI PREFECTURAL ENVIRONMENT
AND TOURIST DEPARTMENT **0286-23-3210/13**

LOCAL TOURIST INFORMATION OFFICES

KIRYU CITY COMMERCE
AND TOURISM DEPARTMENT **0288-46-1111 (EXT. 563)**

AKAGI TOURIST ASSOCIATION **0272-87-8400**

ASHIO TOWN TOURIST DEPARTMENT **0288-93-3111**

KANUMA CITY TOURIST ASSOCIATION **0289-64-2111**

AWANO TOWN TOURIST ASSOCIATION **0289-85-2111**

KOBUGAHARA TOURIST ASSOCIATION **0289-74-2131**

TOCHIGI CITY TOURIST DEPARTMENT **0282-22-3535**

NIKKO CITY TOURIST ASSOCIATION **0288-54-2496**

AZUMA VILLAGE TOURIST DEPARTMENT **0277-97-2111**

PLACES TO STAY   One of the great advantages of Kiryu and Ashio is that, unlike elsehwere in Japan, it is very easy to travel even without reservations. Kiryu, in particular, has many cheap hotels, conveniently located close to the station, where it is almost always possible to find a room. Reservations are required, however, for the three *kokumin shukusha* (people's hostels) — by Lake Kusagi, on the Watarase line; at Ginzandaira, in Ashio; at the top of Akagi — and also at the many campsites and bungalow villages beside the courses described in this book.

In most of Japan, reservations are generally needed for *ryokan* (Japanese-style inns) and *minshuku* (guest houses) as well, but this is not likely to be a problem in Ashio or Kiryu.

While writing this book, I frequently stayed at the Station Hotel, in Kiryu, and Ashikaga Kenko Land, a bath center three stops down the JR Ryomo Line from Kiryu, about twenty minutes' walk from the JR Ashikaga Station or Tobu Ashikaga-shi Station. The Ashikaga Kenko Land has several kinds of baths, a swimming pool, sauna, beer hall, cinema, massage room, and a communal resting room, which all combine as a wonderful salve to the body after the rigors of the mountains. You even get pajamas, toothbrushes, and razors. The admission charge, which includes everything except the massage and food and drink, is just ￥2,000, with various discounts available. There is a surcharge of ￥800 if you stay overnight. The only walks in this book that cannot feasibly be done in a single day from Kiryu or Ashikaga are Hikes 8 and 10.

The other inn that has truly taken my fancy is the Izumiya Ryokan in Ashio, just close to Tsudo Station. This has a beautiful Meiji interior, and the service is superb and utterly genuine. One evening, for example, I said that I'd be leaving at five the next morning, so I wouldn't need any breakfast. Not expecting anything at all, I nonetheless found that a pot of tea and a newspaper had been placed outside my door, without disturbing me, at the unearthly time of four-fifteen! The price for a night with dinner at this marvelous, atmospheric old retreat was a mere ￥5,100!

Nikko, of course, is another matter entirely. The best advice is to go to the excellent Tourist Information Center near the Sacred Bridge (see Short Walk 3), where the friendly, English-speaking staff are used to helping foreigners with pocketbooks and itineraries of all shapes and sizes. Most of the hotels in the Chuzenji Hot Spring are expensive, with indifferent service tailored to the moneyed masses. In fact, they don't even accept bookings for lone travelers, so determined are they to squeeze every last penny from their visitors! Since all the walks in Nikko can be managed even from Ashio, Kiryu, or Ashikaga, I rarely stayed at Chuzenji Hot Spring. The campsites and youth hostels of Nikko, by contrast, do have a good reputation. One should remember, though, that these camps are liable to be overflowing with children and will have a rather noisy, communal atmosphere. The best solution is to slip over the Asegata Pass (Hike 12) and pitch a tent in the lovely woods near the top for free. The following is a representative list of cheap or convenient places to stay in the region:

HOTELS There are many hotels in Kiryu; following is a list of those close to Kiryu Station. All cost about ¥5,000 per night, without meals.

STATION HOTEL　ステーションホテル

2-8-3 MIYAMAE-CHO, KIRYU-SHI **0277-22-0505**

HOTEL MIYAMOTO　ホテルみやもと

2-22 SUEHIRO-CHO, KIRYU-SHI **0277-22-4478**

SILVER HOTEL　シルバーホテル

4-13 SUEHIRO-CHO, KIRYU-SHI **0277-22-7717**

ACE HOTEL　エースホテル

2-1893-9 TOMOE-CHO, KIRYU-SHI **0277-47-4910**

PEARL HOTEL　パールホテル

2-9 SUEHIRO-CHO, KIRYU-SHI **0277-22-0166**

BUSINESS HOTEL NEW MOCHIMARU　ビジネスホテル・ニューモチマル

9-19 SUEHIRO-CHO, KIRYU-SHI **0277-22-3352**

RYOKAN Overnight prices range from about ¥5,000 to ¥8,000, with two meals. Additional information is available from the Kiryu Ryokan Association (Kiryu Ryokan Kumiai), at 0277-22-4624.

RYOKAN KOTOBUKISO　旅館寿荘

1-7-37 MIYAMAE-CHO, KIRYU-SHI **0277-22-4455**

FUKUYA RYOKAN　富久家旅館

1-4-5 MIYAMAE-CHO, KIRYU-SHI **0277-22-3600**

MIYAMAE RYOKAN　宮前旅館

2-5-35 MIYAMAE-CHO, KIRYU-SHI **0277-22-2746**

NISHI KIRYU KAN　西桐生館

4-14 ENRAKU-CHO, KIRYU-SHI **0277-22-2985**

KAGETSU RYOKAN　花月旅館

2-7-10 MIYAMAE-CHO, KIRYU-SHI **0277-22-5051**

RYOKAN OMI　旅館おおみ

5-28 SUEHIRO-CHO, KIRYU-SHI **0277-22-2841**

ETCHUYA RYOKAN　越中屋旅館

3-9 SUEHIRO-CHO, KIRYU-SHI　**0277-22-5780**

TOSEIKAN　桐盛館

7-17 SUEHIRO-CHO, KIRYU-SHI　**0277-22-5421**

FUKUFUMI RYOKAN　フクフミ旅館

7-8 SUEHIRO-CHO, KIRYU-SHI　**0277-22-2458**

KINSEIKAN　錦静館

1-9-26 NISHIKI-CHO, KIRYU-SHI　**0277-44-7666**

RYOKAN IKOI　旅館いこい

6-736 HON-CHO, KIRYU-SHI　**0277-44-6113**

KANAKIYA　金木屋

5-358 HON-CHO, KIRYU-SHI　**0277-22-2046**

This *ryokan,* with rooms in the ¥6,000 to ¥8,000 range, appears in the 1859 guide to Nemoto, *Nemotoyama Sankeiro Hitori Annai,* preserved at Nemoto Shrine.

UMEDA (KIRYU)

SEIFUEN　清風荘

5-7652 UMEDA-CHO, KIRYU-SHI　**0277-32-1181**

This *ryokan*, with rooms from ¥6,000 to ¥8,000 per night, is the nearest inn to the start of Hike 3.

OMAMA

HOTELS AND *RYOKAN*　The following are all located near Omama Station.

HOTEL TOYODA　ホテル豊田

1341 OMAMA, OMAMA-MACHI　**0277-72-1002**

MIHARASHI CENTER　見晴しセンター

1570-170 KIRIBARA, OMAMA-MACHI　**0277-73-3978**

BUSINESS HOTEL SHINSEI　ビジネスホテル新生

1481 OMAMA, OMAMA-MACHI　**0277-72-4188**

MATSUYA RYOKAN　松屋旅館

1117 OMAMA, OMAMA-MACHI　**0277-72-1080**

FUKUZUMI BEKKAN　富久住旅館

962-2 OMAMA, OMAMA-MACHI　**0277-72-1148**

TAKATSUDO RYOKAN　高津戸旅館

918 TAKATSUDO, OMAMA-MACHI　**0277-72-1070**

RYOKAN

KANBAIKAN　神梅館

275-1 KAMIKANBAI, OMAMA-MACHI　**0277-73-0355**

Near Kamikanbai Station

IEYASU RYOKAN　家康旅館

680 SHIOBARA, OMAMA-MACHI　**0277-73-4871**

Near Kamikanbai Station

AKAGI KAKU　赤城閣

125 MIZUNUMA, KUROHONE-MURA　**0277-96-2705**

Will meet guests at Mizunuma Station.

MARUHACHI RYOKAN　丸八旅館

1109 KUSAGI, AZUMA-MURA　**0277-95-6101**

MIDORI RYOKAN　みどり旅館

891 GODO, AZUMA-MURA　**0277-97-2318**

Will meet guests at Godo Station.

TOYOKAN　東陽館

773 KONAKA, AZUMA-MURA　**0277-97-2840**

Will meet guests at Konaka Station.

OGIYA　扇屋

303 HANAWA, AZUMA-MURA　**0277-97-2432**

Will meet guests at Hanawa Station.

OTHER ACCOMMODATIONS

NASHIGIKAN　梨木館

285 SHUKUMEGURI, KUROHONE-MURA　**0277-96-2521**

A large, hot-spring *ryokan*. Will meet guests at Motojuku Station.

KEIRYU GYOEN　渓魚苑

1872 SHIMOTAZAWA, KUROHONE-MURA　**0277-96-3670**

A *minshuku* for fishermen high up on the slopes of Akagi, on the road above Mugikubo (see Hike 6, Route 1 down Akagi). Will meet guests at Mizunuma Station.

SUNLAKE KUSAGI　サンレイク草木

1654-1 OJI KUSAGI, AZUMA-MURA　**0277-95-6309**

A *kokumin shukusha* located halfway around Lake Kusagi between Godo and Sori stations, the hostel accommodates 100, at ￥2,600 per night. Will send a car to meet you from Godo Station. Facilities include a restaurant, coffee shop, and large bath (￥300 for bath only, up to 2 hours). Convenient for Hikes 2, 4, 7, 8, 9, 11, and 12.

KUROSAKA ISHI BUNGALOW TENT MURA　黒坂石バンガロー・テント村

OAZA-SORI 1146, AZUMA-MURA　**0277-95-6611**

Run by the village, this bungalow and camping facility can be reached from either Mount Nemoto or Wannajo (see Hike 3), or Sori Station on the Watarase Keikoku Tetsudo. Tennis, fishing, campfire, showers. Rental of five-person tents about ￥1,000; five-person bungalow ￥2,600, with bigger tents and bungalows available.

OKUWATARASE LOG CABINS　ログキャビン奥渡良

434-1 SORI, AZUMA-MURA　**0277-95-6841**

Rental tents, ￥5,000; with your own tent ￥3,000; cabins ￥10,000. Other camping or cooking equipment available very cheaply, plus bath, shower, and washing machines. Open April into November. Along Hike 8.

SANKEI　山景

923 SAYADO, AZUMA-MURA　**0277-97-2121**

Along Hike 7. *Ryokan* with bungalows, specializing in *ayu* (sweetfish) and wild boar cuisine. Will meet guests at station.

AKAGI

GUNMA KENKO LAND　群馬健康ランド

This public bath *(sento)* is really a bath-food-cinema-bed complex. It also has a

48

limited number of capsule rooms and rental videos. Basic charge ¥1,800 (capsules extra). Near Ino Station between Takasaki and Maebashi on the JR Ryomo and Joetsu local lines; for further information, call 0273-64-1010.

AKAGI ONSEN HOTEL　赤木温泉ホテル

MIYAGI-MURA　**0272-83-3012**

A hot-spring hotel along Hike 6.

AKAGI RYOKUFUSO　赤木緑風荘

AKAGISAN, FUJIMI-MURA　**0272-87-8111**

A *kokumin shukusha* along Hike 6.

RIHEIJAYA SHINRIN KOEN　利平茶屋森林公園

OAZA-SHIMOTAZAWA, KUROHONE-MURA　**0277-96-2588.**

Campsite offering bungalows for ¥4,100; rental tents ¥1,000; bedding ¥360. Open May 1 to October 31. Along Hike 6 (see page 158).

HANAMIGAHARA KYANPUJO　花見ヶ原キャンプ場

OAZA-SHIMOTAZAWA, KUROHONE-MURA　**0277-96-3131.**

Campsite offering bungalows for ¥3,000 and ¥4,100; rental tents ¥1,000 and ¥1,200; with your own tent, ¥510; bedding ¥360. Open May 1 to October 31. Along Hike 6 (see page 156).

MINSHUKU ON MOUNT AKAGI

ONUMA SANSO　大沼山荘	**0272-87-8311**
AOKI RYOKAN　青木旅館	**0272-87-8511**
AOKI BEKKAN　青木別館	**0272-87-8106**
GREEN SO (summer only)　グリーン荘	**0272-87-8028**
MIYAMA SANSO　みやま山荘	**0272-87-8205**
MEIGETSUKAN　名月館	**0272-87-8127**
KOGENSO IMANISHI　高原荘今西	**0272-87-8006**

ASHIO

RYOKAN Overnight charges are about ¥6,000, including two meals.

IZUMIYA RYOKAN　泉屋旅館

MATSUBARA 1-22, ASHIO-MACHI　**0288-93-2001**

Next to Tsudo Station, along Hike 9 (see page 44).

49

ICHIMARU RYOKAN 一丸旅館

MATSUBARA 2-11, ASHIO-MACHI **0288-93-2002**

Another large, old-fashioned *ryokan* with a friendly staff, very close to Tsudo Station.

KAMEMURA RYOKAN 亀村旅館

AKASAWA 15-26, ASHIO-MACHI **0288-93-2109**

Between Ashio and Tsudo stations.

KAMEMURA BEKKAN 亀村別館

GINZANDAIRA 5488, ASHIO-MACHI **0288-93-2218**

Along Hike 9 and close to start of Hike 10.

MINSHUKU These average ￥6,000 per night, with two meals.

MINSHUKU MIKOUCHISO 民宿みこうち荘

1888 MIKOUCHI, ASHIO-MACHI **0288-93-2783**

MINSHUKU YAMAMESO 民宿やまめ荘

1883 MIKOUCHI, ASHIO-MACHI **0288-93-2340**

MINSHUKU ASHIOSO 民宿足尾荘

302 MIKOUCHI, ASHIO-MACHI **0288-93-2747**

MINSHUKU SENZANHAKU 民宿染山泊

3738 MOCHIGASE, ASHIO-MACHI **0288-93-4272**

OTHER ACCOMMODATIONS

KAJIKASO かじか荘

5488 GINZANDAIRA, ASHIO-MACHI **0288-93-3420.**

A *kokumin shukusha* offering a hot spring, pottery classes, and free use of the pool. Overnight charge is ￥2,680; dinner ￥1,440; breakfast ￥830. A ￥1,000 deposit is required with reservations. Along Hikes 9 and 10.

GINZANDAIRA KYANPUJO 銀山平キャンプ場 XXX

5488 GINZANDAIRA, ASHIO-MACHI **0288-22-1111**

A year-round campsite with a free pool, run by Ashio Town. Four-man bungalows ￥4,000–￥7,000; four-man rooms in the lodge ￥5,000; six-man tents ￥1,100. Along Hikes 9 and 10.

KOSHIN SANSO　庚甲山荘

An unmanned mountain lodge also run by Ashio Town, with bedding and water available, for ￥2,000 per night. For further information, call 0288-93-3111 or 4099. Along Hike 10.

OYADO KOTONO IE　御宿琴乃屋

4251 KURASAWA, ASHIO-MACHI　**0288-93-2660**

A hot-spring with lodgings for about ￥8,000 per night. Will pick up at Ashio Station.

AWANO

In addition to the listings below, there are three *minshuku* and one *ryokan* in Awano, but these are not very convenient for the walks in this book. For details, call the Awano Town Tourist Association (Awano-machi Kanko Kyokai) at the town hall at 0289-85-2111. An unmanned mountain hut is also available at Ido Marsh.

YAMA NO KAMI BUNGALOW VILLAGE　山の神バンガロー村

1069 KAMI KASUO, AWANO-MACHI　**0289-82-3518**

With Yama no Kami Drive In, offers bungalows along Hikes 3 and 4.

HOKKOJI NO MORI　発光路の森

762-4 KAMI KASUO, AWANO-MACHI　**0289-82-3546**

Near Kami Kasuo bus stop, offers a campsite and bungalows convenient for Hikes 3 and 4.

SUMIDA-KU AWANO SHIZEN GAKUEN　墨田区あわの自然学園

1041 AZA SHIBATA, OAZA KAMI KASUO　**0289-82-3221.**

This large facility belongs to the Sumida Ward of Tokyo and was built as a kind of country dormitory and activity center for residents of the ward, although nonresidents of the ward are permitted to use the facilities. Along Hikes 3 and 4, between Kami Kasuo bus stop and Yama-no-kami Bungalow Village.

IZURU

MANGANJI　満願寺

288 IZURU-CHO, TOCHIGI-SHI　**0282-31-1717.**

A temple offering accommodations, located along Short Walk 2.

51

IZURU SANSO　出流山荘

943 IZURU-CHO, TOCHIGI-SHI　**0282-31-2060.**

A *minshuku* along Short Walk 2. Reservations essential except on Sundays and holidays.

MINSHUKU IZURU　民宿いずる

231 IZURU-CHO, TOCHIGI-SHI　**0282-31-1975.**

Along Short Walk 2.

KANUMA

HOTELS AND *RYOKAN*　In addition to those listed, all near Shin Kanuma Station, there are several other hotels and *ryokan* in Kanuma. For details, call the Kanuma Tourist Association (Kanuma Kanko Kyokai) at the city hall, 0289-64-2111.

TOBU SHIN KANUMA HOTEL　東武新鹿沼ホテル　　　　　**0289-64-1122.**

A small hotel with small rooms and indifferent service, for ¥5,000 per night, excluding meals. Nonetheless, very convenient for Hikes 3, 4, and 5.

MIYAKO RYOKAN　みやこ旅館　　　　　　　　　　　　**0289-62-2610**

TAMURAYA RYOKAN　田村屋旅館　　　　　　　　　　　**0289-65-0870**

OTHER ACCOMMODATIONS

FURUMINE SHRINE　古峰神社　　　　　　　　　　　　　**0289-74-2131**

About ¥6,000 including meals. Accommodation for eight hundred. Along Hikes 4 and 5.

KANUMA KABOKU CENTER　鹿沼花木センター　　　　　**0289-76-3390**

The Kanuma Flower and Tree Center is a year-round facility with six- and ten-man tents available for ¥600–¥1,000.

NIKKO

Ask at the tourist information center near the Sacred Bridge about hot springs, *ryokan,* and *minshuku*. There are far too many to list.

CAMPSITES

SENJUGAHAMA BUNGALOWS　千手ヶ浜バンガロー

BOAT FROM CHUZENJI HOT SPRING　**0288-55-0690**

Five- to six-man bungalows ¥6,000, larger bungalows available; six-man tents ¥4,500 with bedding. With your own tent, ¥500. Open July 10 to August 31.

SENJUGAHAMA KYANPUMURA　千手ヶ浜キャンプ村

BOAT FROM CHUZENJI HOT SPRING　**0288-54-1078**

Six-man bungalows with bedding ¥6,500; six- to seven-man tents ¥4,500; with your own tent, ¥450. Open mid-July to late-August.

SHOBUGAHAMA KYANPUMURA　菖蒲ヶ浜キャンプ村

BOAT OR BUS FROM CHUZENJI HOT SPRING　**0288-55-0272**

Four-man bungalows ¥5,000, larger bungalows available; with your own tent, ¥500. Open May 1 to October 31.

ASEGATA KYANPUJO　阿世潟キャンプ場

BOAT FROM CHUZENJI HOT SPRING　**0288-54-1111**

Six-man tents ¥1,200; service fee ¥300. Open July 18 to August 21. Along Hike 12 and close to course of Hike 11.

OTHER ACCOMMODATIONS

KOKUMIN SHUKUSHA OGURAYAMA SANSO　国民宿舎小倉山山荘

2823 TOKORONO, NIKKO-SHI　**0288-54-2487**

Lodgings for ¥5,100, with two meals.

NIKKO YOUTH HOSTEL　日光ユース・ホテル

2854 TOKORONO, NIKKO-SHI　**0288-54-1013**

Lodgings for ¥3,630 per night, with two meals. Closed December 29 to January 3.

THE MOUNTAIN WALKS

KIRYU, ASHIO, AND NIKKO

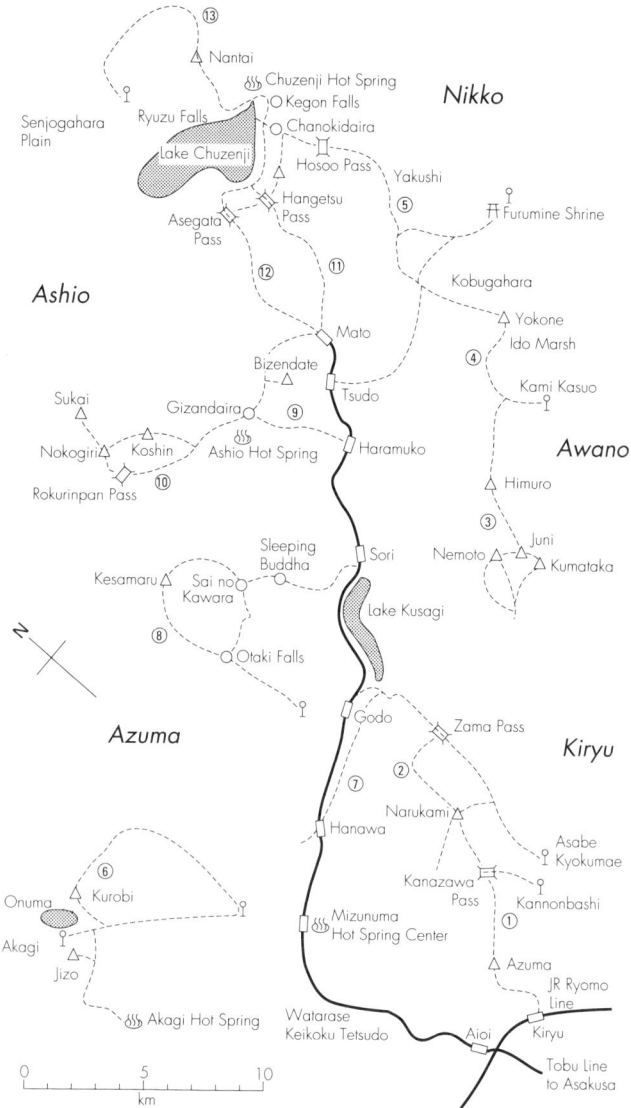

Nikko

⑬

△ Nantai

♨ Chuzenji Hot Spring
○ Kegon Falls

Ryuzu Falls
○ Chanokidaira

Senjogahara
Plain

Lake Chuzenji

Hosoo Pass

Yakushi

Hangetsu
Pass

⑤

Furumine Shrine

Asegata
Pass

Ashio

⑫   ⑪

Kobugahara

△ Yokone
Ido Marsh

Mato

④

Bizendate
△

Kami Kasuo
○

Sukai
△

Gizandaira
○   ⑨

Tsudo

Awano

Nokogiri△   △ Koshin
Ashio Hot Spring ♨

Haramuko

△ Himuro

Rokurinpan Pass
⑩

③

Juni
△

Nemoto △   △ Kumataka

Sleeping
Buddha

Sori
○

Kesamaru △   Sai no ○
Kawara

Lake Kusagi

N

⑧

○ Otaki Falls

Godo

Zama Pass

Azuma

⑦   ②

Kiryu

Narukami
△

Asabe
Kyokumae

Kanazawa
Pass

Kannonbashi
○

△ Kurobi
⑥

Hanawa

①

Onuma

Mizunuma ♨
Hot Spring Center

△ Azuma

Akagi
△
Jizo

JR Ryomo
Line

♨ Akagi Hot Spring

Watarase
Keikoku Tetsudo

Aioi

Kiryu

0   5   10
km

Tobu Line
to Asakusa

SHORT WALK 1 ▲ AZUMA
A VIEW OF KIRYU

KIRYU STATION • SUIDOYAMA PARK, OKAWA MUSEUM OF ART, AND AZUMA BOTANICAL GARDEN • MOUNT AZUMA • TOZENJI, SENJUJI, AND SOZENJI • KIRYU NATURE SANCTUARY

TOTAL WALKING TIME   2 HOURS, 30 MINUTES

MAPS   1:25,000 OMAMA; 1:50,000 KIRYU AND ASHIKAGA. A FREE KANTO FUREAI NO MICHI MAP (FOR COURSES 32 AND 33) IS AVAILABLE FROM THE GUNMA TOURIST INFORMATION OFFICE. A FREE ENGLISH MAP OF CENTRAL KIRYU IS AVAILABLE FROM THE TOURIST DEPARTMENT OF THE KIRYU CITY HALL

One of the best things about starting these hikes at Kiryu is that one enters the mountains in only about a five-minute walk from the station. Azuma lies at the very tip of a range that extends all of the way to Ashio, and at this extreme outpost of the mountains the culture of the plains is dominant. Suidoyama Park has the feel of a typical city park, and its main sight is the excellent but utterly civilized Okawa Museum of Art. From there, the path up Mount Azuma is a popular climb among the local residents. It is a stiff hike, but many people, especially the elderly, climb to the summit every morning for their daily exercise. The peak is particularly crowded on the morning of New Year's Day, when residents gather to see the first sunrise of the year. Later in the day, however, throughout the year one is likely to meet groups of high school students jogging to the top. One of the best times to climb Azuma is from early to mid-December, when the sky is almost always clear, the leaves are still turning, and snow has already fallen on the highest of the nearby peaks.

Azuma also has a wide variety of flora and fauna. The blossoms include *jaketsu ibara (Caesalpinia japonica),* a shrub with beautiful five-petaled yellow flowers that bloom in the rainy season of June; the pink blossoms of the small *edohigan* cherries *(Lycoris radiate)* that brighten up the long, spidery branches in early spring; reddish-pink *togo kumitsuba tsutsuji* azaleas *(Rhododendron wadanum); yamatabako (Ligularia angusta),* a yellow chrysanthemum over a meter tall that flowers in June and in all of Gunma Prefecture grows only at the top of Azuma; and the dogtooth violets, another symbol of the coming of spring. There are also small animals, such as hares and squirrels, and larger creatures stray here occasionally.

Tradition has it that the shrine on the peak of Azuma was once one of the three main shrines of Kiryu. Actually, there were formerly two shrines on Azuma, for the people on the Kiryu and the Kawauchi sides of the mountain prayed to different Shinto gods here. Worship at both mountaintop shrines was discontinued late in the Meiji era, when they were merged with larger ones in the plains, a fate that also befell the shrines of Narukami.

Old records tell us that the mountain was officially opened on March 15 each year (which corresponds to April 15 in the modern calendar). On that day, many citizens would hike this path up from Suidoyama. One landmark now lost was a large wooden shrine that marked the farthest point to which women were allowed to ascend. Such demarcation points were a feature common to all mountain faiths, including Shugendo, for women were widely considered to be spiritually impure. In Nikko, for example, women were not allowed to climb to Lake Chuzenji until 1878, the year that the *shugendo* were discontinued. The bright red hall that marks the old border can still be seen there, on the Iroha Road to the lake.

Descending the other side of Azuma, we leave the city behind for the suburban countryside. There we enter a world of mulberries, vegetable fields, and rice paddies, with the quiet broken here and there by clatter of textile machines from tiny domestic workshops. We find a medieval stone pillar from the time of Nitta Yoshisada, the oldest Koshin stone in Gunma, the sixteenth century Ogura stupa, a grand old cypress tree, and the Koshin Hall of Sozenji. Other sights include modern Jizo, protectors of children, and a golden Amida, both deities deeply rooted in popular faiths all over Japan. The walk ends at the Kiryu Nature Sanctuary, one of several such sanctuaries recently set up around Japan by the Environment Agency.

The first part of this walk largely coincides with the Kanto Fureai no Michi route from the Azuma Botanical Garden to the Kiryu Nature Sanctuary.

KIRYU STATION ▶ AROUND SUIDOYAMA PARK ▶ START OF HIKING COURSE
WALKING TIME: 30 MINUTES

There is much to be said for seeing what a provincial city has to offer before starting to hike out of it. Suidoyama Park is a modest but well-maintained leisure zone with a surprising variety of attractions, ranging from the family-oriented to the frankly highbrow. It is sort of miniature Ueno Park, complete with its own museum, botanical garden, and even a nearby zoo.

To reach Suidoyama Park, leave JR Kiryu Station by the north exit, cross the square, and continue straight ahead past Nishi Kiryu Station (Jomo Dentetsu Railway). Turn left at the nursery school. On the railings there is a sign indicating the Okawa Museum of Art. Immediately, a second sign points up a steep, concrete road to the right. This rises above the houses to a water storage plant, where there is a third sign pointing up another concrete road. The pleasant, brick-faced, European-style building at the top is the Suidoyama Memorial Hall. Fragrant olive and flowering dogwood are planted outside. These are the official trees, respectively, of Kiryu and Columbus, Georgia, Kiryu's twin city in America.

The road down to the right on the far side of the parking lot leads to the museum; the path straight up is the direct route to the top of Suidoyama; and the road to the left leads past the start of the hiking course to the parking lot at the top of the mountain. All of these can be reached in just two to four minutes, while the botanical garden lies about five minutes beyond the summit or the museum. All are worth seeing, and the hiking course can be reached from any of them.

Suidoyama Park is a pretty, landscaped hillside park, with a restful lawn and promenade near the top. These command a good view of the city and are popular destinations for Sunday outings. The start of the hiking course can be reached by descending from just behind the war memorial, located at the summit, to rejoin the road directly opposite the entrance to the course.

The Okawa Museum of Art houses a large private collection of twentieth century works of many different schools. It is one of the best places to view some of Japan's most prominent modern artists, including Shunsuke Matsumoto (1912–48) and Hideo Noda (1908–39), for it is the right size to allow visitors to give each painting the time it deserves. There are also works by Western painters, including Chagall, Dali, Ernst, El Greco, Jasper Johns, Matisse, Miro, Modigliani, and Picasso, plus a quiet tearoom and library on the ground floor. Admission is ¥800. The steps directly up from the museum parking lot lead to Mount Suidoyama; the path to the right, to the Azuma Botanical Garden.

Just as the Okawa Museum of Art houses a private collection, the Azuma Botanical Garden used to be a private garden. It was purchased by the city for conversion into a public park in 1951. It has a fine display of about eighty species of flowering bushes and trees, water plants, fruit, and other specimens for all seasons. Although best seen during the tulip and iris festivals of the spring and early summer, the garden is also well worth visiting for its cherry blossoms and azaleas. The plan is centered on two ponds and a thatched teahouse. There are displays of ferns, deciduous and evergreen trees, and the grasses of spring, summer, and autumn. As if to complete the sense of urban well-being, a "philosopher's walk" winds around the edge of the park, with worthy quotations from such thinkers as the early twentieth-century Chinese writer Lu Xun, Goethe, Galileo, and Hugo. This garden is the official start of the Kanto Fureai no Michi walk to the Kiryu Nature Sanctuary. The route leaves from the top, just beyond the ponds, quickly joining the path along the ridge from Suidoyama to Mount Azuma.

If you are not in the mood for climbing a mountain, however, you may wish to take the short walk from the garden to the Kiryugaoka Zoo and Amusement Park. To reach these, leave the garden past the parking area and the large temple of Komyoji. Continue straight, through three consecutive crossroads. The steep road with steps up the center leads to the south gate of the zoo. The zoo site itself is of some archaeological interest, for many stone and clay implements dating from around ten thousand years ago have been unearthed there. At present, however, none are on display. The zoo has bears, lions, elephants, deer, flamingos, penguins, farm animals, monkeys, and also an aquarium. This is quite a large zoo by provincial standards, and the monkeys are always entertaining. The amusement park, just beyond the far gate of the zoo, has a small Ferris wheel and a number of other rides suitable for small children. Admission to the zoo is free; to the amusement park, ¥100.

START OF HIKING COURSE ▶ MOUNT AZUMA
WALKING TIME: 40 MINUTES

The start of the hiking course up Mount Azuma is marked by a number of large signboards. There are two paths. The one to the right leads directly down to the Azuma Botanical Garden; the one to the left up the mountain. A large map shows the entire route from Mount Azuma to Mount Narukami (Hike 1).

Taking the left-hand path at the entrance to the course, you quickly reach the junction with the Kanto Fureai no Michi. A sign points back to Suidoyama Park, right to the Azuma Botanical Garden, and straight on to Mount Azuma (1.4 km). Soon afterward, the path comes out onto a ridge. Stay on top, first along the path, and then over the final stretch of a road. Take the short right fork at the end. A sign points straight up the mountain. Clamber up the rocky path directly in front of you; don't follow the small trail off to the right.

Then just keep on going, ignoring all paths off to either side. At times, the incline is very steep. The trees are quite mixed, with red pines and *kunugi* oaks *(Quercus acutissima)* in addition to the ubiquitous cedars. In just four or five minutes, the trail reaches one of the best vantage points for viewing the city: a large stone outcrop known as Tonbi Iwa (Kite Rock) on account of its resemblance to the bird. The Kanto Fureai no Michi sign indicates that you are now exactly halfway between the botanical garden and the top of Azuma.

A legend associated with this rock illustrates the importance of not violating the purity of a holy mountain. Mount Azuma was once thought to be inhabited by a Tengu, a mythical creature that belongs less to the world of religion than to that of nursery rhyme and fable. Tengus are said to be half-man and half-bird and to live in the treetops in the mountains. They are generally depicted with long noses and beady eyes and are thought able to fly through the air with ease (in fact, they sound suspiciously like flying squirrels). Although a great deal of mischief is placed at their door, in most cases they come across as pure hearted. When a Tengu does get angry, however, he tends to overreact.

It is told that one day early in the Meiji period, four or five young men were climbing Azuma by this very route for the festival. Just as they reached Tonbi Iwa, the sky suddenly turned black, and the Azuma Tengu swooped down in a terrible fury. One of the young men was violently flung from the side of the rock. The others quickly finished their observances and made their way down as fast as possible, but they couldn't find their friend anywhere. His body wasn't discovered for three days, by which time it was covered with insects. The Tengu supposedly wreaked this terrible punishment because the young man's sandals were dirty! They were the sandals he had worn earlier to dig a ditch, hence he was polluting the mountain.

Having checked your own appearance, just in case, continue up the path from the left side of Tonbi Iwa as you face the mountain. The route soon begins to level out and even to descend slightly. There follows another short, steep stint to the ridge at the top. Suddenly, all of Mount Akagi comes into view on the other side, together with most of the other famous peaks of Gunma, including Haruna, Asama, and Tanigawa. On a clear day, it is possible to see as far as Mount Fuji. The summit lies just three minutes along the ridge to the right. Today, there is only a small stone shrine there, but it is clear from the offerings that prayers are still made. A Kanto Fureai no Michi sign indicates 3.5 kilometers to the Kiryu Nature Sanctuary (Shizen Kansatsu no Mori).

There used to be a bell at the top of Azuma, associated with Tozenji, which the men, at least, could ring when they reached here. It is said to have been forged in the 1660s and recast in 1779. Accounts suggest that this recasting was quite an occasion, with the people of Tsutsumi Village, which lies at the foot of the mountain on the Watarase side, taking turns to work the bellows. Climbers continued ringing that bell through to the 1890s, but then it had to be removed after being damaged twice in quick succession by thieves after the copper. The bell was later recast for use at a nearby temple.

At this point, the view of Kiryu is excellent, but that of the mountains on the other side is still somewhat obstructed by trees. I'd therefore suggest walking two or three minutes farther along the ridge because the scenery improves immediately. Then return for the path down to Tozenji and Sozenji. The route on to Narukami is described in Hike 1.

MOUNT AZUMA ▶ TOZENJI AND SOZENJI
WALKING TIME: 1 HOUR

Descend by the narrow path signposted to Kawauchi and Kannondo, directly from the rear of the summit. Although steep in places, this path is much easier than the way up from Suidoyama, winding down peaceful, wooded slopes. Here, for the first time, one has a feeling of leaving urban settlement behind. As if to affirm this sensation, there is a rather gentler legend on this side of the mountain about a mysterious meeting between the Azuma Tengu and a woman of Kawauchi.

The story goes that the woman had an elderly mother who was suffering from poor eyesight. Late one night, as the young woman was on her way to the shrine, a handsome youth suddenly appeared out of nowhere and landed right on top of her. The youth held her to the ground and demanded to know what she was doing there. The Azuma Tengu in disguise, he was no doubt offended to discover a woman on his mountain. In a great fright, she quickly explained about her poor mother's eye condition and that she was on her way to the shrine to make essential prayers for her recovery. The youth immediately repented his rough behavior and promised to cure her mother himself. At once, his body grew lighter, and in a twinkling he had completely disappeared. The woman quickly completed her prayers and hurried back down the mountain. On arriving home, she found to her delight that her mother was already better. Recognizing the work of the Azuma Tengu, the whole family hastened to give thanks.

The red roofs of Tozenji come into sight beyond a large grove of bamboo after a descent of about fifteen minutes. The path emerges by a small shrine. Pass under the tiny shrine gate, and turn left into the compound, containing a temple belonging to the Rinzai sect of Zen and said to have been founded in 1325. The temple has a fine Japanese garden and belfry, and three Jizos stand in the courtyard. This is the deity to whom one prays for the souls of stillborn or aborted children. The main Jizo has a *shakujo,* a pilgrim's staff, in its right hand and a crystal in its left. The two smaller Jizos also have staffs, but are shown cradling children, a modern innovation in the design of Jizo statues. These Jizos are only about a decade old, though there are several much older ones on the temple grounds.

Jizo, like Koshin, is one of the most common wayside figures in Japan. Jizo is the Japanese characterization of Kshitigarbha, the bodhisattva who cares especially for children and sinners during the time between the historical Buddha's entry into Nirvana and the appearance of the Buddha of the future, Miroku (Maitreya in Sanskrit), at the start of the next cosmic cycle. He wanders through all the six realms of existence (those of hell, ghosts, beasts, warring spirits, men and devas), in order to enlighten and save. In Japan, however, Jizo has also come to be regarded as the bodhisattva who protects children beyond the borders of life and death. Thus the Japanese pray to Jizo both for safe births and for the souls of deceased children.

As a bodhisattva of borders, stone Jizos are also often seen by the roadside, where they are placed to protect both the villagers and any travelers who happen to pass by. In the Nara period, Jizo was typically depicted sitting cross-legged and was only distinguishable from other Buddhist figures by the position of his hands. The last four hundred years or so have witnessed a switch to Jizos portrayed as young, often childish monks, generally adorned with red bibs. These are a very familiar sight to all travelers on foot in Japan.

After passing through the temple grounds and turning right out of the gate just beyond the belfry, continue down the concrete road through the graveyard. About thirty meters from the main gateway, there is a long path off to the right through the graves. The simple white stone sheltered by a red roof at the end of the graveyard is one of the designated cultural treasures of Kiryu City. This modest, eighty-seven centimeter tufa pillar is engraved with the incantation *Namu Amida Butsu,* meaning "I take refuge in Amida Buddha."

Amida (in Sanskrit, Amitabha) was a royal prince of India who became a monk and, through intense self-discipline, was able to attain enlightenment. He estab-lished an eternal paradise for the dead far away in the West, having vowed that through his infinite mercy all who called his name would be saved and could join him there. On the basis of this appealing promise, Amida became a populist Buddha, one willing to save all those lacking the education or strength of will to save themselves. Followers of Jodo Buddhism (Jodo means "Pure Land" or "Paradise") hold that the calling of Amida's name is all that is required of anyone to achieve salvation. The basis of this simple faith is the placing of total reliance in Amida rather than struggling to achieve salvation by one's own efforts. This easy route to paradise, so different from the tortuous path to enlightenment of the mountain ascetics like Shodo Shonin, originated in the Mahayana Buddhism of northern India and swept Japan from the early medieval period.

The presence of the pillar at Tozenji suggests that the temple started out as a Jodo temple and only later switched to Zen. The main interest of the stone, however, lies in the date on the lower left-hand side: March 3, 1338. This is just thirteen years after the temple is said to have been founded and the very day after the death in battle of Nitta Yoshisada, one of the warlords who destroyed the Kamakura shogunate and brought about the Kemmu Restoration under the Emperor Godaigo. It was Yoshisada who sacked Kamakura and exterminated the Hojo family in the early 1330s (no relation of the Hojo mentioned on page 28). Past priests of this temple clearly wished to claim close connections with Yoshisada, who came from the neighboring district now known as Nitta-gun. Only the previous year, Yoshisada is purported to have consecrated a statue of Bishamonten, one of the gods of war, at this temple. This statue is preserved today, although it is certainly not as old as tradition holds. It has further been suggested that the hole in the side of the pillar was used for holding Yoshisada's ashes. If so, the stone would have been both an offering and a grave. Of course, there is no telling whether it was actually erected for Yoshisada himself or for another of the many local nobles who died on that day.

Returning to the main path, turn right toward the gate. There is a row of six more Jizos, dressed in the distinctive red bibs. Jizos are often depicted in groups of six because of Jizo's incarnations in the six realms of existence mentioned earlier. Just after the gate, there is an interesting stone on the right with characters meaning "twenty-third night." It is dated 1828.

Koshin was not the only date for all-night vigils; they were held on other fixed dates as well, generally the same day each month. The dates varied by locality, but the twenty-third-night vigil was especially common in this area. For priests, these nights were associated with rituals for specific Buddhist deities, while for ordinary people, they were probably more like social gatherings, as the night of Koshin.

The twenty-third is generally regarded as a night for the god of birth, hence a night for women-only gatherings. While some groups would stay up till dawn, others would just wait, for example, until the moon had risen. Stone markers were put up to commemorate such occasions. Gunma, however, is somewhat of an exception: here the twenty-third is the night for men and the twenty-second for women. There are said to be 615 twenty-third-night stones in Gunma Prefecture.

This particular twenty-third-night stone, however, was not originally placed where it is now, but was moved here later. Since the Meiji era, there has been a strong movement to relocate wayside stones because they obstruct construction and road-widening projects. The stones are gathered and placed out of the way at temples and shrines. Although this is certainly better than destroying them altogether, one cannot help wishing that more effort had been made to keep them at least roughly where they belong.

The road now leads down into the valley. Turn left at the bottom, and take the second right just three or four minutes later. There is a stone pillar on the corner with the characters for Senju Kannon (Thousand-handed Kannon). Taking the right fork after the workshop, one quickly comes to Senjuji. This temple, although also belonging to the Rinzai sect, could hardly be more different from the last. Founded in 1641, it is, in essence, a house with an altar. It appears to have developed as the temple for the graves of a single noble family. The main image of the goddess Kannon is still maintained, however, and the necessary sutras faithfully recited in front of it.

As noted in the introduction, the bodhisattva Kannon (Avalokiteshvara in Sanskrit) was an especially important deity to Shodo Shonin. It was to Kannon that Shodo's mother had prayed at Izuru before his birth. For Shodo, Mount Nantai was Fudarakusan, the paradise of Kannon. An attendant to Amida and literally one who "hears the sounds" of the world, Kannon is often worshiped as the goddess of mercy. As at Senjuji, Kannon is frequently depicted with one thousand hands to represent the great abundance of this mercy. A passage in the *Lotus Sutra* tells that a man thrown into a burning pit need only to think of Kannon in order to be saved; a man struggling in a sea of serpents has but to remember Kannon and he will never sink or drown; a man beset by thunderbolts will not have a single hair on his head hurt; and so on with goblins, ghosts, giants, and wild beasts.

You will be rather lucky to see the Kannon at Senjuji, however, as the image is displayed to the public only twice each year, on August 17 and January 17. Local legend once held that anyone who set eyes on it would be blinded. The priest no longer thinks that way, but the image is still kept from view, except on those special days. There is a photograph of the statue, however, in the main hall. As this is a house, you will have to ask the priest to be allowed in. And as there are thousands of Kannon representations all over Japan, it might be better not to disturb him unless you are truly interested.

The chief reason for visiting this temple is the stone stupa on the left at the entrance, the oldest known Koshin stone in Gunma Prefecture. Built in the shape of a pagoda, it has six Jizos and one Buddha carved around the top. It stands 1.6 meters high and was erected in 1548. Although an almost identical stupa was erected in 1547, at Jusokuji in Tenjin-cho, Kiryu, the inscription on that one does not identify it as a Koshin stone. Even today the priest of Senjuji reads sutras at the special times for Koshin.

Returning to the main road, turn right at the next junction (there is a tiny noodle and doughnut shop on the corner), and right again at the T-junction. Here, the route rejoins the Kanto Fureai no Michi on its way down from the Kiryu Nature Sanctuary. The Kanto Fureai no Michi sign indicates five hundred meters to Sozenji. Immediately on the right, in a grove of bamboo, is another stone stupa in a small red shelter.

This 1.95-meter andesite stupa, the Ogura Tabutsuto, was set up in 1523. Ogura is the old name of this area. This stupa also has seven figures carved around the top. Stupas like this were set up in many places around this time, generally to request favors or to commemorate ancestors. In addition to the stupa that we have just seen and the one at Jusokuji, there is also another pair of very similar Koshin stupas in Omama, dating from 1573. The inscription on the Ogura stupa indicates only that six Jizos are carved around the side, but as with the Koshin stone at Senjuji, there are clearly seven figures. In the case of the Omama examples, however, on which the inscription also reads that there are six Jizos, the literature identifies the seventh figure as Amida.

Although the Ogura stupa is not a Koshin stone, almost all of the stones in front of it are, making an impressive collection. Most are plain, marked only with the characters for Koshin. However, two monkeys are clearly visible on the fourth stone from the steps. The large central stone shows Shomen Kongo, two monkeys, and two hens. There are also a couple more carvings of Shomen Kongo. Here, the god is depicted with either four hands or six. Only the statue at the end of the row does not appear to be a Koshin stone. This is clearly a Jizo. I could not make out the dates on most of the stones, but some of the readable ones were from the Genroku (1688–1704), Meiwa (1764–1771), and Tenmei (1781–1789) periods.

Sozenji lies off to the left a little farther along this road. A long driveway leads up to the gates, and the temple itself is spread out over a pretty 2.3-hectare site, dotted with paths, in an environmentally protected area. The two prides of the temple are a famous wooden statuette of Amida and the fine *itohiba (Cham-aecyparis pisifera*, a kind of cypress tree) in the main courtyard. There are also Japanese red pines, *konara* oaks, and bamboos.

Tradition has it that the temple's origins date back to the very start of the thirteenth century, when a local samurai went to Kyoto and studied under Honen, the founder of the Jodo sect. He stayed there for six years and was given the name Chimyo, meaning Light of Wisdom. When the time came for Chimyo to return to Kawauchi, Honen is said to have presented him with the statue of Amida that stands in the temple today. Chimyo, who is also known as Ogura Shonin, set up his hermitage a short way from here and stayed until his death at the age of seventy-five. Today, this is a Rinzai temple, but it too was for a long time a Jodo temple after developing from the original hermitage.

Entering the main courtyard, you find the cypress tree and a belfry stand on the right and the red pines on the left. To the far left, there is a pyramid of unnamed graves, and beside it a small Koshin hall. As noted in the introduction, there used to be many Koshindo all over Japan, but these days there are relatively few. Inside is an altar with the name of Shomen Kongo Doji, the Blue-faced Diamond Child.

Shomen Kongo, as related in the introduction, is a god who guards against epidemics. Appropriately, this Koshindo is a place to pray for protection from disease and the health of body and mind. One is also invited to pray for safety from fire, another traditional function of the border gods.

The priest says that there used to be about two hundred Koshin stones scattered around the grounds of the temple and a large Koshindo on top of the hill containing a statue of Shomen Kongo. The hall was moved to the courtyard in the Meiji era and remained quite large until about a decade ago, when the small hall replaced it. The statue, by then in terrible condition, was removed. The Koshin stones also have been largely cleared away, but there is a row of stones behind the hall marked with the characters for Koshin or Shomen Kongo.

The statue of Amida is kept in the strong-walled storehouse just behind the main hall. Again, you'll have to ask the priest to show it to you. The 1.3-meter statue is constructed from five pieces of cypress but lacquered to look like gold. Amida is depicted standing on a lotus plant, one hand raised, head held high, but eyes cast down in a profound gesture of mercy. The statue does appear to date from the Kamakura period, and was restored with a prefectural subsidy in 1979.

SOZENJI ▶ KIRYU NATURE SANCTUARY
WALKING TIME: 30 MINUTES

Continuing along the road up the valley for about twenty minutes, you will arrive at the Kiryu Nature Sanctuary (Shizen Kansatsu no Mori), lying at the very head of the valley on a large 16.25-hectare site. This is a genuine nature sanctuary with rich plant life and wildlife, and with no new species artificially introduced. Part of the site is a recovery zone. There are special huts or viewing areas for such diverse species as dragonflies, buzzards, zelkova, black paradise flycatchers, beetles, fireflies, herons, great tits, and river crabs. In summer, the flowers of the snowbell (*Styrax japonica*) are particularly beautiful. The well-appointed nature center has an exhibition hall, lecture room, and small library. There are also special nature events, such as bird-watching, on Sundays and holidays. It would take one or two hours to walk every path in the sanctuary.

The sanctuary is open from 9:00 to 16:30 from March through October and from 9:30 to 16:00 from November through February. It is closed on Tuesdays and on New Year's Day, and the parking lot closes at 17:00 daily.

It takes well over an hour to walk from here back down the valley to Kiryu Station, so you may wish to call a taxi from the sanctuary. Those returning directly to Tokyo should ask to be taken to Aioi Station, which is closer than Kiryu or Shin Kiryu stations.

USEFUL KANJI

AZUMA BOTANICAL GARDEN	吾妻公園
KANNON HALL	観音堂
KANTO FUREAI NO MICHI	関東ふれあいの道
KAWAUCHI	川内
KIRYU NATURE SANCTUARY	桐生自然観察の森
KIRYU STATION	桐生駅
KOMYOJI	光明寺
KOSHIN	庚申
MOUNT AZUMA	吾妻山
OGURA TABUTSUTO	小倉多仏塔
OKAWA MUSEUM OF ART	大川美術館
SENJUJI	千手寺
SOZENJI	崇禅寺
SHOMEN KONGO	青面金剛
SUIDOYAMA PARK	水道山公園
TONBI IWA (KITE ROCK)	トンビ岩
TOZENJI	東禅寺
"TWENTY-THIRD NIGHT"	二十三夜

HIKE 1 ▲ NARUKAMI
ALONG THE MOUNTAIN RIDGE

**KIRYU STATION • MOUNT AZUMA • KANAZAWA PASS • MOUNT NARUKAMI •
ASABE KYOKUMAE BUS STOP OR SHIRATAKI SHRINE (OR KANAZAWA PASS •
KANAZAWA VALLEY • KANNONBASHI BUS STOP)**

TOTAL WALKING TIMES   3 HOURS, 40 MINUTES TO KANNONBASHI BUS STOP; 5
HOURS, 50 MINUTES TO ASABE KYOKUMAE BUS STOP; 6 HOURS, 10 MINUTES TO
SHIRATAKI SHRINE

MAPS   1:25,000 OMAMA; 1:25,000 BANBA; 1:50,000 KIRYU-ASHIKAGA

This hiking course was created by the youth of Kiryu in 1962. It follows a ridge from
peak to peak through quiet but generally invigorating scenery. To the left, there are
the peaks of Akagi and Kesamaru and the valley of Kawauchi; straight ahead,
Narukami; and to the right, Mount Senningatake, on the other side of the Kiryu
River. At the finish are glorious views. From the outcrop at the top of Narukami, you
see all of the great volcanoes of the Kanto area, including Fuji, Asama, Tanigawa,
Nikko Shirane, Nantai, and Tsukuba. The path is well maintained and in excellent
condition all of the way to Narukami.

In many ways, this is a typical local hiking course, though perhaps a little harder
than many. If you prefer to walk it in two stages, the obvious places to break it are
at the junctions for the paths descending to the Kiryu Nature Sanctuary or the
Kanazawa Pass. The Kanazawa Pass is also an ideal point for starting the section of
Hike 2 from Narukami to Zama Pass and Godo.

There is a local tradition that Mount Narukami should be climbed on the first
Sunday in May, so it is always especially crowded on that day. As at Azuma,
however, the trails here are popular and you are almost sure to meet hikers any day
of the year.

Special points of interest on this course include several Koshin stones; a
mountaintop branch of the Mitsumine Shrine, in Chichibu; a shrine to the god of
thunder, with whom Narukami is particularly associated; and at the finish, the
shrine that was according to legend the birthplace of the Kiryu silk industry.

MOUNT AZUMA ▶ KANAZAWA PASS

WALKING TIME: 1 HOUR, 50 MINUTES

Allow one hour from Kiryu Station to the top of Mount Azuma (Short Walk 1). From the summit, continue along the ridge northward, following the sign to Mount Narukami. The view rapidly improves toward Akagi, Kesamaru, and the Yamada Valley, in Kawauchi. You can also see most of the ridge to be hiked, all the way to Narukami. The path soon descends a long flight of earthen steps. Then the path climbs Azuma's twin peak, or rather mate, known as Onna Azuma (Female Azuma), which has a large radio reflector on top. On the way up, there is a spectacular view back toward Tanigawa, Haruna, and the conical peak of Asama.

The path then winds up and down from summit to summit through pretty woods, mainly of cedar but also of *konara* oaks and mountain cherries. Along with the violets and other flowers mentioned earlier, you find some truly lovely lilies: the *katakuri (Erythronium japonicum),* a dark pink, twenty-centimeter flower that blooms in early spring, mainly on south-facing slopes beneath the *konara,* and also the *chigoyuri (Disporum smilacinum).* The route is extremely safe and easy to follow, with the first fifty minutes a part of the Kanto Fureai no Michi.

There are many paths off to the right and left along this stretch of the hiking course, offering quick descents to the valleys on either side. If you are going down early, it is easier to reach a bus stop by descending a path to the right. The following are the times I took to reach these junctions from the summit of Mount Azuma (only signposted paths are listed):

TIME FROM MT. AZUMA	PATH TO LEFT	PATH TO RIGHT
20 minutes	Kawauchi	Miyamoto-cho
38 minutes		Miyamoto-cho
		4-chome
42 minutes		Umeda-cho 1-chome
43 minutes	Shiyagami Kannon	
	Iriguchi	

About one hour from Mount Azuma, the Kanto Fureai no Michi turns off to the left for the Kiryu Nature Sanctuary. The sign here indicates: straight on to Mount Narukami; 1.4 kilometers left to the Kiryu Nature Sanctuary; or 2.1 kilometers back to Mount Azuma. This path to the left is also signposted for Yanagihara and the Ogura Ridge. It takes about fifteen minutes to walk down to the shelters and benches at the very top of the sanctuary.

The main hike, however, continues a further forty minutes gently up and down along the ridge. Okadaira Plateau is reached in twelve minutes, and Mount Joyama twenty minutes later. There is a path down from Okadaira to the remains of Kiryu Castle. It might be worth wandering down; tradition has it that a treasure of one thousand pieces of gold was buried on this mountain when the castle was built!

The final peak of this stretch is Ogata, where a sign indicates 4.5 kilometers and two hours, ten minutes to Narukami. Soon afterward, the path descends steeply, with a clear view of Kesamaru straight ahead. This descent lasts for a good ten minutes, coming out at the Kanazawa Pass. Here, again, there is a choice of descending: to the left into Kawauchi; to the right, this time to Kanazawa; or continuing straight ahead toward Mount Narukami. The path down to Kanazawa is described in the next section. It is best, however, to continue to Mount Narukami, where the views are spectacular.

KANAZAWA PASS ▶ KANAZAWA VALLEY ▶ KANNONBASHI BUS STOP
WALKING TIME: 50 MINUTES

The path down turns into a narrow, concrete road about eight minutes from the pass. This descends steeply through the forest, reaching the first buildings about thirty-five minutes below the pass. The descent then continues through stepped paddies and vegetable fields. As the valley begins to open up, the rows of high, wooded peaks in places achieve an almost Alpine splendor.

This road is known as the Kanazawa Dori (Kanazawa Road). It is the Omote Sando (main road) to the Mitsumine shrine on top of Mount Mitsumine, the first peak after the pass in the direction of Mount Narukami. It is possible that the name Kanazawa (Metal River) derives from this being the place where the bell for the Mitsumine Shrine was made, though some say that it simply indicates that metals were mined here. The main road is reached in about fifty minutes from the pass, at the confluence of the Kanazawa and Kiryu rivers. The small Kanemiya Shrine stands on the left corner.

This shrine is dedicated to Emperor Jimmu, the mythical first emperor of Japan who supposedly reigned from about B.C. 660 to 585, plus two other gods. Built in 1351, the shrine once flourished under the patronage of the Kiryu family of Kiryu Castle, but then declined with their fortunes. Several stones on the bank to the left of the shrine are noteworthy. One is a ball-shaped stupa that comes to a point, dedicated to Benten (Sarasvati in Sanskrit). In Japan, Benten has become one of the many gods of wealth, but she was originally the ruler of water. The pair of tall, natural stones with characters on the face are unusually large Koshin stones, both some 1.6 meters in height. The engravings indicate that they were set up in December 1788. A smaller Koshin stone to the left bears the characters for Shomen Kongo, the god reputed to have introduced the Koshin faith to Japan. There is also a stone engraved with the characters for Dosojin, the gods of the road.

The Kannonbashi bus stop is just the other side of the main road to the left, though the buses back into Kiryu are very infrequent. If you are unlucky, you can either call a taxi from one of the shops or restaurants, or walk thirty minutes down the road to the main bus station at Tenjin-cho.

KANAZAWA PASS ▶ MOUNT NARUKAMI
WALKING TIME: 1 HOUR, 30 MINUTES

The sign at the pass indicates four kilometers and two hours to Mount Narukami. In fact, though, you will probably reach the top of Mount Mitsumine (easy to recognize by its small shrine) in just twenty minutes. There the distance and time to Narukami are given as 2.9 kilometers and one hour. I found one and a half hours sufficient to walk from the pass to the mountain.

The shrine on Mitsumine is thought to have been the first branch of the main Mitsumine Shrine in Chichibu, Saitama Prefecture, to be established elsewhere in the Kanto area. It was founded as recently as 1826, just at the time that the Nemoto pilgrimages were at their height. This Kiryu branch is rather small, just a couple of stone shrines and a statue of the mountain god dressed as a Shinto priest. It used to have a bell, but that was melted down for the war effort in 1943. A popular belief held that one should not walk under the bell for fear of being turned into a giant snake!

73

Like the main Mitsumine Shrine in Chichibu, this branch had active *shugendo* connections. Supposedly there was a small hall in front of the shrine for use on ascetic retreats, but it was lost at some stage in a mountain fire. There also used to be a hall for ascetic practices on the path up from Kanazawa.

On the lower slopes of the Kawauchi side of the mountain, there are statues of thirty-six children. It is unclear whether these are meant as intermediaries of the gods or were erected by local residents to the spirits of real lost children. There is also a Fudo Myoo image (for information on this deity, see page 82). Unfortunately, none of these can be seen from the path along the ridge. There is a route down, of sorts, along a spur to the left, about forty meters beyond the shrine. The statues of the children are scattered in a number of exposed locations, while Fudo stands in a cave. They can be hard to find in the dense undergrowth.

The route on from the Mitsumine Shrine again follows the ridge up and down a number of progressively higher peaks, reaching the foot of the twin peaks of Mount Narukami in a little over an hour from the shrine. There are more *mizunara* and *isubuna* oaks, and maples as the path climbs higher, as well as an almost continuous view of Akagi off to the left. There are even a few early glimpses of Nantai and the mountains of Ashio. At the base of Narukami, a plateau of giant crags has become a popular spot for family outings. Here is another junction with signs indicating: left for Komagata, 2.2 kilometers and 40 minutes; right for the Umeda entrance to the mountain, 2.23 kilometers, 40 minutes; or straight up through the shrine gate to the top of Narukami, 0.125 kilometers, 5 minutes.

The shrine itself is now gone except for a few ruins. There is no record of when it was founded, but we know a bell was installed here in 1753. This was replaced in 1813 with a second bell which remained until 1943, when it too was melted down for the war. Many of the city's textile machines met the same fate later that year.

Narukami, as noted, has two peaks and also straddles the border of Umeda and Kawauchi. Accordingly, the mountain was revered by the people of both villages, to the point that there was an element of rivalry about who should call it their own. There were two gates and two paths to the top. At the festival on May 5, both villages set up their own stages, right next to each other, for their own separate and simultaneous Shinto Kagura dances. The festival was briefly revived by the people on the Umeda side in 1965. Sadly, since all of the performers were old and there were no successors to replace them, the festival again quickly died a natural death.

The old shrine was dedicated to the god of the mountain, but it is also known as the Raiden Shrine. Raiden is the god of thunder and lightning, usually portrayed as a fierce, red-faced demon, with claws on each foot and several drums hanging by ropes from his hands or belt. Curiously, Raiden also has a taste for eating human navels. Japanese children are frequently told to take care that the thunder god doesn't get their tummy buttons.

Since "thunder" is *kaminari* and "god" is *kami* in Japanese, the mountain's name, Narukami (the Roaring God) appears to be a play on words. A further association with thunder is lent by the belief that a Buddhist hermit called Raijin Shonin (Saint Thunder God) once lived here. I have been caught in a thunderstorm on this mountain, and it was an experience that I am in no hurry to repeat.

The two guardian wolves (not foxes) at the foot of the final path up to the top are clearly messengers of the shrine, placed here by the people of Kozawa. This suggests an association with the Mitsumine Shrine, which is famous for its wolf messengers, although there are no such statues at the Mitsumine Shrine in Kiryu.

Besides lightning and wolves (only divine ones), Narukami is also locally known for its many splendid flowers, including the *kokinreiika (Patrinia triloba)*, a small plant with tiny yellow flowers, which grows fifteen to twenty centimeters high on rocks and blooms in August; the *hotsutsuji* azaleas *(Tripetaleia paniculata)*; *kakkoso (Primula kisoana)*, a primrose that blooms in mid-May at altitudes of four to nine hundred meters; and especially, the stunning violets of early May.

Climb past the gate and up a further couple of hundred meters to the ridge. Turning right, the path immediately comes out on the summit, presenting a fabulous view. To the rear, you can see exactly how far you have come from Mount Azuma. On a clear day, the view extends all the way across to Mount Fuji. As you gaze around, the mountains you will see include Asama, Haruna, Akagi, Tanigawa, and Kesamaru in Gunma, and Nikko Shirane and Nantai in Tochigi. Sukai, Koshin, the Asegata Pass, and Mount Hangetsu can all be clearly made out. Off to the right, one can also see the very top of Yokone, while Sankyo and Nemoto dominate the foreground. Far across to the right, there is the distinctive peak of Mount Tsukuba. The view provides a truly fitting climax to the day.

Those who have come all the way from Mount Azuma should descend here. There will be no further opportunities to go down for another three hours, until the Zama Pass, a lot of hard walking away (and then a one-and-a-half hour walk down from there; see Hike 2). The route crosses some pretty remote mountains areas; anyone who gets lost at night is likely to stay lost.

The best route down Narukami is the one on the Umeda side to the Asabe Kyokumae bus stop. Buses into Kiryu are very infrequent, however, so you'll probably have to call a taxi. If you are going that way, return from the summit to the junction by the rest house, and turn left. This is the route up in Hike 2 and very easy to follow. It takes about one and a half hours to get to the bus stop. For reference, however, the two routes down to Komagata are described below.

MOUNT NARUKAMI ▶ SHIRATAKI SHRINE
WALKING TIME: 1 HOUR, 50 MINUTES

The quickest way down to Komagata is the path from the junction at the rest house. This takes about fifty minutes, and plunges steeply along the bed of a stream. At times the path completely disappears, and it is necessary to clamber as best you can down the rocks. The path leaves the stream about forty minutes from the junction, after which the final ten minutes to Komagata run first along a narrow track and then a short, concrete road.

The better route, however (the two paths join at Komagata), is as follows. Return from the peak to the point where you turned right to the summit, but do not descend the path you came up from the shrine gate. Instead, continue straight along the ridge. At first, this path is unmarked, but within twenty meters, a sign points down to the right to the Zama Pass, Mount Sankyo, and Mount Nemoto. Some eighteen minutes later, at the bottom of the slope, the path arrives at the last junction on this route for the next three hours until the Zama Pass. This is part of the Hike 2 route. The sign to the right is for an alternative route to Umeda, and the one to the left for Komagata.

Follow the sign to Komagata down a steep gully. This opens up into a rough track in about twenty-five minutes. Another fifteen minutes' walk brings you out to a rest house, with a water wheel and trout fishing ponds. The rest house sells noodles, tempura, and beer and is altogether a very relaxing spot — but there is a table charge. The rest house is open from ten in the morning to six at night. It is fifteen minutes from there to Komagata.

Most maps of the hiking course show a bus route to Kiryu Station from Doba, twenty minutes below Komagata, but this stretch has been discontinued, so you will have to call a taxi. Alternatively, you may prefer to walk a further fifty minutes down the pretty valley of the Yamada River to Shirataki Shrine and call a taxi from there. The entrance to the shrine lies off the road to the left, under a large metal gate.

The shrine has some fine trees in the courtyard, but it is not especially interesting architecturally. What it does feature is a living tradition of Shinto Kagura, a performing art of sacred music and dance. This is an officially designated Intangible Folk Treasure of Kiryu City, with annual public performance in early August, coinciding with the Kiryu festival. The origins of the Shirataki Kagura are unclear, but most of the masks date from the Edo period. The performances were briefly discontinued after the war for lack of participants but were happily revived in 1962. This folk treasure is now supported by a society of enthusiasts.

Shirataki is the shrine, as mentioned in the introduction, where legend has it the Kiryu textile industry began. There are several versions of this story, but the one that I like best is said to date from the reign of the Emperor Junnin (758–64 A.D.). Just at that time, the young Shodo Shonin was practicing at Mount Yokone and studying Buddhism in Yakushiji. Another places the story in 782, the year that Shodo finally conquered Nantai. This, however, is a tale of courtly, not religious love between a lowly retainer called Yamada (also the old name of this area) and a princess named Shirataki (White Falls). It is recounted that they first expressed their passion for each other in the form of *waka* poems. This was his despairing plea:

Though the June rice yearns for dew,

Heaven releases not its White Fall threads.

To which the young lady replied:

The White Falls will finally descend from heaven,

Your love is so strong, man of Yamada.

Accordingly, for this tale of courtly love is most unusual in that it has a happy ending, it was decided by the emperor himself that the young couple should be wed. Yamada gave up his job as a retainer, and the couple came here to dwell at Yamada's old home in Kawauchi. Princess Shirataki was already an accomplished weaver, thanks to her education in the palace. Soon she had also taught the craft to people all around. The Shirataki Shrine thus still receives strong support from the grateful Kiryu textile industry.

USEFUL KANJI

ASABE KYOKUMAE	浅部局前
BANBA	番場
DOBA	堂場
DOSOJIN	道祖神
KANAZAWA PASS	金沢峠
KANEMIYA SHRINE	兼宮神社
KANNONBASHI	観音橋
KAWAUCHI	川内
KIRYU NATURE SANCTUARY	桐生自然観察の森
KIRYU STATION	桐生駅
KOMAGATA	駒形
KOSHIN	庚申
MIYAMOTO-CHO	宮本町
MIYAMOTO-CHO 4-CHOME	宮本町四丁目
MOUNT AZUMA	吾妻山
MOUNT JOYAMA	城山
MOUNT MITSUMINE	三峰山
MOUNT NARUKAMI	鳴神山
MOUNT NEMOTO	根本山
MOUNT OGATA	大杉山
MOUNT SANKYO	三境山
OGURA RIDGE	小倉尾根
OKADAIRA	岡平
OMAMA	大間々
RAIDEN SHRINE	雷電神社
SHIRATAKI SHRINE	白瀧神社
SHIYAGAMI KANNON ENTRANCE	釋迦彌観音入口
SHOMEN KONGO	青面金剛
TENJIN-CHO	天神町
UMEDA-CHO 1-CHOME	梅田一丁目
YANAGIHARA	柳原
ZAMA PASS	座間峠

ACROSS THE ZAMA PASS

ASABE KYOKUMAE BUS STOP • MOUNT NARUKAMI • ZAMA PASS • KUSAGI DAM • GODO STATION (OR ZAMA PASS • ASABE KYOKUMAE BUS STOP)

TOTAL WALKING TIMES   6 HOURS, 15 MINUTES TO GODO STATION; 7 HOURS, 10 MINUTES RETURNING TO ASABE KYOKUMAE

MAPS   1:25,000 BANBA; 1:25,000 OMAMA; 1:25,000 KOZUKE HANAWA; 1:25,000 SORI; 1:50,000 KIRYU-ASHIKAGA; 1:50,000 ASHIO

This is a delightful route for getting away from it all. The path rises high up on the ridge, crossing mountains seldom visited by other hikers and offering superb views across to Nemoto, Nantai, and Kesamaru. It is, even so, an official hiking course, so the trail is relatively easy to follow. The course is at its most attractive in late May and early June, when the azaleas are in bloom. There are bears here, so some precautions ought to be taken, but one is far more likely to meet deer. The trees are mainly cedar, but close to the pass these merge increasingly into oaks. Finally, the route crosses a major watershed at the Zama Pass to descend into the valley of the Watarase River just above Godo Station. From there you have the choice of taking the train down the Watarase Gorge, walking up the valley via the Kanto Fureai no Michi to Sori Station and the start of Hike 8 up Kesamaru, or starting straight out on Hike 7 to Hanawa.

Other attractions include the Otaki waterfall, with its statue of Fudo Myoo, one of the gods most beloved by the mountain ascetics, and the huge straw sandals hanging by the Zama Pass, traditionally believed to protect the village at its foot. At the finish, there is a hall and exhibition dedicated to the author of many of Japan's most famous nursery rhymes.

Narukami, the first peak of the course, is one of the true highlights of this region. (The views from the top have already been described in Hike 1.) A fascinating travelogue dating from 1775 tells us what this ascent from Otaki was like back in the late eighteenth century. Its author was Takayama Hikokuro (1747 — 93), an extraordinary man who left records of journeys all over Japan. Hikokuro was born at Hosoya, in nearby Ota City. The son of a samurai, Hikokuro is best remembered as a fanatical emperor-worshiper. In fact, he was so notorious that he was dubbed one of the Three Eccentrics of the Kansei era (1798 — 1801). His more bizarre behavior included whipping the grave of Ashikaga Takauji, who betrayed the Emperor Godaigo, and repeated prostration at Sanjo bridge in front of the imperial palace in Kyoto. The shogunate naturally regarded him as a dangerous subversive; eventually he was hounded to the point of suicide in 1793.

It comes as something of a surprise, therefore, to find his description of the ascent of Narukami a model of good sense and precision. Hikokuro visited the mountain on August 10, 1775. In his account, he refers to the falls both as Otaki (Great Falls) and Fudo no Taki (Fudo Falls), and mentions a Fudo Hall. The details of the Fudo cult are explained on page 82. First, though, part of Hikokuro's record is of sufficient interest to be quoted here:

"From here, I went south down the [Kozawa] valley and came to Otaki on the right. A stone indicated twenty-one *cho* [1 *cho* = 119 yards] to the mountain. I rested at a private home. This was Kozawa. Then I rested and left my lunch at a teahouse. Ascending the small stream another two *cho,* I came to the Fudo no Taki, the rock rising like a wall and the fall very fine. There was a Fudo Hall close by. Climbing then three or four *cho* to the northwest, there was a place to wash my hands in a clear small stream. After drinking the water, I continued up the mountain. It was about mid-day when I reached the top.

"The two peaks lined up side by side, Kiryu peak to the south and Mount Nita to the north [the twin peaks of Narukami]. On a stone tablet the two peaks were together named Mount Raijin. Everything was visible in all four directions. From here, it was just a two *cho* walk to the rocky summit. There was a limit for female worshipers half way up and a bell at the top with an inscription. This had been consecrated by a man named Kosone of Kozawa and bore the mark of the Koenji Temple, whose priest is an ascetic named Kozawain. Everybody strikes the bell. There was a shrine just above, only two *ken* [1 *ken* = 6 feet] to the southeast. That was the highest point.

"To the south, I could see Kiryu New Town [Shinmachi]. Mount Akagi lay to the northwest. Tatebayashi lay to the southeast. It is said that Maebashi can clearly be seen to the west on a clear day. Today, though, the thunder had begun to echo from around the time that I reached the shrine gate. There were clouds in all four directions, so I could only view the scenery in parts. It is said that Tatebayashi Castle and other sights can be seen faintly in the distance. Azami Marsh lay to the southwest.

"I am told that this mountain is named Narukami after a priest, Raijin Shonin, who once dwelt here. It is even said that his inkstone and hand-washing stone lie to the northwest of this peak. This is surely a false theory. The name appears to predate the saint . . . Isn't it probable that they later simply added the name of the famous priest? It is said that the shrine is consecrated to the mountain god.

"Mount Nita stands only two *cho* to the northwest from here. From below, this mountain looks like a single peak but close up there are two, Kiryu Peak and Mount Nita, and it is truly no wonder that people visit this place as sacred ground.

"Returning down, I opened the door of the hall for offerings beside the shrine gate and sat down to rest. I am told that one or two teahouses are set up there in the spring. The gate on the Mount Nita side bears the name Sunaga, who is said to be the lord of Mount Nita. Kozawa is written on the gate on the Kiryu side. On the way down, I met with a thunderstorm and sheltered in a grove of cedars waiting for the rain to stop. Crossing a small peak, I dropped in at the house of Gonpachi and opened up my food. It grew dark."

ASABE KYOKUMAE BUS STOP (UMEDA) ▶ KISHINA
WALKING TIME: 45 MINUTES

There is infrequent municipal bus service to Asabe Kyokumae bus stop. For information, please call the Kiryu City Hall Commerce and Tourism Department (Shogyo Kankokei) at 0277-46-1111 (ext 563). Otherwise, it's only about twenty minutes by taxi from Kiryu Station (thirty minutes from Shin Kiryu Station). If you take a taxi, it would be best to ride all of the way to Kishina and start the walk directly from Otaki.

If you do take the bus to Asabe Kyokumae, after getting off you'll have to return a few paces across the bridge and turn right into the broad two-lane road up the tributary valley. There is a map of the Kiryu hiking courses a short way up on the right, with your present position shown by a red circle. The road narrows sharply about twenty minutes from the bus stop and from here on there are many pleasant places to stop along the river. The gateway to the Otaki waterfall stands about forty-five minutes from the bus stop.

KISHINA ▶ OTAKI WATERFALL ▶ MOUNT NARUKAMI
WALKING TIME: 1 HOUR, 15 MINUTES

Enter the road to the left under the stone gateway. There is another map of the hiking course, with signs indicating a rather optimistic one hour to Mount Narukami and a conversely pessimistic fifty minutes back to the Umeda bus stop.

From here, as Hikokuro informs us, it is a mere two *cho* up the stream to the waterfall. Follow the path through the bamboo up the right bank of the stream. Take the lower (right-hand) path at the fork five minutes later, staying with the stream. The waterfall is just three minutes from there. It is indeed a fine falls. There is no Fudo Hall there now, but Fudo has not been forgotten. First, there is the small stone shrine on the rocks just in front of the pool. Then, just to the right of the falls, beside a second stone shrine, there is an unusually gentle-looking statue of Fudo Myoo himself, dated 1709. Of course, this must have been here when Hikokuro visited the mountain.

Fudo Myoo is always easy to recognize by the sword and rope in his hands and the flames that leap from his hair. Like Kannon and Jizo, Fudo has long been immensely popular in Japan and was especially so with the ascetics on the *shugendo*. It is thought that the Fudo faith was introduced to Japan by Kukai.

Fudo is especially associated with the ascetic discipline of ablution in cold water, particularly beneath waterfalls. One result of this is that the vast majority of falls in Japan that are not called Otaki (Great Falls) are known as Fudo no Taki (Fudo Falls). Here we have an ex-Fudo no Taki, also Otaki, that still has a statue of Fudo. The reason for this association, I read in one source, is that the crashing of the water resembles the fierce sound of Fudo's incantations. The more probable explanation, however, is that Fudo, literally the immovable (Achala in Sanskrit), is revered as the ferocious defender of the faith; hence, he is just the kind of ally one wants while standing under an icy waterfall.

More specifically, Fudo is one of five Myoo, the lords of wisdom and light. Four of the Myoo guard the directions north, south, east, and west, while Fudo holds the center. All of the Myoo are emanations of the supreme Buddha, Dainichi (Vairochana). Fudo is said to be the terrible aspect Dainichi presents when confronted by wrongdoing. Many believe that Fudo and the other Myoo go further back, and have their origins in Shiva, the Hindu god of destruction. The flames are not just representative of fearsome wrath but also of boundless intellectual energy. These flames burn out distress and handicaps and force all devils into submission. Fudo protects the faithful against disease, poison, fire, temptations, and the violence of enemies. He thus represents the kind of intense activity and energy so distinctive of the mountain priests and esoteric Buddhism in general.

Such qualities and resolve must, of course, have seemed especially dear to the ascetics as they pushed their bodies to the limits of human endurance. At Izuru (Short Walk 2), for example, the ascetics had to practice for twenty-one days under the Waterfall of Sorrow before setting out for Nikko. Where waterfalls were not available, buckets would do, as at the Fudo Reisen at Chuzenji, which was also a base for the mountain priests. The center of the Fudo cult in Japan is Shinshoji in Narita.

One other interesting point should be noted about Fudo, and that is his extreme masculinity. This contrasts with the typically feminine portrayal of Kannon, who was originally the male bodhisattva Avelokitashvara, and the obvious childishness of Jizo, who started out as the adult bodhisattva Kshitigarbha. There is strong reason to suppose that the popular Japanese imagination has turned these three into a trinity of mother, father, and child.

Fudo will be a prominent presence in almost all of the remaining walks in this book. Turning our back on him for the moment, however, and resuming the climb, again there are signs: the one to the left points to Otaki, all of ten meters away, the one straight on indicates 1.8 kilometers and fifty-five minutes to Mount Narukami.

The path briefly climbs quite steeply. The first path to the left above the falls is a dead end, so take the next one around, following the red ribbons on the trees. There are also many small wooden signs with arrows pointing out the trail. The path quickly returns to the stream above the falls, then once again follows the river. At times the path is steep, but extremely easy to see. Some thirty-five minutes from the falls is a sign indicating half a kilometer and fifteen minutes on to Narukami and 1.2 kilometers and thirty minutes back to Otaki. The way up from here is very rocky, but there are some beautiful crags towering out from among the trees. It took me another twenty minutes to reach the rest house, which is five minutes below the summit (at the junction of the path for Kawauchi).

The path to the summit then leads up through the stone gateway on the right, as described in Hike 1. The views are superb, commanding a sweep not only toward Tatebayashi, Maebashi, and Akagi, but also toward Nantai and the other peaks of Nikko. Whereas Hikokuro appears to have cast his eyes toward the plain, Shodo Shonin had faced toward the mountains from his hermitage in Izuru. The view of Nantai is no less impressive from Narukami in Kiryu.

MOUNT NARUKAMI ▶ ZAMA PASS
WALKING TIME: 3 HOURS

Those with the time to continue to Zama now enter an extremely attractive stretch along the ridge. As before, the path meanders up and down from one summit to the next, with glorious views to both sides.

First, follow the ridge back from the top of Mount Narukami without turning down the trail from the stone gate. There is no signpost at the junction. Just twenty meters afterward, a sign points down to the right to the Zama Pass, Mount Sankyo, and Mount Nemoto. Heading off to Zama in the direction indicated, after fifteen minutes we reach, at the bottom of the slope, the final junction of trails until the Zama Pass. The path to the left for Komagata is the better way down described at the end of Hike 1. The one to the right descends into Umeda. For the Zama Pass, however, climb the path up the steep slope straight ahead. You will have to cross the narrow, rocky ridge at the top. But again the rewards are immediate, with some fine views from the 978-meter summit. The route here is heading directly for Nikko Shirane and Mount Nantai.

There are frequent signs to the Zama Pass all along the trail, which follows the boundaries of both Kiryu City and the Nemoto-Narukami Park. The next summit is reached in about twenty minutes. A further thirty minutes bring us to a major peak, with a sign that reads one and a half hours back to Mount Narukami and one hour, fifty minutes to the Zama Pass. This is the 1,059-meter mountain at the head of the Nabe Stream.

Here, the trail to the Zama Pass bends around to the right. About fifteen minutes later, along the ridge, a superb, full view opens up down to the left of Lake Kusagi, the Kusagi Dam, and Mount Nantai. The Kusagi Dam was completed only in 1976, but the lake is now an important reservoir for Tokyo. Actually, it is a multipurpose dam. Its other functions include flood control, power generation, water storage for agriculture, and even, according to the promotional literature, a destination for sightseers. There are rowing boats on the lake in summer. The dam was built at the cost, however, of the two hundred twenty-two households of the former village of Kusagi and also the old Kusagi Station. A new 5.25-kilometer tunnel had to be built to reconnect the railway between Godo and Sori stations. The dam has also become well known as a suicide spot. Word has it that it is haunted by the spirits of those who have succeeded!

While the Watarase Valley now looks very close, there are still another couple of summits to climb before it is possible to go down. There is no path either to the forestry road far below on the right or to the paved road far below to the left. Instead, there is soon another tricky ridge, topped by jagged outcrops which have to be crossed. Stay on top. The final peak is reached about fifty minutes from the first sight of Lake Kusagi. A sign there indicates another thirty minutes to the Zama Pass. Actually it is downhill all the way and much more like twenty minutes. The sign at the pass reads four hours back to Mount Narukami, straight on to Mount Sankyo, three hours right to the Asabe Kyokumae bus stop in Umeda, and one and a half hours left to Godo Station.

The route to Mount Sankyo is hard to follow and takes about three hours. The paths to Godo Station and back down the Kozawa River to the Asabe Kyokumae bus stop in Umeda are outlined in the next two sections.

ZAMA PASS ▶ KUSAGI DAM ▶ GODO STATION
WALKING TIME: 1 HOUR, 15 MINUTES

The Zama Pass lies on the watershed between the two major valleys of the Kiryu and the Watarase rivers. If you are walking here in mid-summer, there may be huge straw sandals hung by the side of the path. The custom of hanging giant sandals at the borders of villages was once common throughout Japan, but Zama Village must be one of very few places where it is still practiced today. In fact, sandals are hung at six gateways into the village, at the borders with Godo, Kusagi, Matsushima, Yamaki, Kozawa, and the path in from Narukami. It is said that there was a outbreak of dysentery after the custom was briefly discontinued around 1980, so the villagers quickly started hanging the sandals up again.

There are various theories about the origin of this custom. Some say that the villagers put out huge sandals to indicate that giants live there and thus to scare away the gods of disease. Others see the sandals as an offering to a god who has walked a long way and is no doubt in need of a replacement. This traveling god is sometimes known as Sae no Kami, the god of borders. The villagers take turns making the sandals, of either wheat or rice straw, on June 8 each year.

The path from the pass toward the station drops continuously and sometimes steeply. Fifteen minutes along the trail are more beautiful views of Lake Kusagi and Nantai. About ten minutes later, the path enters and then follows down the side of a stream. A narrow concrete road is reached in roughly ten minutes, and another ten minutes bring us out to a road just below Kusagi Dam. There are hiking course signs on the corner.

Turn right onto this road and left at the T-junction soon afterward. After so much traditional culture, there is now a historical attraction in a very different vein. As the path finally comes out to the road, after all of these deserted, virginal mountains, it is impossible not to notice a decidedly odd-looking building, with red pyramids on the roof, a landscaped garden, and a bright-green parking lot. This is a community hall called the Dowakan, or Nursery Rhyme Hall; its eccentric appearance is thus entirely appropriate. It really is a kind of high tech gingerbread house. Azuma Village was the home of Ishihara Wasaburo (1865 — 1922), who wrote the lyrics of many of Japan's most famous children's songs.

Wasaburo was born near here in a house on the Akagane Kaido (Copper Road) when the road was still busy. He graduated from the school that later became the Education Faculty of Gunma University, and was appointed headmaster of his old school, Hanawa Elementary, at the very young age of twenty-six. There was still no school building at that time, so at first he had to teach the children in a nearby temple. When the school was finally built, Wasaburo donated an organ for the children, a truly remarkable gift in those years, particularly in such a remote area.

His most famous lyrics were those for "The Hare and the Tortoise" *(Usagi to Kame),* which, of course, is the story from Aesop. That was written in 1900. His other well-known pieces included *Kintaro, Urashimataro, Hanasakajiji,* and *Daikokusama* (the Daikokuten described on page 193).

The hall has a small tearoom, an auditorium with a stage, and a souvenir shop that sells mainly charming, old-fashioned children's toys. One item of interest there for the foreign visitor, however, is an inspiring English-language biography of a local artist Hoshino Tomihiro, who wields his brush in his teeth because his arms are paralyzed. A gallery of his works has been opened on the far side of Lake Kusagi, half way between Godo and Sori stations, and is well worth a visit.

There is also an exhibition of items connected with Wasaburo and his songs (admission ¥100). I found the words on the ticket rather intriguing: "Long, long ago, the mountains, the rabbits and the gods were all wonderful friends." Displays include old editions of Wasaburo's works, a shadow puppet play on a large screen, in the style of the old wandering storytellers, and a series of music boxes, which the children turn themselves in order to hear their favorite songs.

It all adds up to an admirable attempt to give small children the chance to enjoy some of the simple pleasures of a more traditional childhood. As the hall also stages some quite highbrow cultural events, it is always a good idea to inquire about its schedule. Generally, the hall is open from 9:00 to 17:00 and is closed on Mondays and the days after national holidays. It is open every day during the summer holidays (Tel: 0277-97-3008).

To reach the station, continue past the sports facilities of the Azuma Athletic Park (Azuma Sogo Undo Koen). This is the official start of the Kanto Fureai no Michi courses around Lake Kusagi to Sori Station, and through Sayado to Hanawa (see Hike 7). A map of these courses is displayed beside the baseball field. There are also basketball, tennis, volleyball, and badminton courts, plus a training room, outdoor pool, and even a hall for practicing Japanese archery *(kyudo).* The prices for using these facilities are all very reasonable. The park, too, is open every day in the summer, but closed on Monday during the rest of the year (Tel: 0277-97-3138).

The Kanto Fureai no Michi branches off to the left a couple of hundred meters beyond the baseball ground, but keep going down. There is a new Jizo on the corner, cradling a child, just like the ones at Tozenji (Short Walk 1). This is known as the Child-rearing Jizo *(Kosodate Jizo)*, to whom one can pray for babies and safe births. It takes about fifteen minutes more to reach the bridge across the Watarase River. On the far side of the bridge on the right, there is a path through a tunnel, leading to a promenade over a short river gorge that goes up to the base of the dam. The views, however, do not especially improve on those from the bridge itself.

The station is about twelve minutes straight down the main road from the bridge. It can be seen from the road bridge over the railway line. This is Godo Station, on the Watarase Keikoku Tetsudo. The train from here follows the gorges and valleys of the Watarase River to the beginning of the Kanto Plain at Omama. When going down the line to Kiryu Station, you will find that the views are best from the left side of the train. The fare to Kiryu is ￥640, and the journey takes about fifty minutes. Trains run roughly once every hour, with the last train leaving at 20:45. Pay on the train.

ZAMA PASS ▶ ASABE KYOKUMAE BUS STOP
WALKING TIME: 2 HOURS, 10 MINUTES

The path to the right from the pass (straight on if you are climbing up from Godo) starts off gently down the head of the valley and then joins the course of a stream. The footing is a little rough at times, but the scenery down to the road is always peaceful and attractive, with some striking crags and caves on the tree-lined slopes. There are countless idyllic spots for a hard-earned rest. After about fifteen minutes, the path suddenly rises high above the valley bottom to cross over the ridge to the stream in the neighboring gully. The route then winds in and out of this stream several times, arriving in ten minutes at a couple of log bridges and at another one approximately five minutes later. The junction with the stony, forest road is only a minute beyond the third bridge. At that junction, a sign indicates that it is two hours to the bus stop and one to the Zama Pass.

Cross the bridge and turn left down the road. This follows down the densely wooded, steep-sided valley of the Kozawa River. In seventeen minutes, there is a road barrier and a parking lot; six minutes later the road becomes properly surfaced; and another four or five minutes bring us within sight of a small group of farmhouses. This is the pretty, isolated hamlet of Nabeashi, where a handful of farmers grow vegetables and tea.

The road then leaves habitation behind once again to pass through more forest and groves of bamboo. At one point, there is a collection of wayside stones, mainly Koshin, on the left-hand side of the road. One has a fine carving of Shomen Kongo, displaying his distinctive six hands, a couple of hens, and a monkey. Soon after, just twenty minutes from Nabeashi, the road reaches Kishina, the turning for the Otaki waterfall. The sign indicates another fifty minutes to the Umeda bridge, where the Asabe Kyokumae bus stop is located. Simply follow the road back down.

USEFUL KANJI

ASABE KYOKUMAE	浅部局前
ASHIO	足尾
AZUMA ATHLETIC PARK	総合運動公園
DOWAKAN (NURSERY RHYME HALL)	童話館
GODO STATION	神戸駅
KANTO FUREAI NO MICHI	関東ふれあいの道
KISHINA	木品
KOMAGATA	駒形
MOUNT NARUKAMI	鳴神山
MOUNT NEMOTO	根本山
MOUNT SANKYO	三境山
OTAKI WATERFALL	大滝
SORI	沢入
UMEDA	梅田
UMEDA BRIDGE	梅田橋
UMEDA 1-CHOME	梅田一丁目
ZAMA PASS	座間峠

HIKE 3 ▲ NEMOTO
A MOUNTAIN FOR GAMBLERS

ISHIGAMO • NEMOTO SHRINE • MOUNT NEMOTO • MOUNT JUNI • MOUNT
HIMURO • KAMI KASUO SHAKO BUS STOP (OR MOUNT JUNI • MOUNT
KUMATAKA • ISHIGAMO)

TOTAL WALKING TIME   6 HOURS, 55 MINUTES; 4 HOURS, 55 MINUTES FOR
CIRCUIT, RETURNING TO ISHIGAMO

MAPS   1:25,000 SORI; 1:25,000 ASHIO; 1:25,000 KOBUGAHARA; 1:25,000 NAKA
KASUO; 1:50,000 ASHIO; 1:50,000 KANUMA

This course first ascends Nemoto, a sacred mountain that once attracted pilgrims
on a route which stretched for 120 kilometers, all the way from Nihonbashi in Edo,
present-day Tokyo. During the Edo period, pilgrims to this mountain ranged in
social class from members of the imperial household to commoners. The shrine
was managed by Daishoinji (precursor of the present Nemoto Shrine in Umeda
1-chome), which used to stand where the Umeda Dam is today. Sadly, many
records were lost in a fire that swept that temple in March 1845. There is, however,
a fascinating pictorial guidebook from the year 1859 that describes all of the
teahouses and inns on the entire route from Nihonbashi to Nemoto. Titled
Nemotoyama Sankeiro Hitori Annai (The Lone Pilgrim's Guide to the Road to
Nemoto), a copy is preserved at the Nemoto Shrine in Umeda 1-chome.

Nemoto's reputation as a sacred mountain is assured by legendary links with
such names as Kukai and even En no Gyoja (see page 10). En no Gyoja is credited
with having named the mountain after espying auspicious clouds here while
gazing to the northeast from Mount Fuji. According to that legend, Nemoto means
"the root of the cloud." Kukai is later said to have climbed the mountain at the time
of his visits to Nikko and Izuru. There is no supporting evidence for either story.

The precise origins of the shrine are unclear, although there is a suggestion that
the Kiryu family may have worshiped the mountain god here from as early as the
Kamakura period, as a means to protect their northern frontier. There is a mainly
Buddhist tradition that northern frontiers, especially, must be defended against the

entry of disaster. The shrine is still dedicated to the mountain god. We also know that Daishoinji was founded as a Tendai temple in April 1573, immediately after the fall of Kiryu Castle (see page 28). Tradition has it that the remaining nobles of the Kiryu army retreated there and became mountain ascetics. Daishoinji was thus likely founded as a kind of front for these aristocratic refugees. The mountain became a sacred place for Yakushi, the Healing Buddha, and the shrine was then either developed or established as the Oku no In (remote annex) of the temple. Mount Nemoto was to flourish for many years as a base for *shugendo* priests.

The pilgrimages from Edo and elsewhere appear to have begun in the early nineteenth century. These so-called Nemoto Ko were especially associated with the Ii family of Hikone in Kansai, one of the most powerful clans in Japan. The Ii had given important support to Tokugawa Ieyasu in the wars of the sixteenth century and been richly rewarded with territory in Kanto as well as in Kansai. The Ii were to become one of the pillars of the Tokugawa shogunate. During the last one hundred years, almost until the Meiji Restoration, the Ii house generally held the position of Great Councillor (Tairo), equivalent to a prime ministership in the councils of state.

As it happened, the Ii family's territory in Kanto included Sano in Tochigi Prefecture, which lies in the eastern foothills of Nemoto. The mountain itself, moreover, stands almost due north of the capital, at the northern edge of the Kanto Plain. As noted, northern boundaries were considered especially vulnerable. That was one of the chief reasons why Toshogu was built at Nikko, and by the same logic, Nemoto too was an ideal location for guarding Edo. There is thus no mystery about why this remote mountain briefly attracted pilgrims from so far away: it was thought to be protecting the capital from fire and disease. There was, of course, also a route up from the Sano and Kuzu side of the mountain. This led first to Kumataka and then along the ridge from Juni to Nemoto. The path still exists, but the way up from Kiryu became more popular.

There is an interesting legend about the Ii and the Black Tengu of Nemoto. According to the famous artist Watanabe Kazan, who visited Kiryu in 1831, the Black Tengu of Nemoto came to the rescue of the Hikone house in Kojimachi, Edo, when it was threatened by fire. While all the samurai of the Ii household were working feverishly to put out the conflagration, a strange warrior flitted about like a bird between east and west, helping to extinguish the flames. When they later asked his name, he told them that he was the Black Warrior of Nemoto and immediately disappeared. Accordingly, in 1830, the Ii family are said to have erected a stone shrine on the mountain for the protection of the nation.

Nemoto is still associated with the Black Tengu. Interestingly, Mount Zanma, a peak between the Zama Pass and Sankyo, is said by local residents to be the home of the Red Tengu. There is also a tradition of five Tengus, each of a different color, occupying mountains along the border of Gunma and Tochigi. According to this tradition, the Black Tengu lives on Nemoto; the Red Tengu, on Himuro; the White Tengu, in Tanuma; the Yellow Tengu, on Mount Ode, in Awano; and the Blue Tengu, at Sori, in Azuma.

A legend has also been passed down in Kiryu related to that very same night when the Ii house in Edo was threatened by fire. A sake seller in Umeda is said to have been awakened by the sound of knocking. When he opened the door, a warrior pressed a bottle into his hands and asked him to fill it with three *sho* of sake (1 *sho* = 1.8 liters). The man could only laugh, for the bottle was big enough for only one. The warrior impatiently insisted, however. True enough, the three *sho* of sake did all fit in! When asked his name, the visitor answered that he was the Black Warrior, on his way to fight a fire in Edo.

The last of the Ii family to hold power in Edo was Ii Naosuke (1815 — 60), one of the two lords who in 1853 and 1854 had urged that Japan capitulate to Commodore Perry and end its long period of seclusion. Naosuke became the virtual dictator of Japan from 1858 to 1860, signing the Harris Treaty in 1858. He had not referred his decision to the emperor, and he dismissed, arrested, or executed many opponents of the new open policies in the famous Ansei Purge. Those placed under house arrest included members of the Mito and Satsuma families. The pilgrimages to Mount Nemoto ended with Ii's assassination outside the imperial palace in Edo in 1860. That came at a particularly unlucky time for the shrine, as a plan had just been approved for a major reconstruction. Not only was this rescinded, but the priest then died soon afterward. The temple-shrine was to enter the turbulent period of the Meiji Restoration in the charge of a little boy.

In addition to its religious and samurai connections, one other aspect of the history of Nemoto should certainly be noted: its notoriety as a place for gambling. Local people say that the mountain became popular among gamblers because it lay on the borders of the territories of different warlords. Hence, Nemoto was outside any specific domain, and gamblers who climbed the mountain entered a kind of no-man's land, beyond the reach of the law.

There are now two main paths to the top from the Kiryu side: one up the valley via the shrine, and another which bypasses the shrine and instead follows the ridge directly to the summit. The shrine route is longer and perhaps even a little bit dangerous, with one stretch of ten chains in a row. It is, however, also much the more rewarding route to follow. The trail ascends through beautiful woods of oak and maples, including the tall *oniitaya (A. mono),* the medium-sized *iroha momiji (A. palmatum),* and the short *chidorinoki (A. carpinifolium).* Other trees include *sawagurumi* walnuts *(Pterocarya rhoifolia)* and *shioji (Fraxinus spaethiana),* a kind of ash. The straight-trunked *shioji,* upwards of twenty meters tall, appear about twenty minutes up from the entrance to the stream route and continue to an altitude of around eight hundred meters. In addition, just close to the summit, Nemoto has original *tsuga (Tsuga sieboldii)* and a few surviving woods of *buna* oaks *(Fagus crenata).* The *tsuga* trees are reddish pines, growing to a height of twenty to twenty-five meters, quite unique to Japan. They are thought to be a survivor from the warmer, more humid Tertiary Cenozoic period.

The route then continues on to Mount Juni, where it divides. The right fork heads for the fine lookout point at Mount Kumataka. This path then goes back away from the pilgrimage route up from Kuzu to return to Ishigamo. The left fork continues through the remote, natural mixed forests between Juni and Himuro, where there are far more bears than people, and on past the isolated Himuro Shrine to descend finally to a holiday village beside the Omoi River in Awano, Tochigi Prefecture. You can take the bus to Kanuma, where the route also picks up the trail of Shodo Shonin, at a tiny wayside shrine near Shin Kanuma Station.

ISHIGAMO ▶ NEMOTO SHRINE
WALKING TIME: 1 HOUR, 45 MINUTES

Ishigamo lies at the very top of the valley of the Kiryu River. There is a very infrequent municipal mini-bus service that links Kiryu station with the Ishigamo bus stop. For details, phone the Kiryu City Hall Commerce and Tourism Department

(Shogyo Kankokei) at 0277-46-1111 (ext. 563). Otherwise, the twenty or so kilometers can be covered by taxi for about ¥4,000. For those using public transport, I'd recommend doing the full walk across to Kami Kasuo because it's not so easy to call a taxi to take you back into Kiryu if you descend back down to Ishigamo. If you do have a car, however, the Kumataka route is also an attractive option.

Getting off the municipal minibus at Ishigamo, first follow the road up the stream. This quickly reaches Tenmangu Shrine, which has several Koshin and other stones outside. The simple square post with characters stating "Thirty-six *cho* to go," is perhaps the most interesting. Dated 1828, this is a distance marker to the Nemoto Shrine, a *cho* being a little over one hundred meters. It is the first of several such stones that still mark the route up the valley. Later ones include numbers twenty, fourteen, thirteen, ten, nine, two, and finally number one, a short way from the top. Similar stones also extend backward from Tenmangu toward Kiryu and ultimately Nihonbashi. It would be interesting to walk the entire course sometime to find out how many still survive.

The road ends at a traffic barrier, twenty minutes from the bus stop, at the confluence of two streams. The sign indicates that it takes two hours to reach Mount Nemoto via the ridge and three via the stream. Cross the bridge to look at the map, on which your present location is indicated by a red circle.

Here, there is straightaway a choice of paths, for it is possible to start the stream route up to the shrine from two different places. The best way is to turn up the right bank of the stream at the yellow road barrier. The path climbs steeply and quickly comes to a branch with signs: straight on for the Nemoto Shrine, and right for the ridge course, which is described on page 96 below. Going left, the route to the shrine quickly descends to and crosses the river, recrossing it again almost immediately afterward over the stones in the stream. The path then rises steeply up the right bank and comes to another junction at the top of the river cliff. A sign points straight on (left) for the Nemoto Shrine, while the path up to the right reaches the road up from the traffic barrier in just a few meters.

Turning left away from the road, the path returns to the river and again crosses to the left bank. Take the left fork at the large black nature reserve sign. The route climbs for about ten minutes up a splendid river gorge to a bridge at a confluence of streams. Don't follow the path up the left bank of the smaller stream. Cross the bridge, and ascend by the left bank of the main stream.

This may sound a bit complicated, but it is not. The path then crisscrosses the river for the next fifty minutes. If you are uncertain of your direction, look for the red arrows or ribbons that point out the way. You know that you are coming to the end when you reach a metal ladder. There used to be a hermitage here in the days when pilgrims came to the mountain. Be sure to follow the stream at the top of the ladder, not the rope. You are now only about ten minutes from the shrine. A chain has been fixed to the rock to assist walkers up the final steep climb to the shrine.

The shrine itself is amazing, a wooden structure perched high above the cliff. The platform up to it has fallen away, but it is quite easy to swing over the edge of the cliff to get inside. Those who survive this feat can record their names for posterity in the visitors book. Don't be put off, though. Even the names of children can be found in the book. One day, no doubt, it's all going to rot away and fall down the cliff. Just hope that this doesn't happen when you visit.

NEMOTO SHRINE ▶ MOUNT NEMOTO
WALKING TIME: 50 MINUTES

The first ten minutes up from the shrine are steep, with long falls if you should miss your footing. You will need both hands. Certainly, you shouldn't attempt this climb in the rain. Happily, a long series of chains has been fixed to the rocks. There is a fine view of Nantai from the top.

The path then follows a narrow ridge for thirteen minutes to a minor peak. I am told that this stretch between the shrine and Mount Nemoto used to be the place for trapping one of the great local delicacies, the dusky thrush, which is a common winter visitor. A sign on this minor peak indicates sixty minutes to the entrance to the hiking course at Ishigamo and fifteen minutes to the junction of the paths down to Ishigamo (ridge route), up to Mount Nemoto, and across to Mount Kumataka.

Take the path down to the left for Mount Nemoto. The descent is steep, but fortunately not as steep as some of the slopes you have just climbed. There is also a chain here to help you down. The path then climbs again, forking about five minutes after the peak. A tiny, wooden sign indicates ten minutes to the *bunki* (junction). Take the left fork up. From here the path is very easy along the ridge. About ten minutes later, there is another unmarked path off to the left. A sign points onward to Mount Kumataka and the junction, which is reached in another three minutes. The signs at this major junction tell you it is twenty minutes to the left to Mount Nemoto, twenty minutes straight on to Mount Juni, and sixty minutes down to the right to Kiryu.

In fact, it takes only about forty-five minutes to descend to the road barrier from here and sixty minutes to the Ishigamo bus stop. If you are going down by this route, however, be warned that there are two or three places where the path forks confusingly. Follow the direction signs carefully, and watch for ribbons on the trees. If in doubt, it is probably best to take the left forks.

Turning left at the signs, the top of Mount Nemoto can be reached in only ten minutes. The summit is a bit of a disappointment after the glorious views from Mount Narukami. It is so overgrown with trees that you'd hardly know you were on top of a mountain at all. There is a good, unmarked path along the ridge to the left and a path to the right signposted for Mount Juni.

ISHIGAMO ▶ MOUNT NEMOTO VIA THE RIDGE COURSE
WALKING TIME: 1 HOUR, 40 MINUTES

The ridge course avoids the difficulties of the chains above the Nemoto Shrine and is much the faster way to the top. It is significantly less interesting, however, with long stretches of man-made forest and quite wide areas of felling.

Starting at the junction just a short way up from the yellow traffic barrier, the trail climbs back up to the road in about five minutes. Turn left, and the path up the ridge leads off to the right just ten meters farther on. It is signposted for the ridge course.

The path climbs fairly continuously, but at a comfortable gradient. The trail passes a stone shrine at a small peak about ten minutes from the road. Later on, there is a long, twenty-minute stretch up a ridge, where all the trees have been felled. Across the valley, there are clear views of Mount Kumataka and the ridge across from Juni. At this point, Mount Kumataka does not look so attractive, because the forestry plantations tend to dominate the scenery. On the ridge itself, however, there is no sense of the destruction just a short way below. The views from the top of Kumataka are superb.

It takes about one hour from the road to the four-way junction ten minutes below the summit of Mount Nemoto, where the ridge route joins the path up from the shrine (see previous section).

MOUNT NEMOTO ▶ MOUNT JUNI
WALKING TIME: 30 MINUTES

The path to Mount Juni leads through dense woods, descending quite steeply at one point, but is quite easy to follow. If in doubt, stay on the ridge. The trees are mostly cedars and obviously planted by man. There is a small shrine and shelter midway between the two peaks, the Juni Nemoto Shrine, dedicated to the mountain god Oyama.

This shrine is said to have been founded in 1771, when a certain Ono Seiun erected a small stone shrine here. Two large wooden buildings were then put up by the village in 1789. In 1806, Ono Kiyonori installed the twelve warriors of Yakushi. According to the inscription on the large, black monument, this is the origin of the mountain's name, Juni, meaning Twelve.

Just as Amida is thought to dwell in a paradise in the west, Yakushi, the Healing Buddha, is believed to inhabit an emerald mountain paradise in the east, called Rurisen. Yakushi became popular in Japan in the eighth century, just before the time of Shodo Shonin. Yakushi remains one of the most worshiped gods in the country today. Clearly, as were the Koshin deities, this Buddha was perceived to fulfill a definite need. Yakushi is almost always enshrined together with these twelve fierce warriors, who are known as the Juni Shinsho (Twelve Divine Generals). They serve him in the battle against disease, and are each customarily identified with one of the twelve branches of the Chinese horoscope.

Despite that plausible explanation, however, it is worth noting that Juni is also a common name for the mountain god in many places. In some areas, Juni is also thought of as the god of safe birth. The Juni cult was obviously very popular in this area at one time. Along the Watarase, too, there is a shrine dedicated to Juni in

Matsushima (very close to the course of Hike 7). Also, there is a tradition that a disinherited prince of the imperial family, who died young while traveling in the area, himself became Juni. This prince is worshiped at the Tomiya Shrine in Sori.

There are several theories about why the mountain god should be called Twelve. One is that the number comes from the date of the mountain god's festival, which is held on the twelfth of the month in many parts of Japan. On that day it is thought wrong to fell trees, and offerings of sake are made in cups of cut bamboo stalks. It is also common practice to offer the god twelve rice cakes. These cakes are reserved for the men. Women are generally forbidden to eat them, and sometimes even to make them.

The key to the god's name, however, seems to lie in those twelve branches of Chinese astrology. The fact is that there are two types of mountain god, represented in animal form by either a snake, the sixth branch of the horoscope cycle, or a wild boar, the twelfth branch. In other words, the snake and the wild boar are diametric opposites in the twelve-year cycle. According to Chinese divination principles, the sixth branch further corresponds to the father and husband, and the twelfth branch to the mother and wife. Now the connection becomes clearer, for while the snake is perfect yang, the boar is perfect yin. To put it simply, Juni, the wild boar, is the female mountain god, while the snake is the male. And that explains why Juni is regarded as a god of safe birth while at the same time there are the prohibitions on the activities of women — the mountain god, whether male or female, is above all known for its intense jealousy.

A priest of the shrine, Nagasawa Sojiro, and his son lived here from 1896 to 1928. The shrine burned down the following year and another small, wooden shrine was erected in its place. The son, who was born and brought up here, returned in April 1986 at the age of seventy-two and arranged for the shrine's restoration. A new stone shrine was brought here in September of that same year, and a new gate erected in 1987, with the assistance of the Omama Forestry Office. The annual festival, traditionally held on the tenth day of the tenth month, has also been resumed. October by the modern calendar (one month earlier than the old tenth month) has been chosen for the ceremonies, though it seems that the precise date is no longer fixed. The new priest is a nephew of the son, the priest of Tenmangu at Asahimori in Sano City.

There are signs from here on to Mount Kumataka and Mount Himuro and back to Kiryu. The path from the shrine to Mount Juni is very good. About thirty minutes from Mount Nemoto, there is a path down to the right marked with red ribbons. Ignore it! You reach the main junction just two minutes later. The path to the right is posted for Mount Kumataka and Mount Nomine, the one to the left to Mount Himuro and the Kasuo Pass. Both are described below. The actual peak is about one minute on from here, but it is no better than the top of Mount Nemoto. After viewing it, it is necessary to return to this junction.

MOUNT JUNI ▶ MOUNT KUMATAKA ▶ ISHIGAMO
WALKING TIME: 1 HOUR, 50 MINUTES

The path sets out along a very level ridge with thin mixed woods and thick bamboo grass. It runs first one side of the ridge, then the other, and finally along the top, all very easy but overgrown. Actually, I missed the direct path up the summit of Kumataka the first time I came here on account of the bamboo grass, for there is also a fork around the right side of the peak that rejoins the main path a few meters beyond it. This does not really matter, for there is a rickety wooden shrine gate at the point where the paths rejoin. If you make the same mistake, turn left up here. You will reach a tiny stone shrine in a couple of minutes and the summit about a minute later. The total walking time from Juni to Kumataka is twenty to twenty-five minutes.

A wooden lookout post has been built on the summit, commanding a splendid 360-degree panorama that takes in all of Azuma, Narukami, Sankyo, Nemoto, Juni, Akagi, and the mountains of Nikko, plus the range extending from Ashikaga down toward Tochigi. The valley of the Kiryu River cuts a broad, twenty-kilometer swath all the way down to the Kanto Plain. The traditional day for climbing Mount Kumataka is November 3.

Return (or continue) down to the gate, keeping right at two apparent forks, to reach a junction with signs just three minutes from the gate. The path ahead is posted for Mounts Maruiwa and Nomine, leading on toward Ashikaga, while the one to the right heads toward Umatate, Kiryu, and the entry to the Nemoto hiking course. Go right.

The path down is excellent, a far cry from the overgrown route on the ridge, making one wonder why on earth it is not shown on the map. There are views of Nemoto on the right and of the range all the way down to Mount Azuma. The path forks to the left about five minutes down from the junction, joining the pretty valley of a tiny stream another eight minutes later. The stream is lined with mixed woods, including cypress, cedar, and *karamatsu* larches *(Larix leptolepis)*. Toward the bottom, however, there are places where the trail is not very clear and that might be very difficult to see coming up. The important thing to remember is that it stays with the stream all of the way to the road. Sometimes it runs along on one bank, sometimes on the other, and at times right down the middle, but it never rises far above the valley bottom. There are also several rather slippery log bridges, but they are fairly easy to avoid if you don't trust them (or yourself on them). There is, however, really nothing to worry about on this route. It reaches the forest road up from Ishigamo about forty minutes from the junction just below Kumataka.

There is no sign up for this path to Kumataka. To be honest, the path looks altogether a bit unlikely, so it might be hard to find if you are starting from here. Looking up, it starts at a bend in the road, going up the left bank of the stream, soon after the second red-on-white ditch warning sign as you come up the forest road from the roadblock above Ishigamo.

From here, it is a twelve-minute walk to the first junction, where you keep left; a further six minutes to the traffic barrier; and eighteen minutes from there to the Ishigamo bus stop.

MOUNT JUNI ▶ MOUNT HIMURO ▶ KAMI KASUO SHAKO BUS STOP
WALKING TIME: 3 HOURS, 50 MINUTES

This path is extremely little used, and there are frequent traces of bears. It is quite possible that no one else will walk along it on the same day as you. Sensible precautions must therefore be taken. The path is initially very narrow, running along the mountainside at a rather awkward angle that quickly begins to tire the feet. The path soon evens out, however, and the gradients all of the way are very gentle. There are occasional red arrows and pieces of red tape stuck on the trees to confirm that you are on the right track. In some ways, this is possibly the easiest path described in the book so far. The woods here are mixed, with many *buna* oaks. The only problem apart from this route's remoteness is that the path is sometimes difficult to see. However, it is always there somewhere. If you think that you have lost it, be sure to go back and find it again before continuing. The maps show a turnoff for the Kurosakaishi River about five hundred meters down the trail, but I could not find it.

An official wild bird survey conducted on this path four times in May and June and once in December of 1986 shows sightings of the following birds: black kite, gray-faced buzzard-eagle, common pheasant, great spotted woodpecker, Japanese pygmy woodpecker, brown-eared bulbul, winter wren, Japanese robin, short-tailed bush warbler, bush warbler, crowned willow warbler, blue-and-white fly-catcher, long-tailed tit, coal tit, varied tit, great tit, Japanese white eye, Siberian meadow bunting, jay, and carrion crow.

Almost exactly one hour along the trail, there is an old and virtually unreadable sign on the right-hand side. This is almost certainly the sign for the path shown on the map that follows down the border of Tanuma and Kuzu. Ignore this and keep straight on. Three minutes later, the path forks. The right fork is posted for the Himuro Shrine, while the left fork is unmarked except for a blue ribbon on a tree.

First, turn right here for the shrine. You reach it in only about one minute. In Japan, you will probably never see such an isolated spot again. This shrine, too, used to be the center of a mountain faith among the people of Kuzu, Awano, Sano, and Ashio. Its festivals are on the third days of May and November. The god is variously said to offer protection for people who work on the mountain and also safety against fire. Just as the Black Tengu of Nemoto is said to have protected the house of the Ii against fire, the Red Tengu of Himuro is believed to have saved the house of the lord of this district during the great fire of 1834 in Edo. And like Nemoto, this is said to have been a popular spot for gambling in the Edo period.

There is no path onward from the shrine, so it is now necessary to return to the junction and take that left fork marked by the blue ribbon. In just a few minutes, this comes out onto a narrow ridge. Far across to the right, you can see a proper road. This is the Kuzu side of the road you have to join, first by following the path to the end of the ridge, then by turning right down the spur to the top of the road. There is still quite a long way to go, however, before this can be accomplished.

A little over ten minutes from the shrine, a path branches off to the left, signposted for Mount Wannajo. This leads across to Kurosakaishi, in about five kilometers, and Sori, on the Watarase Keikoku Tetsudo, in ten or so kilometers. For Kami Kasuo, however, follow the unmarked path straight on.

The trail now traverses some open hillside left bare by felling. At one point, there is a fork backward down to the right, but ignore this track. About twenty-five minutes after the turning for Wannajo, the path appears to fork again. This time, however, it is actually a T-junction, for this is the end of the ridge. Both paths seem to be in good condition at the fork. According to the map, the route to the left heads toward Mount Jizo and Ashio. In fact, though, the path was in a very poor condition when I tried it, and I was forced to give up.

The path down to the right comes out to the road in just eight minutes, at the very top of the pass. This is the Kiura River Forest Road, which leads down to Kuzu to the right and Kami Kasuo to the left. The path we have just come down is unmarked except for some ordinary forestry signs, so those trying to walk this course in the opposite direction may have difficulty finding it. Supposing one approaches the pass from Kami Kasuo, the path climbs up to the right immediately after a cutting lined on both sides with concrete. There is a map on the other side of the road (your position is shown by a red dot inside a red circle). When I was there, this was also the point where the road became surfaced again after a short unpaved stretch.

Turn left in the direction of Kami Kasuo. This is an extremely pleasant road to walk down after all the exertions in the mountains, with fine views of Mount Yokone opposite. There are only a few cars out for a drive and no buildings at all. It takes a little over one hour from here to the bottom of the valley at the Kiura bridge, where the Kiura River joins the Omoi River. Here, it is possible to turn left up the main road to Ashio, now a little over ten kilometers away (but there aren't any buses), or right to Kami Kasuo in Awano-machi.

Turning right, we reach the road up to the left to the Ido Marsh (Ido Shitsugen, the route up in Hike 4) in just seven minutes. This, too, is a stretch of the Kanto Fureai no Michi, so there are plenty of signs. It is just over 8 kilometers from here to Ido Marsh, and 2.3 kilometers straight down the road to Hokkoji, where the Kami Kasuo Shako bus stop is located. There is also a drive-in at this junction, with fishing ponds and the Yama no Kami bungalows. It's an ideal place to stay for those intending to continue straight on with Hike 4 the next day.

It is now easy to follow the Kanto Fureai no Michi signs all of the way to the bus stop, about thirty-five minutes down the road. On the way down, you will also pass the country lodge of Sumida Ward in Tokyo. There are five buses a day from Kami Kasuo to JR Kanuma Station. The last bus leaves at 17:25. There is a pleasant log-house coffee shop just opposite the bus stop, where one can wait.

For those returning to Kiryu, this is where the journey really begins, for now it is necessary to go right around the mountains to get back to where we started. First, it takes a little over an hour (¥1,020) by bus to Shin Kanuma Station on the Tobu Nikko Line. This is cheaper and more convenient than the JR station at the terminus of the bus route, not only for Kiryu but also for Tokyo (Asakusa) and Nikko. Ask the driver to let you off at the Torii Ato-cho stop, because the bus stops close to, but not in front of, the station. Next, take a Tobu Line train in the Asakusa direction to Tochigi (thirty minutes, about three hundred yen). At Tochigi, change for a JR train to Kiryu (forty minutes, a little over seven hundred yen).

There is, however, one tiny surprise lying in wait at the Torii Ato-cho bus stop that certainly should not be missed. Just behind the police box at the junction, there is a small shrine, surrounded by a stone wall, with a single low tree rising up to one side. Almost invisible today, it is easy to imagine what a commanding position this must once have had on the road before the police box was built. This is a Futarasan shrine. Futara is one of the old names of Nantai, and the shrine is thus dedicated to the god of that mountain. As related elsewhere, the original Futarasan Shrine was founded by Shodo Shonin. The year was 782, when he had finally succeeded in scaling Nantai after fourteen years of effort. The present-day Futarasan Shrine in Nikko is spread out over several major locations, as described in Hike 13.

Tradition has it that Shodo Shonin himself planted four lotuses here after opening Nikko. Later, Minamoto no Yoritomo (1147–1199), the first Kamakura shogun, gave this land (the sixty-six villages of Oshihara) to Nikko, and an outer gate to Nikko was erected on this spot. Yoritomo is one of the three deities enshrined at Toshogu. Today, only the shrine remains. The stone monument just inside, dated April 10, 1957, lists the names of the people who contributed to its rebuilding.

USEFUL KANJI

"DITCH CROSSING"	横断溝あり
FUTAWATARI	二渡
"HIKING COURSE ENTRANCE"	登山口
HIMURO SHRINE	氷室山神社
HOKKOJI	登光路
IDO MARSH	井戸湿原
ISHIGAMO	石鴨
"JUNCTION"	分岐
JUNI NEMOTO SHRINE	十二根本神社
KANUMA STATION	鹿沼駅
KAMI KASUO	上粕尾
KASUO PASS	粕尾峠
KIRYU	桐生
KOBUGAHARA	古峰原
KUZU	葛生
MOUNT HIMURO	氷室山
MOUNT JUNI	十二山
MOUNT KUMATAKA	熊鷹山
MOUNT MARUIWA	丸岩
MOUNT NEMOTO	根本山
MOUNT NOMINE	野峰山
MOUNT WANNAJO	椀名条山
NAKA KASUO	中粕尾
"NEMOTO HIKING COURSE ENTRANCE"	根本登山口
NEMOTO SHRINE	根本神社
RIDGE COURSE	尾根コース
SERUSHI	猿石
SHIN KANUMA STATION	新鹿沼駅
SORI	沢入
TENMANGU	天満宮
"THIRTY-SIX *CHO* TO GO"	是ヨリ三十六丁
TORII ATO-CHO	鳥居跡町
UMATATE	馬立

IZURU BUS STOP • MANGANJI • MOUNT SENBUGATAKE • IZURU BUS STOP

TOTAL WALKING TIME   2 HOURS

MAP   1:25,000 SENBA. ALTHOUGH NOT TO SCALE, THE FREE MAP GIVEN OUT BY THE TOURIST OFFICE AT TOCHIGI STATION IS THE MOST USEFUL

The starting point for Shodo Shonin was not Kiryu but Izuru in Tochigi City, which until the Middle Ages was the start of the Nikko *shugendo*. Izuru was not only the site of Shodo's first mountain retreat but, as related below, was also connected with the story of his birth. Later ascetics, conscientiously following in his footsteps, would spend twenty-one days at Izuru at the start of the spring and autumn pilgrimages before setting out on the journey from peak to peak, all the way to Ashio and Nikko. Special rites for the repose of Shodo's soul are still performed here every year on his birthday, April 21.

The mountains of Izuru are low, rising only to a maximum of 644 meters. In time, this stretch of the pilgrimage route became disused and now is virtually forgotten. Instead, Sanmaiishi, described in the next hike, became the southernmost outpost for the *shugendo* priests. Today, no mountain trail exists between the two. Izuru, however, should certainly be visited, for it is an ancient place of truly diverse attractions. First, there is huge Manganji, virtually a hiking course in itself. The temple grounds have many old Buddhist relics, cliffs, waterfalls, long wooded paths, cedars, wild ferns, and grottoes. Manganji is one of the old names of Shodo's temples at Nikko (present-day Rinnoji, Shihonryuji, and Chuzenji). These temples were jointly called Manganji by Emperor Saga in the year 810, during Shodo's lifetime.

Exiting at the top of the present-day Manganji, there is a short climb up a family hiking course to the summit of Senbugatake for a magnificent view of the sharp cone of Nantai, rising above the gentle curves of the surrounding hills. The view is reminiscent of the one from Narukami or the top of the chains above Nemoto Shrine. It is said that this was the sight that set Shodo Shonin off on his travels. And, in truth, anyone gazing upon the mountain from here might feel that it is sacred.

105

Kukai also came to Izuru, in the year 820, apparently out of respect for Shodo. The one-thousand-armed Kannon in the main hall dates from that visit. The temple's main festival is a once-in-twelve-years placing of this Kannon image on public view. The last time was in 1990, so users of this book will unfortunately have to wait a long time for the next opportunity. Manganji still belongs to Kukai's esoteric Shingon sect.

The temple is also number seventeen of thirty-three on a pilgrimage route to the famous Kannon images of the Kanto area: the Bando Sanjusansho. This well-known course was founded in the Kamakura period (1185–1333), connecting eight temples in Sagami, six in Musashi, three in Kazusa, three in Shimousa, two in Kozuke, four in Shimotsuke, six in Hitachi, and one in Awa. The first Kamakura shogun, Minamoto no Yoritomo, was a devotee of Kannon and this pilgrimage route may well have been his own device for spreading the faith. It was mainly a course for the nobility during the Kamakura period, but it also became popular with the masses during the Edo period (1600–1868). The most famous temples on the route are Haseji in Kamakura (number four); Sensoji, at Asakusa, in Tokyo (number thirteen); and Chuzenji, in Nikko (number eighteen), described in Hike 11.

Izuru also gave its name to an armed rebellion in 1867: the Izuru Incident. This was part of a major plot led by Sagara Sozo (1839–68), a disaffected samurai who sought to overthrow the shogunate, restore the emperor, and oust the foreigners. His plan was to organize a series of uprisings in the Kanto area in order to distract the shogunate, then to seize power in Kyoto. Most of the planned uprisings failed even to break out, but in Izuru the banners of revolt were at least unfurled. Depending on the source one consults, between one hundred fifty and three hundred samurai gathered at the temple toward the end of November 1867. Their somewhat pitiful demise began with serious financial difficulties, and were then compounded when many members of a small band sent to seize funds from the office of the Ashikaga Han were killed. The main force was soon surrounded by the army of the shogunate, and eventually gave up without a fight. More than forty of the rebels were executed in Sano on December 15, 1867.

Returning to lighter topics, it is worth noting that this is one of the few walks described in this book that can easily be managed in a day trip from Tokyo. If you are staying the night, on the other hand, Tochigi City has many other attractions, including museums, tumuli, a beautiful urban waterfront with old wooden warehouses on the Uzuma River, and the Ohira Shrine on Mount Ohira. Tochigi was, in fact, the prefectural capital from 1871 to 1884, and some fine buildings remain from that period. There also are several interesting Kanto Fureai no Michi courses leading from and around the city and a well posted walking course in the city center. An English map and brochure about this course, as well as bicycle rentals, are available from the Tourist Information Office (Kanko Annaisho) outside the station. Tochigi, like many other cities in Japan, ambitiously describes itself as a little Kyoto. In this case, however, the description is indeed somewhat apposite.

MANGANJI
WALKING TIME: 1 HOUR

It would actually take rather more than one hour to walk around every path in the compounds of the temple, but this is a reasonable time for making one's way from the bus stop to the top.

Izuru can be reached by buses which run four times a day from Tochigi Station on the JR Ryomo and Tobu Nikko lines, at 10:40, 13:00, 15:40, and 17:40. The journey takes about fifty minutes and costs a little over seven hundred yen. Return buses in the afternoon leave at 14:30 and 17:00. On the way, the road passes through some dramatic limestone quarries, where the dust adheres to everything, turning the vegetation a most peculiar, creamy shade of green. Izuruhara, Nabeyama, and especially the neighboring town of Kuzu have long ranked among the major quarries of Japan. Kuzu is said to have eighty percent of the dolomite reserves of all Japan. Just as Ashio produced copper tiles for Edo Castle and the mausoleums of Nikko, this region produced much of their stone. Here, however, the work still continues apace, so it comes as all the more of a pleasure to break through this twilight world and arrive at the unspoiled and sleepy little temple village of Izuru.

Taking the left fork at the bus stop, you reach the gate of Manganji in just five minutes. This vast temple, which is said to have been founded by Shodo Shonin, spreads over a total area of 390,000 square meters. Entering by the mid-eighteenth century gate, you are greeted by two ferocious sentinels, the statues of the Kongo Rikishi guardian deities. These Kongo Rikishi, as their name suggests, belong to that diamond Kongo world so important to the mountain priests. Their

Sanskrit name is Vajradhara. In their hands they wield pestle-shaped weapons known as *kongosho vajra,* which esoteric Buddhists often carried to ward off evil.

There are several small halls just beyond, including the Yakushido on the left and Hokoin on the right. Then, crossing the bridge, there is large, five-storied pilgrims' lodge built in 1966. This has a capacity of two hundred, and anyone is welcome to stay or rest there for a meal.

The cedar-lined path continues from here to the main hall of the temple itself, which also dates from the mid-eighteenth century, and then bends up the gorge around to the right. There are many fascinating statues and monuments, both old and new, including images of the priests who walked the *shugendo,* Jizos, and some fine old stone stupas. In the main hall, a fire ceremony is performed every day to purify the desires of supplicants in readiness for presentation to Kannon. The temple charges two hundred yen to continue up the path from here.

I would suggest climbing up the steep flight of steps to the left a short way past the main hall. This leads up to the Seitendo and the first main grotto, the Daishi Reikutsu. The temple forbids you to enter the grotto without a guide, but the path is safe just near the opening if you have a flashlight.

Then, continue in the same direction down to the grotto Oku no In, high up on the side of a cliff. It is recorded that the path up to this grotto used to be extremely treacherous. These days, there is a flight of firm, stone steps. The centerpiece of this grotto is a tall pillar, more than three meters high, that is thought to resemble a rear view of the goddess of mercy, Kannon. This pillar, in fact, figures prominently in the story of Shodo's birth.

It is recounted that the wife of Wakata Kosuke, the governor of Shimotsuke Province, was sorely troubled because she was unable to bear a child. She prayed day and night for seven days at this Kannon cave where Shodo later founded Manganji. On the last night, Kannon took mercy on her. A snake appeared in a dream with a golden, eight-leafed bowl in its mouth. Inside the bowl there was a white jewel wrapped in threads of wisteria. The child born in answer to those prayers was Shodo Shonin, who was hence given the childhood name of Wisteria Thread. Ever since, this Oku no In has been a pilgrimage destination for women wishing to bear children.

Of course, given the slow growth of stalagmites, it no doubt looks pretty much the same today as it did when Shodo's mother-to-be prayed before it in the 730s.

The pretty, eight-meter waterfall below Oku no In is known as the Fall of Great Sorrow (Daihi no Taki). Ascetic priests used to purify themselves by ablution beneath this fall in winter. It is said that priests first had to practice for twenty-one days beneath this fall before even being allowed to set foot on the *shugendo* across the peaks to Nikko. These days, people still come here to punish their bodies under the waterfall in winter. It is quite popular with a certain breed of university student and businessman. Actually, some priests say that it is really more agonizing in summer, because in winter the water is warmer than the surrounding air, whereas in summer it is much colder.

The third main grotto, the Dainichi Reikutsu, lies just a short way farther up the path from here. There is no notice in front of this one saying not to go in, but again you'll need a flashlight. This is a deep cave that used to be known for bats. A very safe path has been laid almost all of the way to the top. Here there is a pillar said to resemble Dainichi, the Great Sun Buddha, the key object of worship for Kukai.

Most visitors assume that this is the end of the path. In fact, it continues past a small dam and another grotto, the Fudo Reikutsu, to a forest road. The Fudo Reikutsu is a deep hole with a small waterfall inside. There is a ladder down. About ten meters up on the other side of the road, you will see a new-looking map and sign. This is the start of the family hiking course over Mount Senbugatake.

TOP OF MANGANJI ▶ MOUNT SENBUGATAKE ▶ IZURU BUS STOP
WALKING TIME: 1 HOUR

This path climbs steeply up the forested hillside for about twenty minutes. The path is new and well posted, but as it climbs through a monotonous forestry plantation, one does begin to wonder what it is all for. The effort is richly rewarded, however, by the view at the top toward Yokone, Nikko Shirane, and above all Nantai, which rises majestically on the horizon. It is said that this was the view that began it all for Shodo Shonin. Anyone who sees it will easily understand why. The name Senbugatake means One Thousand Volumes Mountain. The story goes that Shodo Shonin chanted one thousand volumes of sutras here in supplication to the mountains of Nikko.

The path continues mainly downward along this ridge for about seven minutes to a lookout point. The view from here is not nearly as good as that five minutes back, and Nantai itself is completely hidden by the trees. The only real view to be seen is across toward Awano. So, if you are walking this course in the other direction, be sure to keep going. From here the path drops down quite steeply toward the valley bottom. Again, it is well posted, and the steepest parts are neatly stepped. At one point on the left, there is a small wooden shrine to the mountain god.

Turn right onto the road at the bottom. It takes about six minutes from the end of the path to the bus stop. Here you should drop in at one of the many restaurants for a bowl of the highly regarded Izuru *soba* (buckwheat noodles). (Turning left at the bottom of that path, there is also a campsite, a zoo in the shape of a map of Japan, a botanical garden, and a small woodland park, collectively known as the Izuru Fureai no Mori.)

Travelers with cars might also be interested in visiting the Hoshino dig just a few kilometers from Izuru. Starting in the 1960s, the excavations there have unearthed Stone Age tools dating back more than ten thousand years, plus the remains of dwellings from the Jomon (ca 8000–300 B.C.) period and later. There are now reconstructed Jomon-period huts on the site, plus a park, museum, memorial hall, craft center, lookout point, and campsite, the Hoshino Nature Village (Hoshino Shizen Mura). This can also be reached by bus from Tochigi Station. Take the bus to either Ohata or Hoshino and get off at Hoshino Iseki Koen Iriguchi Shita. The journey takes about forty minutes. There is also a hot spring not far from Izuru at Kashiwagura.

USEFUL KANJI

DAIHI NO TAKI	大悲の滝
DAINICHI REIKUTSU	大日霊窟
FUDO REIKUTSU	不動霊窟
IZURU	出流
IZURU FUREAI NO MORI	出流ふれあいの森
OKU NO IN	奥の院
MANGANJI	満願寺
MOUNT SENBUGATAKE	千部ヶ岳
SENBA	仙波

MOUNTAIN MARSHES AND HERMIT RETREATS

KAMI KASUO SHAKO BUS STOP • IDO MARSH • MOUNT YOKONE • MOUNT HOSAI • SANMAIISHI • KOBUGAHARA MARSH • FURUMINE SHRINE (OR KOBU-GAHARA MARSH • ASHIO STATION)

TOTAL WALKING TIMES   5 HOURS, 20 MINUTES TO FURUMINE SHRINE; 6 HOURS, 25 MINUTES TO ASHIO STATION

MAPS   1:25,000 KOBUGAHARA; 1:25,000 ASHIO; 1:25,000 NAKA KASUO; 1:50,000 KANUMA; 1:50,000 ASHIO. FREE KANTO FUREAI NO MICHI MAPS (FOR COURSES 2, 3, AND 4) ARE AVAILABLE FROM THE TOCHIGI TOURIST INFORMATION OFFICE

The main walk now continues on the other side of the valley from Himuro, rising high up the flanks of Mount Yokone to the dairy farm beside the Ido Marsh. The forests and bears are temporarily left behind as we enter a different world, of cattle and azaleas. This, and the route from here on, lies within the Zen Nikko Kogen Prefectural Park. The walk continues with cattle to the left, forest to the right, to Yokone and the great rocks of Sanmaiishi — both places where Shodo Shonin used to practice — and then descends to another upland marsh at Kobugahara. It is said that Shodo Shonin first saw Kobugahara in a dream at Izuru when he was twenty-three years old and immediately set out across Yokone to reach it. He spent a year there during that first visit, at Kobugahara and Sanmaiishi, returning again when he was thirty-one. Just as some say that Shodo first conceived his idea of walking to Nantai when he saw that beautiful view from Izuru, others aver that the inspiration came to him on Mount Yokone. Either way, he was to leave for Nikko the following year.

Sanmaiishi and the Jinzentomoe Lodge at Kobugahara were to become important stops on the *shugendo* even during the time of Shodo Shonin, who recognized them as ideal places to pass his vision and the hardships of his regimen on to his disciples. The Nikko *shugendo* were to flourish in the Kamakura period and continue on a major scale right up until Meiji. One is still likely to meet long files of ascetics, dressed in distinctive white garb, climbing to Sanmaiishi today.

Finally, the path divides, left down to Ashio and right to the Furumine Shrine. This shrine is an old gathering point for pilgrims, with accommodations for up to eight hundred people and the largest landscaped garden in Japan.

This entire route lies along the Kanto Fureai no Michi and is consequently very well signposted. The Kanto Fureai no Michi guide notes that this is one of the most popular spots for bird watchers in Tochigi Prefecture. According to the guide, the following birds may be spotted along the route: great spotted woodpecker, Japanese pygmy woodpecker, gray wagtail, brown dipper, white eye, willow tit, coal tit, great tit, bush warbler, Siberian meadow bunting, rufous turtle dove, jay. It further notes that there are narcissus flycatchers, Japanese robins, and crowned willow warblers in spring and early summer, and dusky thrushes, siskins, and rustic buntings in autumn and early winter.

KAMI KASUO SHAKO BUS STOP ▶ IDO MARSH

WALKING TIME: 2 HOURS, 35 MINUTES

If you are starting from Shin Kanuma Station on the Tobu Nikko Line, go straight down the road directly opposite the station. The bus stop, Torii Ato-cho, is just on the left after the T-junction, on the other side of the road. As explained at the end of the last hike, it is worth noticing the small shrine tucked behind the police box. This shrine has interesting connections with Shodo Shonin (see page 103). The first bus for Kami Kasuo leaves at 7:18. The ride costs just over one thousand yen and takes a little over an hour.

This entire hike lies along a stretch of the Kanto Fureai no Michi. There are plenty of signs, and the path is very easy to follow. However, those walking the path in the opposite direction should note that there are no signs indicating the Kami Kasuo bus stop; they should follow the signs to Hokkoji.

The views from the top of Yokone are superb, but first there is a long climb up the road. Continuing along the road from the bus stop, you quickly come to an 850-year-old *kaya* tree *(Torreya nucifera)*, a kind of yew, on the left. There is a small fork soon afterward, with a sign in Roman letters. Keep right for Nikko, Ashio, and Yokone. Next comes a small shrine on the right, with stones bearing the names of the Great Sun Buddha Dainichi and the mountain god Oyama. It takes altogether about twenty-five minutes to the holiday bungalows and noodle shop of Yama no Kami. The Kanto Fureai no Michi branches up a road to the right just afterward. Notice the cherry tree on the corner. The trunk has completely split a giant boulder and raised the top half right up into the air, making it look a bit like a gaping mouth. The sign here indicates another 8.1 kilometers to the Ido Marsh (Ido Shitsugen). It is not a bad idea to try hitching a lift up this part, because the road is very new and not particularly interesting.

Note that several trees at this junction are labeled. These include: *konara,* an oak; *dakekanba (Betula ermanii),* a birch; *ryobu (Clethra barbinervis); honoki (Magnolia obovata);* and *yamazakura (Prunus jamasakura),* a mountain cherry. Twelve minutes from the junction, a large sign indicates that the road is passing above the-seven-meter-high, three-meter-broad Okufukazawa Fudo waterfall. It cannot be seen from the road, but you can clamber down a rather nominal sort of path soon afterward.

Another six minutes bring the road to the final junction. The maps seem to suggest that the best way up to the marsh from here is to turn right and follow a path up to the left, after a couple of bends in the road. In fact, however, this direct route is very hard to find; I would strongly advise taking the Kanto Fureai no Michi up the left fork instead. The sign here reads 6.9 kilometers to the marsh.

The forest road turns into a broad, rough track twenty-five minutes from the junction, 5.7 kilometers from the marsh, and ends at a parking lot twenty-five minutes later. The final 2.7 kilometers wind up a pleasant and very well-maintained trail through woods of *mizunara* oaks and *momi* firs. There are picnic tables and benches at the parking lot and again some twenty minutes up the trail.

Finally, thirty-five minutes from the parking lot, there is a fence across the path which has to be crossed. Here, the ascent is almost done. The sign on the fence says to beware of the cows. You will probably wonder why the path goes straight back into the woods. In fact, it is only six minutes from here to a splendid lookout over the seventy-hectare dairy farm. There is even a public toilet. After the adventures of Hike 3, we are well and truly back on the beaten track.

This lookout gives a grandstand view of most of the area covered in this book. First, of course, there is the range up from Kiryu. Then come full views of Akagi, Kesamaru, Nokogiri, Sukai, and Nikko Shirane. One can easily make out virtually the whole of Hikes 5 and 11 across to Nikko, and Nantai, of course, rises up behind. These splendid views continue virtually all of the way to Kobugahara. In clear weather, this vista leaves an unforgettable impression. The great crags beside the lookout point are known as Zo no Hana — the Elephant's Nose — on account of their shape. These, like the entire mountain, are made of granite that cooled between sixty and a hundred million years ago.

Given the very settled look of the dairy farm, it comes as something of a surprise to learn that the advance of modern settlement into this area was only recent. Its history really goes back only to 1897, when the first dairy farm opened with a little over one hundred cattle. That operation closed down in 1937. During the Second World War, there was a proposal to use Yokone for growing potatoes. That idea also had to be abandoned, because of the labor shortage. Farming was then restarted in 1948, by settlers returning from Manchuria after the war. This new agricultural community started out with fifty-nine households, but the mountain quickly proved unable to support that many. Accordingly, the number was reduced to twenty-four the following year. Others drifted away later, with the result that there were only seventeen households left by 1963. They grew giant radishes and cabbages. Cultivation was finally abandoned completely in 1973. The new dairy farm, however, has become a popular tourist attraction, where young children from the towns can come to enjoy a taste, both figurative and literal, of the countryside. It is still quite a long walk from here, though, to the rest house on the other side of the mountain that sells fresh milk.

From the lookout point, the path crosses another fence and follows it a short way before descending in about seven minutes to the marsh. Just at the point where the path turns down to the right from the fence, there is a giant rock known as the Buddha Rock, another name from the days when Yokone was an important base for the mountain priests. There is a small stone shrine just beside it.

Again, many of the plants are labeled, including: *yama ajisai (Hydrangea macrophylla); yama tsutsuji (Rhododendron kaempferi),* a wild azalea; *miyama ibota* (genus: *Ligustrum*), a type of privet; and *beni sarasa dodan (Enkianthus campanulatus),* an azalea. Just before the marsh, there is a three-way junction with signs. There are several paths around the marsh, so it is worth wandering around a few of them. The main route, however, is straight on down and across. It is only about thirty seconds from here to the edge of the marsh itself.

The Ido Marsh lies at an altitude of thirteen hundred meters and boasts about two hundred species of marsh plant. Around the edge, there are larches *(Larix leptolepis)*, firs *(Abies firma)*, rhododendron, and birches. The main flowering plants include many types of azalea, plus *maizuruso* lilies in spring; the small white flowers of the *kobaikeiso* lilies in early summer; *gomana* chrysanthemums and *koniyuri* lilies in summer; plus *rindo (Gentiana scabra)* and *aki no rinso* chrysanthemums in autumn. The autumn colors are also very beautiful.

To continue the hike, follow the signs to the rest house (Shitsugenso), crossing the marsh on the wooden walkways. It is, of course, dangerous to leave the path. Hikers can stay the night at this lodge, although be forewarned that it is quite run down. Although you can likely stop the night without bookings, to make sure there will be room contact the Awano Town Hall beforehand at 0289-85-2111. Water and cooking utensils are available.

IDO MARSH ▶ MOUNT YOKONE ▶ MOUNT HOSAI ▶ SANMAIISHI ▶ KOBUGAHARA MARSH
WALKING TIME: 1 HOUR, 50 MINUTES

Turn right about a minute up the path from the rest house at the signs to the Kobugahara Marsh (5.4 km), the Furumine Shrine, and Mount Yokone (600 m). Again, quite a few trees along this path are labeled, including: *shina no ki (Tilia japonica); tori kabuto (Aconitum japonicum),* a poisonous wolf's bane; *momi (Abies firma),* a fir; *karamatsu (Larix leptolepis),* a larch; *togokumitsuba tsutsuji (Rhododendron wadanum),* a kind of azalea; *noriutsugi (Hydrangea paniculata);* and *akamatsu (Pinus densiflora),* Japanese red pine.

The first small summit is reached in only seven minutes. One of the signs here mischievously indicates another twenty-five minutes to Mount Yokone. Actually it is more like ten, but the view from the top is not all that special. The path then descends to the left. It briefly looks as if the path will join the road just below, but it does not. Instead, it follows just above the fence of the dairy farm. In fact, there is so much barbed wire that it soon begins to feel like a footpath in England. The trail is literally a border between two worlds, the forest on the right, the farm on the left.

Some fifteen or so minutes from the summit of Mount Yokone, the path passes just above the visitors center of the dairy farm. It is impossible to descend to the farm just here. But if you are desperate for a cup of Nikko Milk, you will get a chance to go down to the road just a few minutes later, and you can then walk back up to the buildings. Soon after, the trail begins to ascend the next summit. The climb takes about fifteen minutes, but there are benches on the way up with more good views back toward Akagi and Kiryu. The top of Mount Hosai, by contrast, is covered with natural forest and does not command any view at all. The trail straight on from here is signposted to the Kasuo Pass. Take the path to the right, marked 2.6 kilometers to the Kobugahara Marsh and 6.8 kilometers to the Furumine Shrine.

This is a narrow woodland path, along which the trees increasingly blend into azaleas as the walk goes on. After a small peak about ten minutes from Mount Hosai, we enter the Azalea Plateau itself. A sign with pictures identifies the *renge tsutsuji (Rhododendron japonicum); yama tsutsuji (R. kaempferi);* and *sarasadodan tsutsuji (Tritomodon campanulatus).* From here, the three huge rocks and Oku no In of Sanmaiishi are clearly visible, just four minutes away.

Sanmaiishi was one of the principal landmarks on the *shugendo* route from Izuru to Nikko. It is said to have been opened by Shodo Shonin himself as one of his ascetic retreats and dedicated to Kongo Doji. Today, however, it belongs to the Kongosanji (see page 138) and is dedicated to Fudo Myoo (see page 82). Pilgrims still travel to Sanmaiishi today, dressed in traditional white clothes, and perform ritual purifications with fire. The fireplace lies under a metal cover, just in front of the sacred cave in the rocks. I have run into such pilgrims here in mid-June and again in mid-September.

The path forks at the shrine. The route down to the right is the direct way to the Furumine Shrine and bus stop, while the left fork goes first to the Kobugahara Marsh. Some maps indicate that the right-hand trail should be used only by worshipers. The guide issued by the Tobu Railway Company indicates that this trail is quite dangerous. Left or right the slope is continuously downhill from here.

The path to the left now goes down to Kobugahara. Just at the point where it gets considerably steeper, there is an area strewn with large rocks, known as Tengu's Garden. Tengu, as we shall see, figures very prominently at the Furumine Shrine. This area, too, was used as a dairy farm. In the Taisho period, in the early twentieth century, the cows grazed here from spring to autumn. The path descends continuously along the top of the ridge, with Nantai straight ahead and the mountains of Hike 5 looming large in the foreground. Finally, it passes under three silver gates, reaching the parking lot at the marsh in just thirty minutes. There is yet another sign with pictures to identify the many types of azalea: the peach-colored *aka yashio (Rhododendron pentaphyllum); renge tsutsuji (R. japonicum); shiro yashio (R. quinquefolium); murasaki yashio tsutsuji (R. albrechti); kome tsutsuji (R. tschonoskii); togokumitsuba tsutsuji (R. wadanum);* and Nikko *kisuge (Hemerocallis fulva),* a golden yellow day lily.

As far as the walk is concerned, it is far better to take the road to the right from the marsh as described in the next section. If, however, you are too late for the bus (the last bus from the Furumine Shrine to Kanuma leaves at 17:40) or else you especially want to descend on the Ashio side, the easiest route down to Ashio is to follow the Kanto Fureai no Michi toward Tsudo Station. This road is described in the final section.

KOBUGAHARA MARSH ▶ FURUMINE SHRINE
WALKING TIME: 55 MINUTES

The sign here indicates 4.2 kilometers to the Furumine Shrine. Starting down the stony road to the right, the path immediately branches down through the woods above a roaring stream. There are quite a few steps and several junctions with other paths, but all are adequately signposted. If in doubt, just remember to keep going down. The path is broad, but really quite rugged, so it has to be treated carefully. At times it crosses beautiful boulder-strewn streams; at others it is left behind by the gradient and ends up quite high above the valley. Finally, it comes out onto a narrow road some fifteen minutes from the marsh.

Five minutes later, at a roadblock, the Kanto Fureai no Michi again branches off down a path to the right. First, though, notice the small Jizo shrine on top of the outcrop above the roadblock. This is known as the Hetsuri Jizo. It is said that it was erected in the Edo period after a young man was murdered here. He had apparently been trying to escape from the Jinzentomoe no Yado, just on the other side of the marsh (see page 120), a school where the ascetic practices were particularly severe.

After passing down a short but pleasant wooded slope back beside the stream, the path again emerges at the road in just four minutes. The final three kilometers are down this road to the shrine. It is a fine, broad road with a good all-weather surface, but since it does not go anywhere except to the foot of the marsh, there is very little traffic. The valley is also pretty, so it is a relaxing way to wind down at the end of the hike. It takes about thirty minutes from the point where the path joins the road to get to the shrine. Eight minutes before the shrine, a road off to the left is signposted for Mount Jizo. This is the route up to Hagatatedaira in the next hike.

The Furumine Shrine offers cheap board and accommodation for eight hundred people in large, *tatami*-matted rooms. This is the obvious place to stay for those who wish to continue on Hike 5 the next day. Do remember, however, that it is a religious foundation and not a hotel.

The shrine has a history of around thirteen hundred years. It is dedicated to Yamato Takeru, a legendary prince who plays a leading role in both the *Kojiki* and the *Nihon Shoki*, the ancient chronicles of Japan. The prince was not so much an actual historical figure as a kind of Arthurian archetype, who combined all the noblest qualities of the traditional hero. There are many stories about him all over Japan, but above all he is known as the general who subjugated the aboriginal Kumaso people, in Kyushu, and the Ezo, of northeast Honshu. Some say that his armies penetrated as far as modern Miyagi Prefecture. It is very hard to fix his dates, for obvious reasons. He is supposed, however, to have lived sometime in the early centuries A.D. Actually, Yamato Takeru no Mikoto is also one of the two gods worshiped at Mount Azuma in Kiryu.

The Furumine shrine is associated with success in trade and protection against fire, shipwreck, poor harvests, and other disasters. Worshipers come here from all over Japan, especially from farming and fishing villages in the Tohoku district. A central place is given to Tengu, a long-nosed goblin who, among a very diverse range of other activities (see Short Walk 1, Hike 3, or Hike 8 for some examples) provides protection against fires and other calamities. The story of the Black Tengu of Nemoto, related in Hike 3, will no doubt immediately spring to mind for those who have walked that route. There are two Tengu masks in every room, one of the Bird Tengu and the other of the Great Tengu. The Jinzentomoe no Yado hermitage is the purification place for this shrine.

The relationship between Tengu and the *shugendo* is both intricate and obscure. Clearly, this shrine draws heavily on both of these apparently very different mountain faiths: the one Buddhist and magical, and the other a folk belief in a god or messenger of the gods. It was long a center for the *shugendo* and only arrived at its present form after the separation of Buddhism and Shinto in the early Meiji period. Reading through the literature for this area, one finds suggestions that the sounds of boisterous revelings by Edo-period *shugendo* ascetics were blamed on Tengu parties! It is, at any rate, certain that coexistence was not always easy. In 1825, for example, the shogun himself had a sign erected on Yokone ordering any Tengu to move elsewhere while he was visiting the area. Two reasons were given for this order: to demonstrate the power of the spirit of Ieyasu at Nikko, and to make sure that his journey would pass without incident.

The shrine also has a fine garden, the Kohoen. This is actually the largest landscaped garden in Japan. Opened in 1978, it covers a total area of 82,500 square meters. There are three tearooms within the grounds, together with a rest house, which serves refreshments, and a hermitage. The centerpiece of the garden is a lake with a sixteen-meter waterfall. There are azaleas, pines, maples, irises, and a long wisteria trellis. The season for plum blossoms is late March and early April; cherry blossoms, late April and early May; wisteria, yellow rose, and azalea, May; rhododendron and *satsuki* azalea, June; iris and hydrangea, late June and early July; bush clover, August and September; and the turning leaves, October and November. The garden is open from 8:00 to 17:00 from April 1 to November 15, and from 8:00 to 16:00 from November 16 to March 31. Admission is three hundred yen. Photography is not permitted within the garden. If you don't have enough time to visit the garden properly at the end of this hike, it can always be fitted in at the start of Hike 5.

The bus stop for JR Kanuma Station is just in front of the gate of the shrine. It takes about fifty-five minutes from here to the stop for Shin Kanuma Station on the Tobu Line and costs ¥880. Buses depart in the afternoon at 14:30, 15:40, 16:50, and 17:40. The points of interest along this bus route are described at the start of the next hike.

119

KOBUGAHARA MARSH ▶ ASHIO STATION
WALKING TIME: 2 HOURS

The route to Ashio follows an unpaved road down a gorge that is really quite pretty in places. If you are tired, however, you will probably be past savoring its very low-key charm. It is the sort of road that really should be walked in the morning rather than the evening. That said, though, it is certainly more attractive than the road up to the Ido Marsh, and there is a certain satisfaction in descending to a town like Ashio at the end of a long day. It is the route that I tend to choose.

Take the lower of the two unpaved roads to the left along the side of the marsh. The sign indicates 8.4 kilometers to Tsudo Station. It is about eight kilometers from the marsh to Ashio Station. There is a small shrine on the left, set in a pretty location in the woods, about ten minutes down the road. This is the Jinzentomoe Hermitage (Jinzentomoe no Yado, also known as Tomoe no Yado), another place where Shodo Shonin used to practice and which later became one of the main stops on both the spring and winter *shugendo*. Shodo is said to have spent three years here from 757. Later, this hermitage was especially known for the severity of the training conducted here in mid-winter. The lodge is no longer there, but the shrine stands on its old site. We are here just inside Ashio, across the border from Kanuma.

The small stone shrine itself clearly displays its complex Shinto-Buddhist origins. To the right, there are statues of two Buddhist figures, Jizo and Fudo Myoo. Behind, with paper sacred branches hanging from the rope, there is a Shinto sacred tree. On the left, there is a five-storied pagoda dedicated to Shodo and his disciples on the Buddhist *shugendo*. Today, this old ascetic hermitage belongs to the Furumine Shrine, which, as described in Section 3 above, is especially associated with Tengu. As usual, it is probably hopeless even to try to disentangle this web of converging traditions and beliefs.

The road becomes paved almost immediately afterward. But just five minutes later, at a three-way junction, take the unpaved road straight on to Tsudo Station (7.4 km). This route has been used since ancient times, but the road itself is quite new, having been constructed only in 1938. The sign to the left points back to the dairy farm (5 km).

The most remarkable sight on this route comes fifteen minutes later: a house! It even has a public telephone. Soon after, there are picnic tables by the river at the halfway point between the station (6.2 km) and Furumine Shrine (6.2 km). The road now follows down first the valley and then the gorge of the river, at times rising quite high above it. The road becomes paved again at a junction some thirty-five minutes from the midway point. The sign here reads 3.2 kilometers to Tsudo Station. This area is known as Utsu no Komori. There was once a house here called Urushiya that was famous for its peaches, and parties would come up here from Ashio in the season. Turn right at the T-junction thirteen minutes later (2.6 km to Tsudo Station). There are some rather fine views of the gorge during this final stretch. Then, go straight on under the road bridge at the junction at the bottom (1.1 km to Tsudo Station). You soon come to a bridge over the river, which you must cross. This is the Ashio bridge. There are four buses a day to Nikko from here, the last at 18:12. The Kanto Fureai no Michi sign points left for the final eight hundred meters to Tsudo Station. Unless you feel like going straight down to the copper mine (see page 245), you will probably do better to turn right and walk the three hundred meters or so to Ashio Station.

The area on the opposite bank of the river just beyond Ashio Station is called Watarase, the same as the name of the river. This is the official start of the Watarase River at the confluence of the Matsugi and Mikouchi rivers. It is said that Watarase, meaning "easy-to-ford" rapids, was named by Shodo Shonin himself. Hozoji was also originally built here either by Shodo or one of his disciples, but moved to Akakura in 1865 (see page 193). Tradition has it that the temple was founded in 807. That is now impossible to confirm, because all of its ancient records were lost in a series of fires. Later, Watarase was to develop as the shipping and reception point for goods from Nikko after the horse-drawn railway to the Hosoo Pass (see Hike 5) was completed in 1891. Watarase was also once famous for its cherry blossoms, as noted in the song on page 186.

USEFUL KANJI

ASHIO STATION	足尾駅
BUDDHA ROCK	仏岩
FURUMINE SHRINE	古峰神社

HOKKOJI	発光路
IDO MARSH	井戸湿原
JIZENTOMOE NO YADO	深山巴の宿
KANTO FUREAI NO MICHI	関東ふれあいの道
KANUMA	鹿沼
KOBUGAHARA MARSH	古峰原
KOHOEN	古峰園
MOUNT HOSAI	方塞山
MOUNT JIZO	地蔵山
MOUNT YOKONE	横根山
NAKA KASUO	中粕尾
NIKKO	日光
OKUFUKAZAWA FUDO FALLS	奥深沢不動の滝
KAMI KASUO	上粕尾
KASUO PASS	粕尾峠
SANMAIISHI	三枚岩
SHIN KANUMA STATION	新鹿沼駅
SHITSUGENSO	湿原荘
TORII ATO-CHO	鳥居跡町
TSUDO STATION	通洞駅
ZO NO HANA	象の鼻

HIKING MAPS

KEY

卍	Temple	◯	Other Destination
开	Shrine	- - - - -	Path
♨	Hot Spring	———	Paved Road
△	Peak	—▭—	Rail Line
♀	Bus Stop		with Station

SHORT WALK 1
MOUNT AZUMA

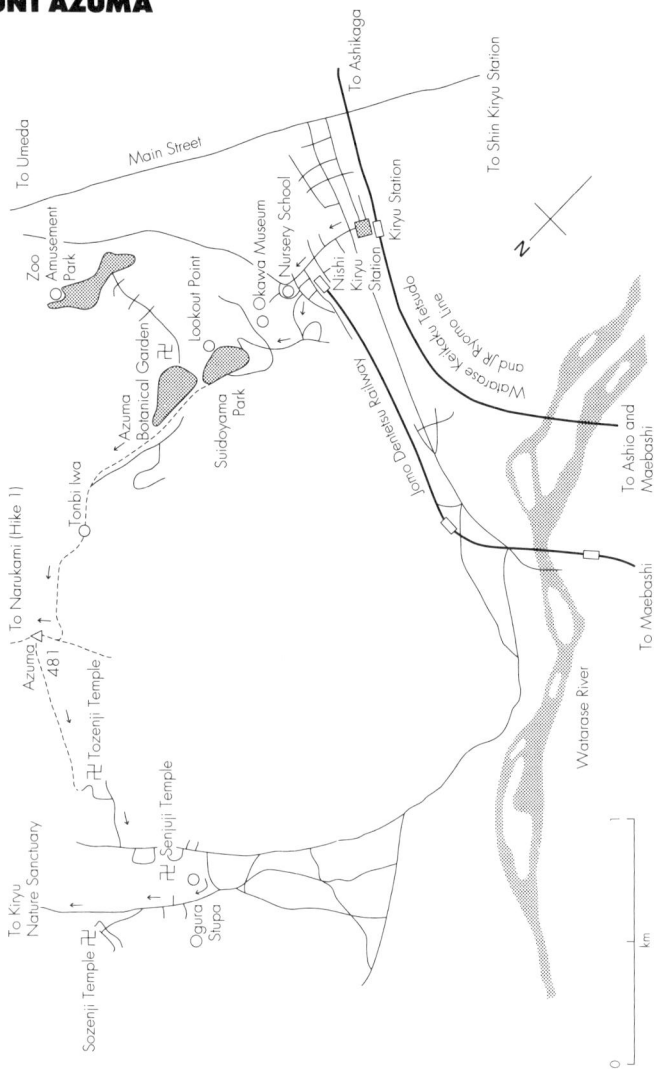

To Ashikaga

To Shin Kiryu Station

To Umeda

Main Street

Kiryu Station

Zoo

Amusement Park

Nursery School

Okawa Museum

Lookout Point

Nishi Kiryu Station

Azuma Botanical Garden

Suidoyama Park

Watarase Keikoku Tetsudo and JR Ryomo Line

Tonbi Iwa

Jomo Dentetsu Railway

To Narukami (Hike 1)

Azuma 481

To Ashio and Maebashi

Tozenji Temple

To Maebashi

Senjuji Temple

To Kiryu Nature Sanctuary

Ogura Stupa

Watarase River

Sozenji Temple

N

km

0

124

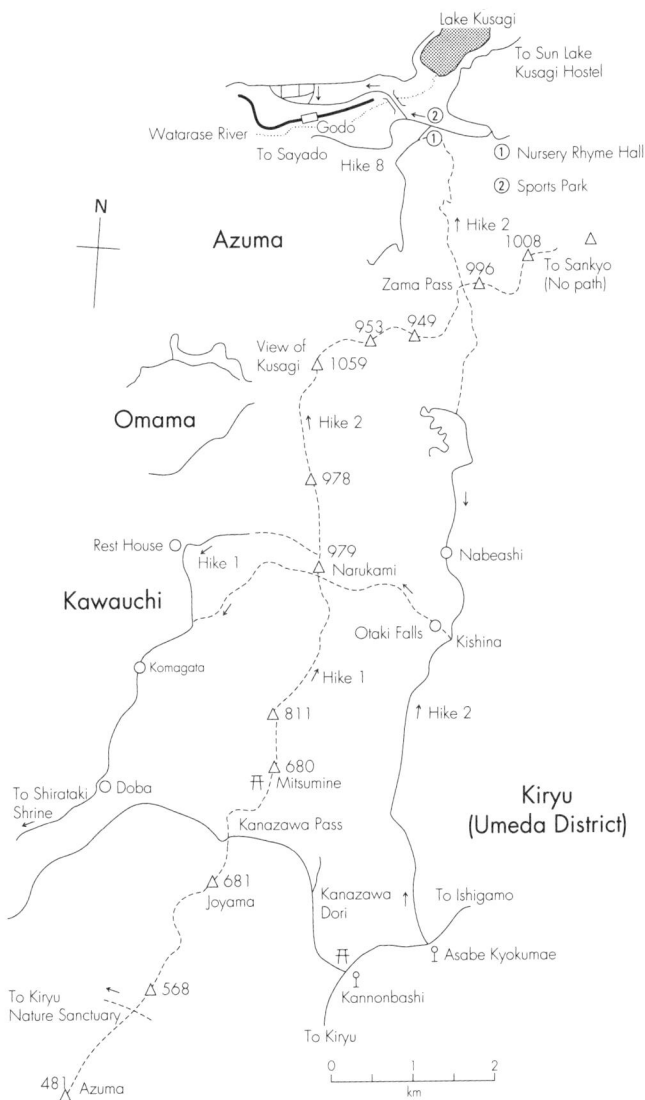

Lake Kusagi

To Sun Lake
Kusagi Hostel

Watarase River

Godo

To Sayado

Hike 8

② ① Nursery Rhyme Hall

② Sports Park

N

Azuma

↑ Hike 2

1008 △

Zama Pass △ 996

To Sankyo
(No path)

953 △ 949 △

View of
Kusagi △ 1059

Omama

↑ Hike 2

△ 978

Rest House ○

Hike 1

△ 979 Narukami

Nabeashi ○

Kawauchi

Otaki Falls ○ Kishina

Komagata ○

↑ Hike 1

↑ Hike 2

△ 811

△ 680
Mitsumine

To Shirataki
Shrine

Doba ○

Kanazawa Pass

Kiryu
(Umeda District)

△ 681
Joyama

Kanazawa
Dori ↑ To Ishigamo

To Kiryu
Nature Sanctuary

△ 568

Asabe Kyokumae

Kannonbashi

To Kiryu

481 △ Azuma

0   1   2
km

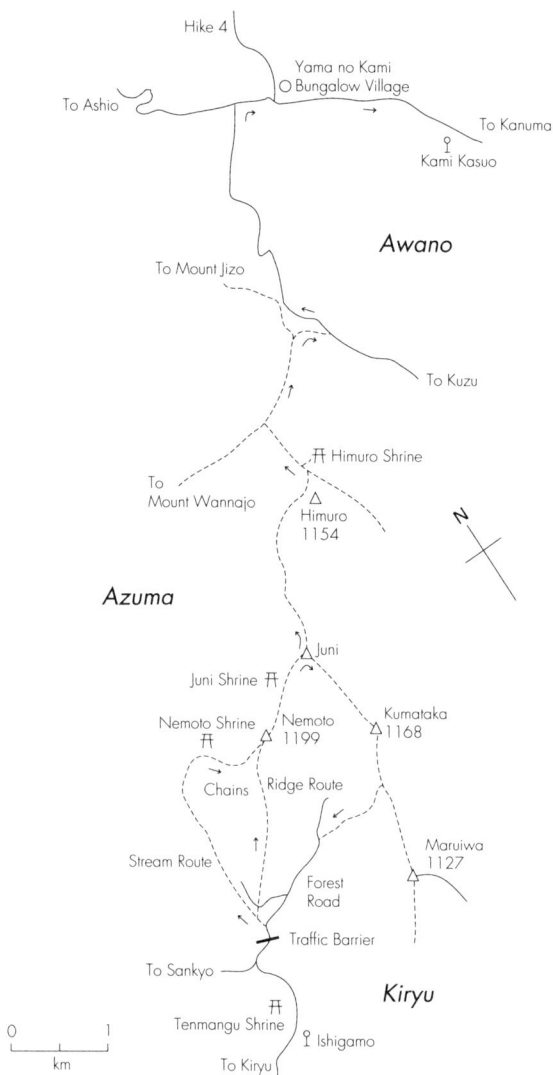

Hike 4

Yama no Kami
Bungalow Village

To Ashio

To Kanuma

Kami Kasuo

Awano

To Mount Jizo

To Kuzu

Himuro Shrine

To
Mount Wannajo

Himuro
1154

Azuma

Juni

Juni Shrine

Kumataka
1168

Nemoto Shrine

Nemoto
1199

Chains

Ridge Route

Stream Route

Maruiwa
1127

Forest
Road

Traffic Barrier

To Sankyo

Kiryu

Tenmangu Shrine

Ishigamo

To Kiryu

N

0   1
km

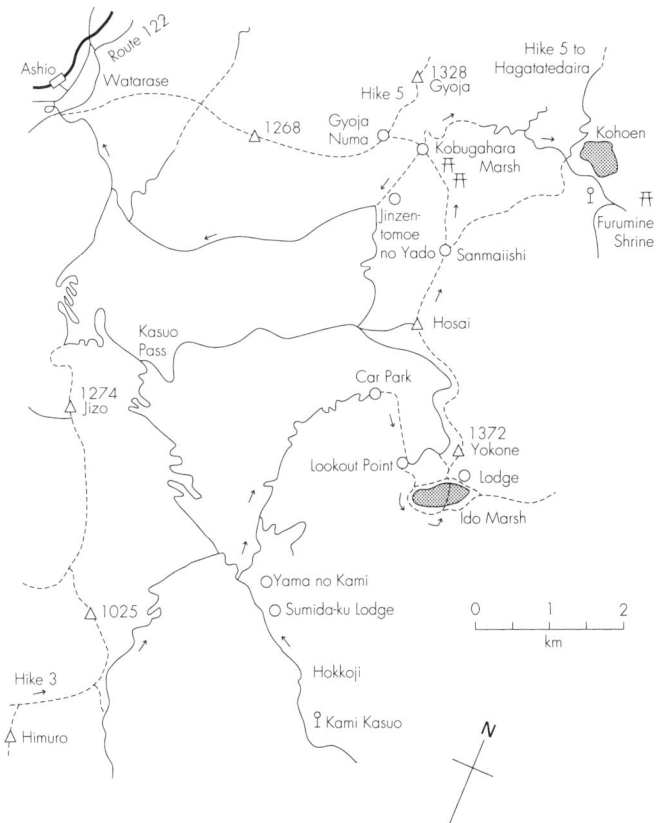

Ashio
Route 122
Watarase
△ 1268
Hike 5
△ 1328 Gyoja
Gyoja Numa
Hike 5 to Hagatatedaira
Kohoen
Kobugahara Marsh
Jinzen-tomoe no Yado
Sanmaiishi
Furumine Shrine
△ Hosai
Kasuo Pass
△ 1274 Jizo
Car Park
△ 1372 Yokone
Lookout Point
Lodge
Ido Marsh
△ 1025
Yama no Kami
Sumida-ku Lodge
0   1   2
km
Hokkoji
Hike 3
Kami Kasuo
△ Himuro
N

Hike 13

Futarasan Shrine

Iroha Road

Bus Stop

Lake Chuzenji

Kegon Falls

Byobu Iwa

Akechidaira

Cable Car

Hike 12

Lookout Point

Hike 11

Chanoki-daira

Komori Iwa

Kiyotaki

1753

To Nikko

Hangetsu

Hosoo Pass

Tunnel

1420 Yakushi

Route 122

Mikouchi

N

To Ashio

1526 Yuhi

Mitsume

Hagatatedaira

1483

1281 Jizo

Karanashi

Oiwa

1328 Gyoja

Tengu Shrine

Kohoen

Furumine Shrine

Kobugahara Marsh

Bus Stop

Jizentomoe no Yado

0   1   2
km

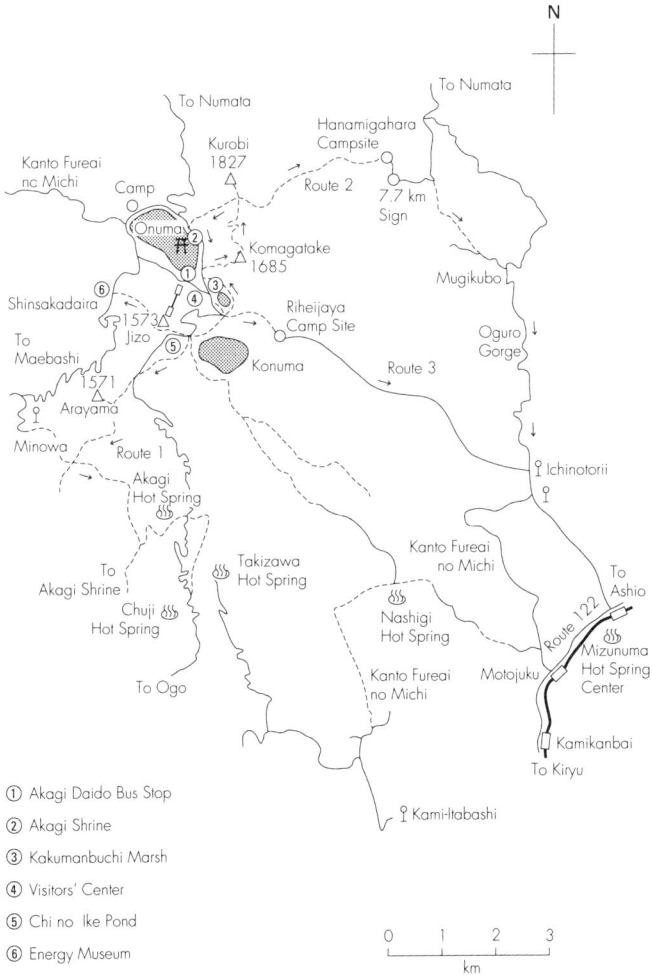

N

To Numata

To Numata

Kanto Fureai
nc Michi

Kurobi
1827

Hanamigahara
Campsite

Camp

Route 2

7.7 km
Sign

(Onuma)

Komagatake
1685

Mugikubo

Shinsakadaira

Riheijaya
Camp Site

1573
Jizo

Oguro
Gorge

To
Maebashi

Konuma

Route 3

1571

Arayama

Minowa

Route 1

Ichinotorii

Akagi
Hot Spring

To
Akagi Shrine

Takizawa
Hot Spring

Kanto Fureai
no Michi

To
Ashio

Chuji
Hot Spring

Nashigi
Hot Spring

Route 122

Mizunuma
Hot Spring
Center

Motojuku

To Ogo

Kanto Fureai
no Michi

Kamikanbai

To Kiryu

Kami-Itabashi

① Akagi Daido Bus Stop

② Akagi Shrine

③ Kakumanbuchi Marsh

④ Visitors' Center

⑤ Chi no Ike Pond

⑥ Energy Museum

0   1   2   3

km

129

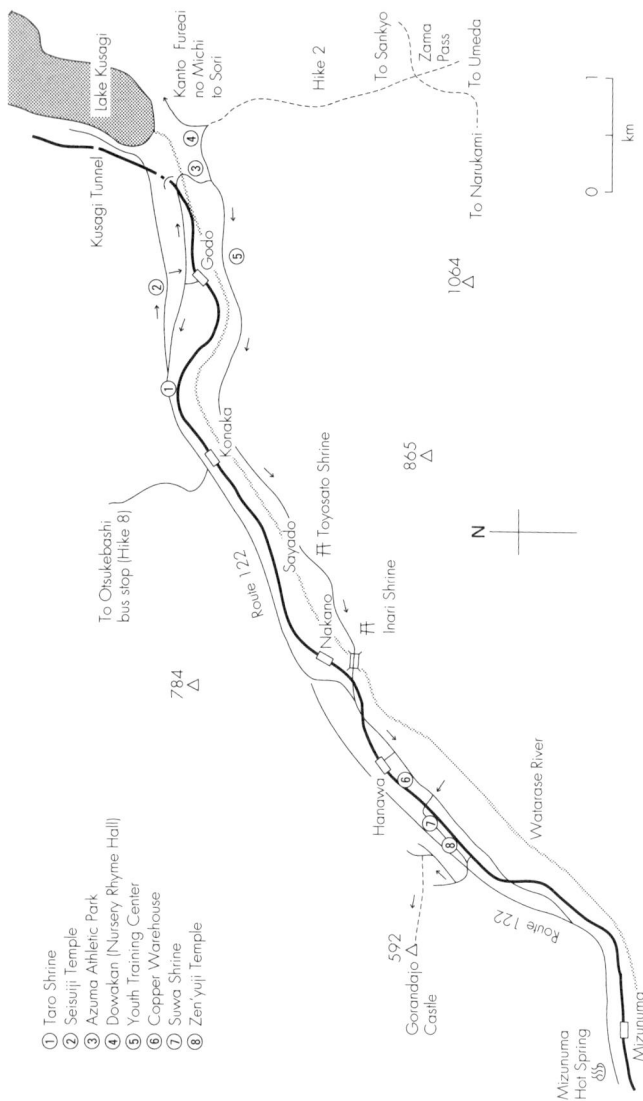

HIKE 7
THE WATARASE VALLEY

Lake Kusagi

Kusagi Tunnel

Kanto Fureai
no Michi
to Sori

To Sankyo

Zama
Pass

To Umeda

Hike 2

To Narukami

km

Godo

To Otsukebashi
bus stop (Hike 8)

Konaka

Route 122

Sayado

Toyosato Shrine

1064
△

865
△

Inari Shrine

Nakano

784
△

N

Hanawa

Watarase River

592
△
Gorandaijo
Castle

Route 122

Mizunuma
Hot Spring

Mizunuma

① Taro Shrine
② Seisuiji Temple
③ Azuma Athletic Park
④ Dowakan (Nursery Rhyme Hall)
⑤ Youth Training Center
⑥ Copper Warehouse
⑦ Suwa Shrine
⑧ Zen'yuji Temple

N

To Rokurinpan Pass
△ Ato Kesamaru
↑ 1878
△ 1676
Mae Kesamaru   △ Komaru

△ 1415 (Flag)

1556

Sai no Kawara ○
Lookout Point ○
Sorinto ○   ○ Sleeping Buddha

To Tone and
Numata

1164
△

To Ashio

1215
△

Daitakuji
卍

○ Otaki Waterfall

○ Sori
Okuwatarase
Log Cabin

Muresugi ○ ⛲ Otsukebashi

Lake Kusagi

Kusagi Tunnel

○ Sunlake Kusagi
Kokuminshukusha
Hostel

784
△

Route 122

Konaka   Godo
To Kiryu   Hike 7   Hike 2

0   1   2   3
km

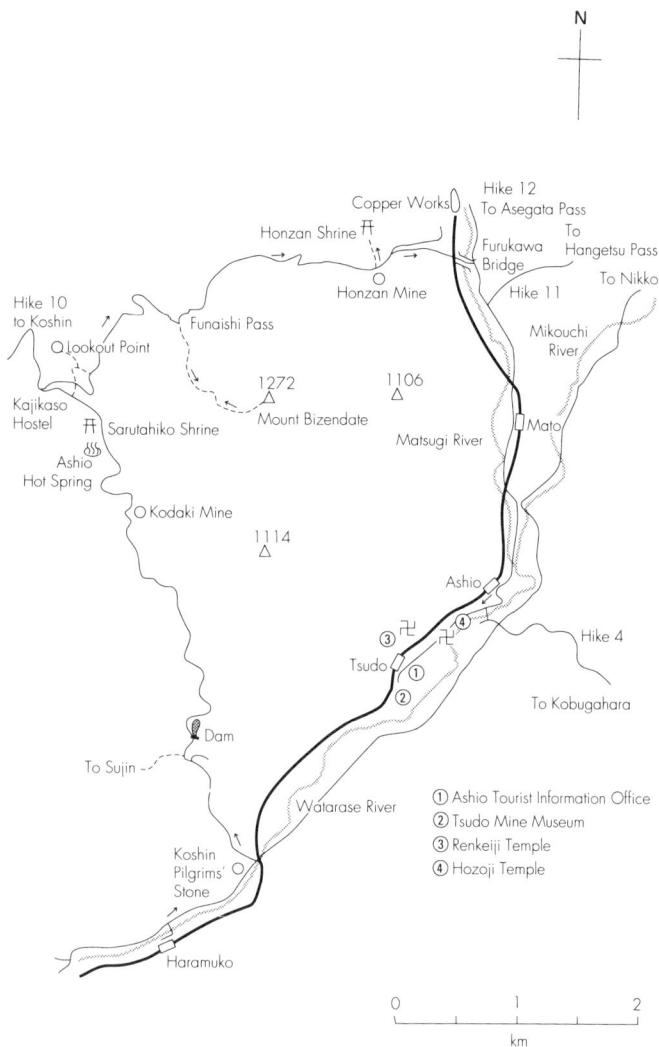

N

Copper Works

Hike 12
To Asegata Pass

Honzan Shrine

To
Hangetsu Pass

Furukawa
Bridge

To Nikko

Honzan Mine

Hike 11

Hike 10
to Koshin

Funaishi Pass

Mikouchi
River

Lookout Point

Mato

Kajikaso
Hostel

1272

1106

Sarutahiko Shrine

Mount Bizendate

Matsugi River

Ashio
Hot Spring

Kodaki Mine

1114

Ashio

Hike 4

Tsudo

To Kobugahara

Dam

To Sujin

Watarase River

Koshin
Pilgrims'
Stone

① Ashio Tourist Information Office
② Tsudo Mine Museum
③ Renkeiji Temple
④ Hozoji Temple

Haramuko

0   1   2
km

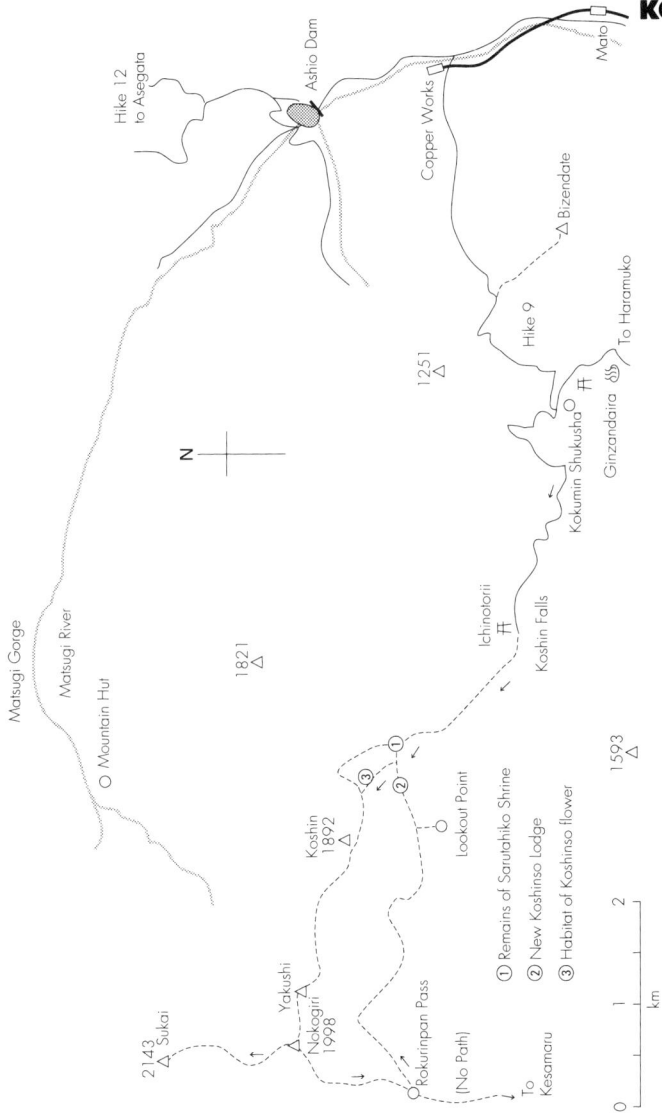

HIKE 10 KOSHIN

Hike 12 to Asegata

Ashio Dam

Mato

Copper Works

Matsugi Gorge

Matsugi River

Mountain Hut

○ Mountain Hut

△ Bizendate

Hike 9

1251 △

To Haramuko

Kokumin Shukusha ○

Ginzandaira

1821 △

Ichinotorii

Koshin Falls

Koshin 1892 △

③

① ②

Lookout Point ○

1593 △

Yakushi △

Nokogiri 1998 △

Rokurinpan Pass ○

2143 △ Sukai

To Kesamaru

(No Path)

① Remains of Sarutahiko Shrine
② New Koshinso Lodge
③ Habitat of Koshinso flower

N

0 1 2
km

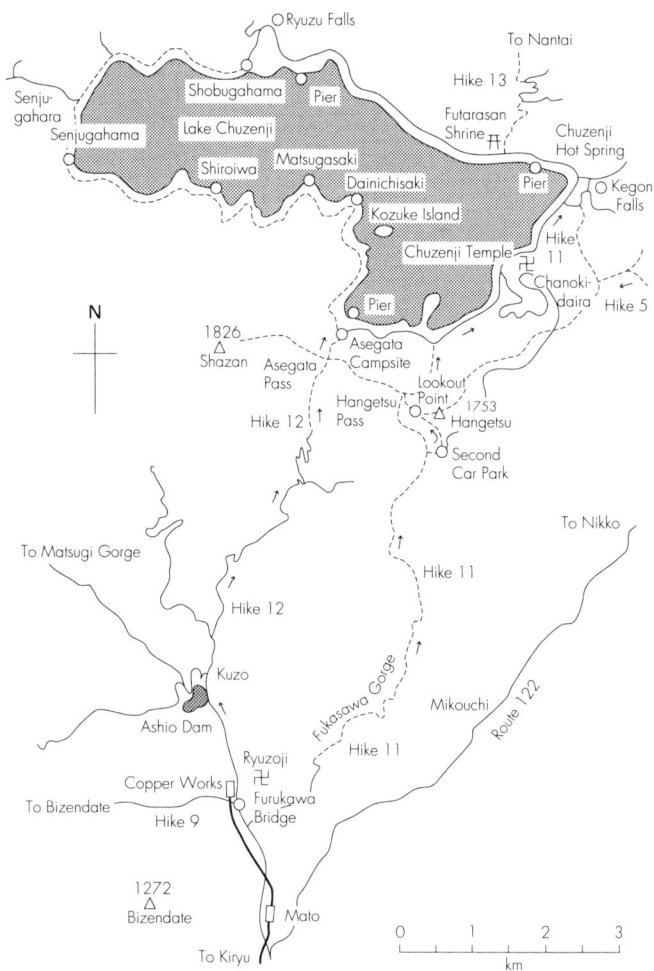

Ryuzu Falls

To Nantai

Hike 13

Senju-gahara

Shobugahama

Pier

Futarasan Shrine

Chuzenji Hot Spring

Senjugahama

Lake Chuzenji

Shiroiwa

Matsugasaki

Pier

Kegon Falls

Dainichisaki

Kozuke Island

Chuzenji Temple

Hike 11

Chanoki-daira

Hike 5

N

Pier

1826 △ Shazan

Asegata Pass

Asegata Campsite

Lookout Point

1753 △ Hangetsu

Hike 12

Hangetsu Pass

To Matsugi Gorge

Second Car Park

To Nikko

Hike 11

Hike 12

Fukasawa Gorge

Hike 11

Mikouchi

Route 122

Kuzo

Ashio Dam

Ryuzoji

Copper Works

To Bizendate

Furukawa Bridge

Hike 9

1272 △ Bizendate

Mato

To Kiryu

0   1   2   3
km

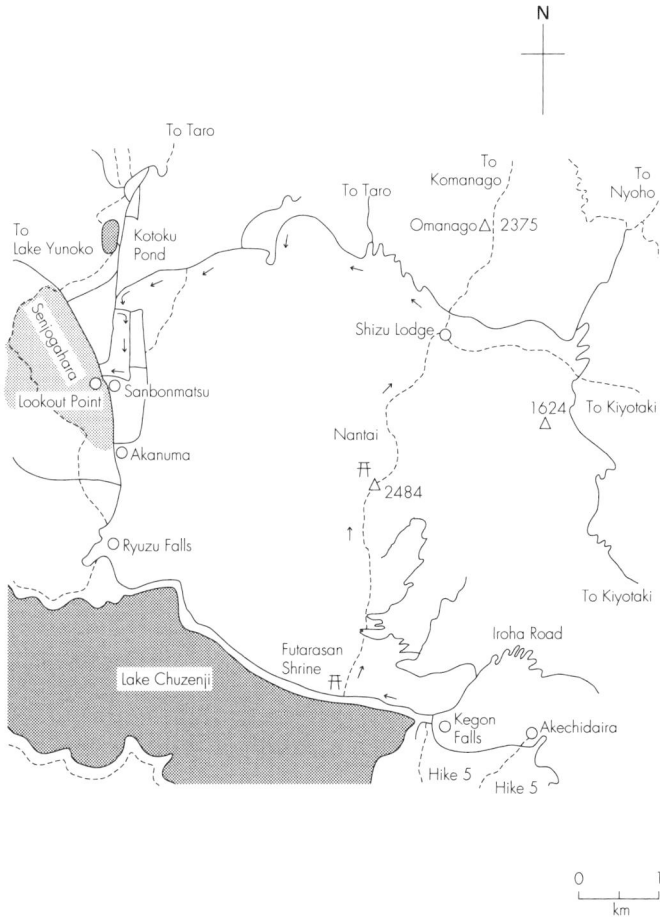

N

To Taro

To Taro

To Komanago

To Nyoho

To Lake Yunoko

Kotoku Pond

Omanago △ 2375

Senjogahara

Shizu Lodge

Lookout Point

Sanbonmatsu

1624 △

To Kiyotaki

Akanuma

Nantai

卍 △ 2484

Ryuzu Falls

To Kiyotaki

Lake Chuzenji

Iroha Road

Futarasan Shrine 卍

Kegon Falls

Akechidaira

Hike 5

Hike 5

0   1
km

SHORT WALK 3
ANCIENT NIKKO

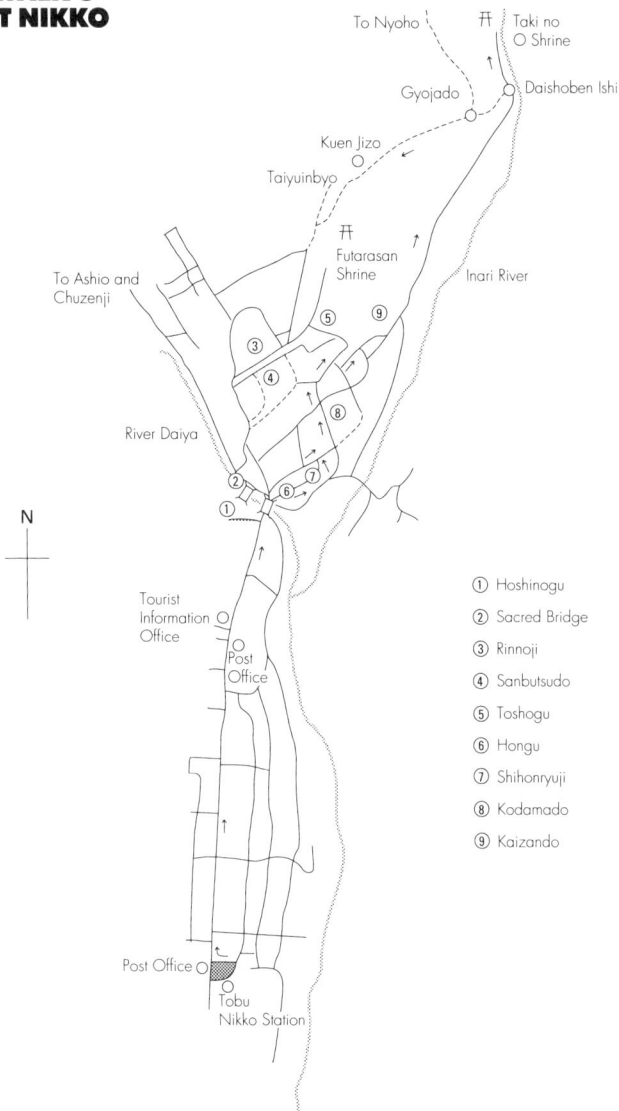

To Nyoho

Taki no O Shrine

Gyojado

Daishoben Ishi

Kuen Jizo

Taiyuinbyo

Futarasan Shrine

To Ashio and Chuzenji

Inari River

⑤
⑨
③
④
⑧
⑦
②
⑥
①

River Daiya

N

Tourist Information Office

Post Office

① Hoshinogu

② Sacred Bridge

③ Rinnoji

④ Sanbutsudo

⑤ Toshogu

⑥ Hongu

⑦ Shihonryuji

⑧ Kodamado

⑨ Kaizando

Post Office

Tobu Nikko Station

HIKE 5 ▲ JIZO, YAKUSHI, AND CHANOKIDAIRA
THE PILGRIMS' WAY TO NIKKO

FURUMINE SHRINE • HAGATATEDAIRA • MOUNT JIZO • MOUNT YAKUSHI
• HOSOO PASS • CHANOKIDAIRA • LAKE CHUZENJI AND THE KEGON FALLS OR
AKECHIDAIRA (ALSO HAGATATEDAIRA • MOUNT KARANASHI • MOUNT OIWA
• MOUNT GYOJA • KOBUGAHARA MARSH)

TOTAL WALKING TIMES   6 HOURS TO KEGON FALLS; 5 HOURS, 20 MINUTES TO
AKECHIDAIRA; 4 HOURS, 5 MINUTES TO KOBUGAHARA MARSH VIA HAGATATEDAIRA
AND BACK TO FURUMINE SHRINE

MAPS   1:25,000 KOBUGAHARA; 1:25,000 NIKKO NANBU; 1:25,000 CHUZENJIKO;
1:50,000 KANUMA; 1:50,000 NIKKO. A FREE HIKING MAP OF THE ZEN NIKKO KOGEN
PARK IS AVAILABLE FROM THE TOCHIGI TOURIST INFORMATION CENTER

This hike begins at the Furumine Shrine and continues from peak to peak along the
ridge to the Hosoo Pass and on up to Lake Chuzenji. It offers fine views of the
mountains of Ashio and beyond to Nantai and the other famous peaks of Nikko,
and here again are countless azaleas and beautiful autumn leaves. Also a section
of the Nikko *shugendo,* the path keeps well away from any roads, striking through
the very heart of the mountains along much the same course as Shodo himself
took to Nikko in 766, at least as far as Mount Yakushi. At the finish, this walk takes
in some of the most famous sights of Nikko: the beauty spots of Akechidaira and
Chanokidaira (both served by cable cars), Lake Chuzenji, and Kegon Falls. There is
also a shorter option that returns to the Kobugahara Marsh and the Furumine
Shrine. This route offers the chance to visit Kongosanji and the excellent Kanuma
Nature and Bonsai Park, which are described at the start of the first section.

FURUMINE SHRINE ▶ HAGATATEDAIRA
WALKING TIME: 1 HOUR, 40 MINUTES

The first bus to Kobugahara from Shin Kanuma Station on the Tobu Nikko Line
leaves at 6:46. The journey costs a little under one thousand yen and takes about

fifty-five minutes. There are several places of interest along the route, and some or all of these can be visited on the same day as the main hike. This is no problem if you are choosing the shorter walk around the mountains from Furumine Shrine to Kobugahara Marsh.

At Shin Kanuma Station there is a choice of bus stops. The closest stop to the station is just a short way down the station road, close to the hamburger shop. Only about one hundred meters farther on, however, turning left at the junction with the main road, there is the Torii Ato-cho bus stop and Futarasan Shrine, which are described at the end of Hike 3. Buses also leave from there to Kobugahara.

Twenty minutes along the bus route, we reach the Kanuma Nature and Bonsai Park (Kanuma Shizen Bonsai Koen). The park is laid out very tastefully, with exhibition halls, natural woods, lakes, wetland, *bonsai,* restaurants, and teahouses, all combined to good effect. There is even a huge fossilized tree trunk, with a circumference of 4.3 meters, the largest plant fossil in Japan. This and the Rokkakudo Museum are surrounded by an astonishing number of Koshin stones. The park is also the place to buy Nikko craft souvenirs more cheaply than in Nikko. It is open daily from 9:00 to 17:00 (9:00 to 16:00 from November 25 to the end of February). Admission is ¥720, and there is a free English pamphlet and map. Tel: 0289-62-7333.

The bus then passes through some stunning countryside, tempting one to ask the driver to stop for photographs. The farms are evidently old, for many have fortresslike stone storehouses on their grounds, each with family crests emblazoned over the doorway.

Some ten minutes before the shrine, the bus passes under its huge outer gate (Ichinotorii). Soon afterward, it arrives at the brightly painted Kongosanji, which has large modern statues of Shodo Shonin and Fudo Myoo on the roadside. The statue of Shodo was erected in 1974, that of Fudo in 1990. The temple itself is a sacred point on the old *shugendo.* The small Oku no In at Sanmaiishi, founded by Shodo Shonin and described in the previous hike, is the original temple of Kongosanji. This sacred ground was developed as a major center for ascetic practices by Dochin Hoshi, a disciple who learned the secrets of the Kongo world from Shodo himself.

Kongosanji was later made a branch of Katsuragi Kongosanji, in Nara Prefecture, by the Emperor Godaigo in the 1330s. This was at the time of the Kemmu Restoration, which ended the Kamakura shogunate in 1333. A statue of Kongo Doji was brought here from Nara. Kongo Doji (Vajra Kumarah in Sanskrit), the Diamond Child, is traditionally depicted with a blue face, six arms, and three eyes, although in another portrayal he is yellow. The god of a secret *sutra* who gives protection against disease, Kongo Doji became known as one of the main protective deities of the *shugendo* priests of both the Shingon and Tendai sects. In his blue form, he is also remarkably similar, if not identical, to Shomen Kongo of the Koshin faith.

Kongosanji belongs to Kukai's esoteric Shingon sect and is dedicated to both Kongo Doji and Fudo Myoo. According to the temple's literature, Kongo Doji is another incarnation of Fudo, and he is also often regarded as a kind of retainer of Fudo. There is another fine statue of Fudo together with a Tengu in front of the main hall.

The temple remained a center for *shugendo* practice right through to the end of the Edo period, but then declined with the political changes of the Meiji Restoration. That decline was completed by massive flood damage in 1919. The temple has since been relocated and is clearly once again flourishing. I can't help wondering, however, whether it is quite safe even now, for the day that I visited it rained heavily and the place was like a waterfall!

Kongosanji is temple number seventeen on a thirty-six temple course for worshiping the famous Fudos of the northern Kanto area. This pilgrimage route has twelve temples in each of Gunma, Tochigi, and Ibaraki prefectures. This is the only one of those thirty-six temples, however, to fall within the area covered by this book. Prayers here can be offered for all of the usual things, including prevention of fire, safety in the home, a good marriage partner, prosperity in trade, road safety, and general good fortune.

Most interesting, however, is that the temple is still a base for pilgrims entering the mountains, with all of the accompanying ceremonies. It is a very pretty, highly decorated temple, with a great range of Buddhist images and monuments on the grounds. It is clearly well worth a visit and can also be reached on foot in just thirty-five minutes from the Furumine Shrine. The bus route terminates just outside the Furumine Shrine, which is described on pages 118.

To start the hike, walk up the road from the shrine following the Kanto Fureai no Michi sign for Furumine Kogen (4.1 km). In six minutes you reach a white sign pointing up a path to your left. This is the direct route down from Sanmaiishi (see Hike 5). Ignore this path, and continue on up the road. Five minutes from here, turn right onto an unpaved road blocked by a traffic barrier. There is a white sign for Mount Jizo. The road forks twelve minutes later. Take the left fork with the blue forestry sign. In seven minutes, there is a turning down to the right to a flood and landslide barrier, but keep straight on. Twenty minutes from here, you will reach a building at the end of the vehicular road. There is a small bridge and a second sign to Mount Jizo.

At first, the path is a fairly easy climb through the woods. It crosses a stream fifteen minutes from the second road barrier, and three minutes beyond this you must turn left at a sign for Nikko and the Hosoo Pass. The path crosses streams a couple more times in the next twenty-five minutes, then forks a little confusingly. Don't take the apparent path straight on across a tiny trickle of a stream, but follow the sign up to your left. The right-hand side of this sign reads Furumine Shrine, but the left-hand side for the route up is no longer legible. There are white and red ribbons on the trees showing which way to go.

The junction at Hagatatedaira, the Hagatate Plateau, is just ten minutes from here. At the junction, there are signs pointing left to Kobugahara Pass (6 km), right for the Hosoo Pass, and back for the Furumine Shrine. The path to the left leads down to the Kobugahara Marsh via Mount Karanashi, Mount Oiwa, Mount Gyoja, and the Gyoja Pond. There appears to be a path all of the way to Ashio.

HAGATATEDAIRA ▶ MOUNT KARANASHI ▶ MOUNT OIWA ▶ MOUNT GYOJA ▶ KOBUGAHARA MARSH

WALKING TIME: 1 HOUR, 30 MINUTES

The path to the left begins with a welcome gentle slope downward, but starts climbing again steeply within about four minutes. After a couple of minor peaks, it arrives at a large outcrop known as the Tatsujuku (or Ryu no Yado, literally, Dragon Lodge), another stop on the old pilgrimage route, and two minutes later the first major peak, Mount Karanashi. This is densely wooded, so there isn't much of a view.

From here, the path descends quite a long way, followed by a long climb back up again to Mount Oiwa. This peak, too, is wooded, but there are nonetheless fine views across toward Mount Hangetsu and the course described in Hike 11. The path on from here again starts easily, but soon descends steeply. On the way down, there is a second large outcropping, a natural feature that held importance for the mountain priests. This one is dedicated to Kongo Doji. There is a small stone shrine beside the rock.

The path starts climbing again soon afterward, reaching the top of Mount Gyoja in five minutes. Gyoja is another name for the priests who followed these sacred routes. This peak commands excellent views all around, but especially toward Yokone and Kanuma. There is a bright red-and-white ordnance flag on the summit. From here it is four minutes to the beauty spot of Gyojadaira, and a further fifteen minutes up and down (but mainly down) to the Tengu Shrine, where the main track turns down to the left toward the Kobugahara Marsh. This small shrine has obviously been renovated quite recently. It is a white painted wooden structure, with an ink print of Tengu posted behind the glass doors.

According to the map, the path straight on leads to Ashio. This path appears little used, although it would probably be fun to try it. The path down to the left is signposted for the Furumine Shrine, and the path back for the Hosoo Pass. Turning left, there is a small lake immediately on the right known as Gyojanuma, with a splendid sacred tree at the side of the path. The marsh is reached in just eight minutes from here. The marsh and the route down to the Furumine Shrine are described in Hike 5.

HAGATATEDAIRA ▶ MOUNT JIZO ▶ MOUNT YAKUSHI ▶ HOSOO PASS
WALKING TIME: 2 HOURS, 10 MINUTES

Turning right at Hagatatedaira, the path at first runs level along the ridge but gradually starts to climb. Soon you find yourself going up quite a steep slope. Eight minutes from the junction, when it looks as if you have only just begun a particularly long and steep climb, the path suddenly veers off to the right at a red ribbon. The route follows around to and across a gully and crosswise up a steep, forested mountainside, which is falling away in places. The path reaches and bends backward up the corner of a ridge about ten minutes from the gully. A further eight minutes bring you to the top of Mount Jizo, twenty-five minutes from the junction at Hagatatedaira. A stone shrine and a Jizo stand at the tree-covered summit, and a sign points back to Hagatate Pass and onward to Mitsume.

The path onward begins with a welcome slope downward, just about the first so far. It follows up and down along a ridge for about fifteen minutes to the peak at Mitsume. Here you can turn right for the short, twenty-minute climb to Mount Yuhi, but then you have to return to the main trail to continue to the Hosoo Pass.

The path descends quite sharply from here before running gently up and down along the ridge. You know that you are approaching Mount Yakushi when you see a small statue of a fierce Fudo Myoo, with stone flames rising from behind his head, about forty minutes from Mitsume. At this point you are only six minutes from the junction just below Mount Yakushi. At the junction, signs point straight on for the final three or four minutes to the top of the mountain and left down to the Hosoo Pass. There is another small stone shrine at the top. Again, you must return to this junction after climbing to the summit.

The pass is just thirty minutes from here, and the path is downhill all the way. It crosses over the 2,765-meter road tunnel to Nikko, which was completed in 1976, after about three years of construction work. This is the most difficult part of the course, for the path runs diagonally across some very steep slopes and is falling away in places. At one point, it has already slipped quite dramatically, and there is a diversion to the other side of the narrow ridge. There are also a couple of unmarked forks. The paths rejoin immediately after the first one. Go right at the second fork, twenty-five minutes below the junction. This soon brings you out to the old road at the Hosoo Pass. You can turn right here to walk down into Nikko, left to Ashio, or climb the path immediately opposite signposted to Chanokidaira (Chanoki Plateau). There is also a map posted at this junction, but it is not very useful. Your present position (not indicated) is at the extreme top of the map.

The Hosoo Pass was used on both the summer and autumn *shugendo* and became very busy after the opening of the Ashio mines. For a time, the mines came under the administration of Toshogu, in Nikko. The road here was widened to a minimum of two meters by Furukawa Ichibei in 1884, for transporting both copper and general goods going to the mines. In 1890, Japan's first steel cableway was built across the pass. This pass remained the main route out for the copper until 1912, when the Ashio line was opened to Kiryu. After that it was seldom used, except by residents of Ashio for private trips to Nikko or by students on school outings. The present auto road took two and a half years to build and was opened with great ceremony on May 17, 1936. Tobu bus service between Ashio and Nikko was started in 1947, but the new road also proved far from satisfactory; it had sixty-two sharp bends and was closed during the winter. So it was in turn replaced when the tunnel was completed in 1976.

HOSOO PASS ▶ CHANOKIDAIRA ▶ LAKE CHUZENJI ▶ KEGON FALLS
WALKING TIME: 2 HOURS, 10 MINUTES; RETURNING VIA AKECHIDAIRA, 1 HOUR, 30 MINUTES

The path up to Chanokidaira is very easy for the first twenty minutes. The route runs across gentle, lightly wooded slopes, with many *karamatsu* larches and a lot of bamboo grass. It passes under some power cables, just three minutes from the road, and to the right of a concrete rainfall observatory for the Kusagi Dam, four minutes later. At a second set of power cables, turn right under the double pylon. You will see the path continuing up to the left on the other side. The route forks fifty meters later. Follow the sign to the left for Chanokidaira and Chuzenji. Now you have to pay for all that altitude you have lost since Mount Yakushi. The path climbs for thirty minutes, through *buna* oaks *(Fagus crenata)*, *nanakamado (Sorbus commixta)*, a kind of mountain ash, plus the ubiquitous *renge tsutsuji* and *shiro yashio* azaleas, up to some rocky crags dubbed Komori Iwa or Kago Iwa. The character *komori* is usually read *kago* and means "cage," but here it has the special meaning of "hermit's retreat." The rock is reached in about fifty minutes from the pass. There are views of Mounts Nantai and Tanze, and another statue, which appears to be of Fudo Myoo.

Five minutes further bring us to the final peak of the route, with views back to Yakushi, Jizo, and out across to the mountains on the far side of the plain, plus a glimpse of the Iroha Road up from Nikko to Chuzenji. There is a T-junction four minutes later. The path to the right is posted for Akechidaira (1.9 km), that to the left for Chanokidaira (0.8 km).

Even if you are continuing to Chanokidaira, it is worth turning right to the observation point for the Kegon Falls, just three minutes below here. This gives a panoramic view of Chuzenji Hot Spring resort, Lake Chuzenji, Nantai, and the very top of the falls. The falls are nearly one hundred meters high, descending from the lava flow that forms the lip of Lake Chuzenji. It was this lava flow from an eruption of Nantai that blocked the valley and formed the lake. Now, the falls are steadily eroding a channel back through it. It is estimated that the falls will reach the lake shore in about two thousand years.

The *Kegon* (Flower Garland) *Sutra* is said to have been taught by the historical Buddha immediately after he attained enlightenment. The central figure of this sutra is Vairochana, the Buddha represented by the great bronze statue at Todaiji in Nara, dedicated during Shodo's youth. The *Kegon Sutra* teaches the importance of every single speck of life, however insignificant it may appear. All life, it preaches, is a manifestation of the truth.

It seems curiously ironic, therefore, that just like the Kusagi Dam, the Kegon Falls are now known throughout Japan as a popular suicide spot, quite possibly the most famous of all. The deaths apparently began in April 1903, when a seventeen-year-old boy killed himself by jumping into the falls. With his last words, which he left inscribed on a nearby tree, he ridiculed life as a meaningless torture that was not worth the pain, a riddle with no solution in either religion or philosophy. Many young people were intensely impressed by his resolve and followed his appalling example. The crater of Mount Asama, in Gunma Prefecture, was also later to become a chosen place for such suicides. Happily, however, not everybody saw it through. The story of one of the fortunate who was saved from the so-called Kegon Disease is related on page 211.

If you are continuing down to Akechidaira, you'll find many fine vantage points for viewing Nantai and the mountains beyond. The path is particularly picturesque in May and June, when the peach-colored *aka yashio* and white *shiro yashio* azaleas are in bloom. The trail drops steeply for about ten minutes, then reaches a T-junction, with a sign indicating a left turn for Akechidaira. Soon after, the path comes to a bare ridge with a pylon, where there are more excellent views of Nantai and Chuzenji. The drive-in at Akechidaira is visible below on the right. The route lastly climbs up and down a small peak, arriving at the observation platform of Akechidaira in just twenty-five minutes from the junction with the path up from the Hosoo Pass. This is the best place for viewing not only Kegon Falls, but also, on the other side, the impressive cliffs known as Byobu Iwa. A *byobu* in Japanese is a "folding screen." It is easy to understand how these perpendicular cliffs got their name. The cable car down to the Akechidaira bus stop is very short. It takes only five minutes to walk down the stepped path that leads directly from the very entrance of the cable car station (on the right-hand side). From there, you can catch a bus up to Lake Chuzenji, but not down to Nikko.

Turning left at the junction with the path down to Akechidaira, the route on to Chanokidaira is flat, through woods of birch, pine, and hemlock. After six hundred meters, there is a junction with the path along the ridge to the Hangetsu Pass, now three kilometers away. Another two hundred meters bring you to the tea shop at the Chanoki Botanical Garden and the cable car down to the Kegon Falls. This cable car, built in 1960, descends the three hundred meters to the top of the falls in just six minutes, and runs from March 18 to December 14. The garden displays some 150 species of mountain plant and is especially noted for its many azaleas. There are fine views of Mount Nantai to the north and Lake Chuzenji down below.

Those who have walked all of the way from the Furumine Shrine will almost certainly wish to descend here. However, it is possible to continue along the ridge above the lake to Mount Hangetsu, the Asegata Pass, and Mount Shazan. This is a popular hiking course that commands fine views of Nantai, Shirane, and Chuzenji on the right, and Yakushi, Yokone, Fuji, Kesamaru, Koshin, Nokogiri, and Sukai on the left. The ridge goes up and down several times quite sharply, so it is not such an easy walk as it may appear from Chanokidaira. Going via the two lookout points just beyond Chanokidaira, it takes thirty-five minutes to the next main peak, Mount Tanuki, five minutes from there to the first parking lot on the toll road up Mount Hangetsu, and a further twenty-five minutes to the peak of Mount Hangetsu. The walks down from Mount Hangetsu to the Hangetsu Pass and on from there to the Asegata Pass are described in Hike 11. If you are starting from Akechidaira or Chanokidaira, it is fun to continue into Ashio, using either the path from the second parking lot on Mount Hangetsu or the Asegata Pass.

To walk down to the lake from Chanokidaira, turn down the path to the left through the gap in the fence, just before the map in front of the cable car station. There is a small sign for Lake Chuzenji. It takes about thirty minutes to reach the road. At one point, the path forks, but the branches rejoin farther down. The path comes out by a low wall at a bend in the road. There is just a tiny, red-and-yellow sign pointing up to Chanokidaira. The quickest way to the bus stop is to turn right here, but it is better to turn left. You can take a short walk, at least, by the side of the lake. You reach the T-junction at the lake shore just four minutes from the end of the path, beside the boat-rental piers. Turn right, cross the bridge, and turn right down the main street of Chuzenji Hot Spring. The bus station is four minutes down on your right; the entrance to the Kegon Falls, one minute further on.

There are many buses from here to Nikko Station (last bus 20:29). Those hikers returning to Kiryu or Tokyo should take the bus as far as the Tobu Nikko Station. This takes about one hour when the road is not congested, but up to about three hours when it is. The ride costs about one thousand yen. The bus also passes in front of Toshogu (forty minutes). Those hikers returning to Ashio can change buses at Kiyotaki (twenty minutes), but remember that there are only four buses a day to Ashio, leaving Kiyotaki at 7:36, 13:37, 15:40, and 19:15. Check at the Chuzenji bus station whether you can make the connection.

USEFUL KANJI

AKECHIDAIRA	明智平
CHANOKIDAIRA	茶の木平
CHUZENJI	中禅寺
FURUMINE KOGEN	古峰高原
FURUMINE SHRINE	古峰神社
GYOJADAIRA	行者平
GYOJA POND	行者沼
HAGATATE PLATEAU	八ヶ岳峠
HANGETSU PASS	半月峠
HOSOO PASS	細尾峠
KANTO FURERAI NO MICHI	関東ふれあいの道

KANUMA NATURE AND BONSAI PARK	鹿沼自然盆栽公園
KEGON FALLS	華厳滝
KOBUGAHARA MARSH	古峰原
KOBUGAHARA PASS	古峰峠
KONGOSANJI	金剛山寺
LAKE CHUZENJI	中禅湖
MITSUME	見ッ目
MOUNT GYOJA	行者岳
MOUNT JIZO	地蔵岳
MOUNT KARANASHI	唐梨子山
MOUNT OIWA	大岩山
MOUNT TANUKI	狸山
MOUNT YAKUSHI	薬師山
NIKKO NANBU	日光南部
TATSUJUKU (DRAGON LODGE)	竜宿

AROUND THE CALDERA

AKAGI DAIDO BUS STOP • KAKUMANBUCHI MARSH • MOUNT KOMAGATAKE • MOUNT KUROBI • AKAGI SHRINE AND LAKE ONUMA • AKAGI DAIDO BUS STOP (INCLUDING MOUNT JIZO, SHINSAKADAIRA, LAKE KONUMA, AND THREE ROUTES DOWN MOUNT AKAGI)

TOTAL WALKING TIME   UP TO 6 HOURS, DEPENDING UPON WHICH ROUTE DOWN THE MOUNTAIN IS CHOSEN

MAPS   1:50,000 NUMATA; 1:50,000 ASHIO (FOR ICHINOTORII); 1:25,000 AKAGI-SAN; 1:25,000 KOZUKE HANAWA (FOR ICHINOTORII). FREE KANTO FUREAI NO MICHI MAPS CAN BE OBTAINED FROM THE GUNMA TOURIST INFORMATION OFFICE. THE RELEVANT PAMPHLETS ARE THE ONE FOR ROUTES 20, 21, AND 22 AND THE ONE FOR ROUTES 26, 27, AND 35. A SIMPLE TOURIST MAP OF AKAGI IS ALSO AVAILABLE

Mount Akagi is an ancient sacred mountain and the recognized symbol of Gunma Prefecture. Clearly visible from Tokyo, the mountain commands the entire sweep of the Kanto Plain, which spreads out in a fan at its feet. The Akagi Shrine has the distinction of being the only institution in this book associated with Shodo's name that is thought to have been rebuilt, rather than founded, by him. The mountain's prehistory undoubtedly reaches far back. Stone swords, mirrors, and jewels discovered at archaeological sites in the foothills of Akagi can all be identified with magical symbols once used to lure the mountain god down from his fastness into the world of men. As related below, the belief that the spirits of the dead rise up to Akagi has survived in communities along the Watarase Valley to the present day.

There are many fine paths on this holy mountain, but the best are concentrated in the caldera at the top. This is a complex volcano, with three crater lakes. The two main lakes are known variously as Onuma and Konuma or Ono and Kono (written with the same characters for either pronunciation). The recommended hike leads principally around the rim above Onuma. This very attractive lake is a popular destination for families on weekend outings, and you may wish to avoid it on Sundays during the school summer holidays. If nothing else, the constant racket of the power boats is enough to drive one crazy. At most other times, however,

Onuma is quiet and peaceful. The lake opens for skating in early December, the first in all Honshu. There are also three family ski slopes inside the caldera. These are the closest ski grounds to Tokyo.

Akagi's caldera is enormous, measuring four kilometers across by three wide. Onuma lies at an altitude of thirteen hundred forty meters, and the highest peak, Kurobi, rises to eighteen hundred twenty-eight meters. It is thought that the mountain once reached a height of about twenty-five hundred meters. Beyond the caldera, Akagi has the broadest flanks of any volcano in Japan except Mount Fuji. The first eruptions here occurred in the late Tertiary period, forming the caldera around Onuma. A later eruption inside the caldera raised the Jizo peak in the center, dividing the caldera into three: Onuma, Chi no Ike pond, and Shin-sakadaira. A third big eruption formed Konuma, close to the main rim. The final eruption occurred to the west of Konuma, forming Jigokudani (Hell Valley). Volcanic activity ended a little over twenty thousand years ago.

Today, the mountain is still new enough to have retained its dramatic shape, but also old enough to support a rich vegetation and wildlife. The areas around Shinsakadaira and Arayama Kogen, in particular, are noted for the beauty of their azaleas in mid-June, and the autumn colors can be stunning around October 10 through 15. Akagi is noteworthy, in addition, for its many silver birches.

The connection with Shodo Shonin derives no doubt from his position as religious leader of Kozuke, present-day Gunma Prefecture. Shodo is credited with having rebuilt the Akagi Shrine, at Daido, just below where the bus stop is today (the shrine was formerly located elsewhere). However, his role in this may have been more that of an administrator than an ascetic. Again, it is interesting to note, however, how easily his beliefs merged with those of more ancient faiths.

MAEBASHI STATION ▶ AKAGI DAIDO BUS STOP
TIME EN ROUTE: 1 HOUR

The best way to reach the top of Mount Akagi is by bus to Akagi Daido. You can catch the bus at the Maebashi Station on the JR Line or at the Chuo Maebashi Station on the Jomo Dentetsu Line. Both trains run direct from Kiryu, but at just under five hundred yen, the JR train is the cheaper. If you are coming from Tokyo, take either an ordinary train, direct to Maebashi from Ueno Station, or the bullet train from Ueno to Takasaki, and change there for the last three stops to Maebashi. The bus to Akagi Daido leaves from bus stand number six on the north side of the station. The first bus leaves at 8:30 on weekends and holidays, from April 29 to November 3, and daily during the summer holidays. Otherwise, the first bus is at 9:30. The journey takes one hour and costs a little under fifteen hundred yen. The last bus down the mountain leaves at 16:35 in summer, and at 15:30 in winter.

The bus passes beneath a huge, red gate about twenty minutes from the station. This is the Kogure Ichinotorii, the first gate of Akagi Shrine. It stands a little over twenty-one meters high. From here, the top of the mountain is a little over twenty-one kilometers. Ten minutes later, the bus enters the mountain toll road, and the entire journey from there winds up the forested slopes of the volcano. Ten minutes from the toll gate, the bus comes to the stop at Minowa, the entrance to a couple of hiking courses in Akagi Woodland Park (Akagi Shinrin Koen). The bus stop for Shinsakadaira is another ten minutes after that. Then the bus begins its descent through a forest of glistening silver birches to Lake Onuma. The Akagi Daido bus stop is located a short way above the lake, right next to the Hotel Akagi and the chair lift and cable car to the top of Mount Jizo.

AKAGI DAIDO BUS STOP ▶ AKAGI VISITORS' CENTER
▶ KAKUMANBUCHI MARSH
WALKING TIME: 25 MINUTES

First, it is worth walking the five or so minutes on up the road to the Akagi Visitors' Center. Here are fine displays of the birds, animals, plants, fish, and insects of the mountain, together with geological information and some historical photos from the Meiji period. There are also several videos showing different aspects of the mountain, such as its seasons. The center is open from 9:00 to 16:00, and is closed Mondays. Admission is free (Tel: 0272-87-8402).

Then follow the Kanto Fureai no Michi sign on the other side of the road to the Kakumanbuchi Marsh. The path descends in just one minute to the small lake and marsh, where you should turn right. The Kakumanbuchi Marsh has a total circumference of only about five hundred meters, but it is very pretty and quite different from anything else on the mountain. It was once a part of Onuma, but became a marsh when the water level dropped. The area by the north bank around the small peninsula is a first-rate swamp, with peat to a depth of two and a half to three meters. The representative marsh plants include sphagnum (bog moss) and bogberry.

There is a rather curious notice by the side of the marsh, which recounts its history. All is well up to the point where it explains the origin of the name Kakumanbuchi. We are told that the marsh is named after the priest Kakuman of Mount Hiei. Kakuman, according to a medieval source, the *Shindoki*, conducted a seven-day-and-seven-night Buddhist high memorial service here during the reign of the Emperor Ingyo (412–53). This sounds a little fishy, as there are no records of Buddhism's presence in Japan at such an early date.

The path runs around the shore of the marsh on wooden plank walks, forking in ten minutes at the tip of the marsh. From here, it is just a five-minute, five-hundred-meter climb up to the right to the Torii Pass, the top of the pilgrimage route from Mizunuma (see Route 3 down Akagi below), and also the foot of the short path from Konuma. There are good views of the marsh from the pass.

On this hike, however, it is recommended that you turn left at the tip of the marsh and return down the other side toward Onuma. In seven minutes, there is a small fork. Either path is fine. The left fork leads to another short stretch on plank walks. Just beyond the junction on the right fork is a monument commemorating the visit of Emperor Showa to the Kakumanbuchi Marsh in October 1983. The paths then rejoin just one minute further on and come out onto the road. Turn right. A sign indicates one kilometer to Akagi Shrine.

KAKUMANBUCHI MARSH ▶ MOUNT KOMAGATAKE ▶ MOUNT KUROBI
WALKING TIME: 1 HOUR, 20 MINUTES

Four minutes from the right turn above, just as the road is about to descend to the lake, there is narrow path up to the right and another Kanto Fureai no Michi map and sign. This is the start of the route to the Hanamigahara Campsite. The sign indicates 6.4 kilometers to Hanamigahara and 1.4 kilometers to Komagatake.

The path begins with a steady climb up through the mixed woods on the side of the caldera, gradually getting steeper. The path is in excellent condition, with many good views of Onuma. About twelve minutes up from the road, there is a long stretch of metal steps over a steep, rough patch. There are more steps a little over ten minutes later. These bring the path out onto the rim of the caldera, with broad views on either side. There are few trees here, but many flowers. Turn left for Komagatake, now four hundred meters away. The path is still climbing, but up a much gentler slope than before. It takes twelve minutes to reach the peak. The path is at times overgrown, but easy to follow. For the last four minutes it is fenced off on the right, because of a hidden cliff just below.

Continuing on to Kurobi, there are steps leading down from the other side of Komagatake. The path descends for eight minutes, goes up and down a small peak, and then the stiff climb up to Kurobi begins. Sixteen minutes of steep, wooden steps lead to the T-junction for the path to Hanamigahara Campsite, now four kilometers away to the right, and to the top of Kurobi, to the left. The path to Hanamigahara and the Ichinotorii bus stop is described in the first route down Akagi, below.

If you turn left for the top of Kurobi, the lower of the two peaks is reached in just one minute. This peak commands a fine view, but not as good as that from the main peak, only a short way farther on. Ten meters beyond the first peak, there is a three-way junction: straight on for Kurobi and left for Daido and Onuma. First continue straight on. The view from the top, three minutes later, is magnificent, encompassing Kesamaru, Koshin, Sukai, Nantai, and the mountains of Kiryu, plus Tanigawa, Mikuni, Haruna, Myogi, and even Yatsugatake and Fuji. It is also possible to see the skyscrapers of Shinjuku.

MOUNT KUROBI ▶ AKAGI SHRINE ▶ AKAGI DAIDO BUS STOP

WALKING TIME: 1 HOUR, 5 MINUTES

There is no path down the far side of Kurobi, so it is necessary to return to the junction for the path down to Daido and Onuma. Turning right, the way is steep and rocky, but very refreshing to walk down. Not being part of the Kanto Fureai no Michi, this route, thankfully, has no more steps. After passing an outcrop known as Neko Iwa (Cat Rock), the path descends more gently down wooded slopes and is not always easy to see. There is little chance of getting lost, but keep an eye open for the ribbons on the trees. The path comes out at the road in fifty minutes. Turn left here for the five-minute walk to the Akagi Shrine.

The shrine is located on a small promontory in the lake, distinguished by the bright-red bridge that extends from the tip of the peninsula back to the lake shore. The main shrine festivals are the opening of the mountain on May 8 and the summer festival in August. In high season, however, the shrine itself is sadly overshadowed by the souvenir shops, refreshment stalls, and the various boats, some shaped like helicopters and swans, on the lake.

Akagi, as noted earlier, is a sacred mountain of long standing, and this shrine is a very old one, dedicated primarily to the god of the mountain. In fact, there are countless Akagi shrines in Gunma Prefecture. Old as this particular shrine may be, it was actually moved to this promontory (formerly the site of Itsukushima Shrine) only in 1970. Before this it was located just below the bus stop at Akagi Daido, where it had stood for nearly twelve hundred years, since 806. Still, that was not its original site. It was moved there from elsewhere, but the name Daido comes from this relocation; 806 was the first year of the reign of the Daido Emperor. There are various theories about where the Akagi Shrine stood before 806, including both Kurobi and Jizo, but the Jizo theory appears the most likely. Some pertinent remains are said to have been excavated there, but the records have now been lost.

Akagi was a popular destination for pilgrims bent on ascetic practices. The older mountain faith and Buddhism, here as elsewhere, mixed to the point where they were indistinguishable. Shodo Shonin was the religious leader of this district, Kozuke, from 782 to 809, and he is said to have supervised the construction of the shrine at Daido from 806 to 809.

Leave the shrine by the red bridge, and turn right down the road. It takes about ten minutes from here to the bus stop. Descend to the beach just after the tennis courts of the *kokumin shukusha* hostel (the large three-story building). There are many restaurants, and this is also the place to hire boats. It all feels very vulgar after the mountains, however. Walk all of the way to the end of the beach to the small shrine on a stone platform in the lake. This is the site of the old shrine at Daido. Climb up through the stone gate, cross the road, and ascend the steps on the other side to come back out at the bus stop.

CABLE CAR TO MOUNT JIZO AND PATHS DOWN TO KONUMA
AND SHINSAKADAIRA

The Akagi Daido bus stop stands right next to the chair lift and cable car to the top of Mount Jizo, so the hike can be rounded off with a ride up to the top of Jizo for a view of Konuma and, of course, Kurobi and Onuma. Then you can descend the short paths, either to Konuma and back around to the Akagi Daido bus stop via the Torii Pass, or to the bus stop at Shinsakadaira. The combined one-way lift and cable car ticket costs about six hundred yen. The word for "one-way" is *katamichi*.

There is a very new Jizo on the summit, together with a number of extremely battered old ones. An unusual story about this site concerns a Jizo that was placed here in 1406 on the lid of a cauldron. Tradition in the foothills of Akagi apparently held that the spirits of dead ancestors were confined in this cauldron. Each year on July 1, with the approach by the old calendar of the Bon Festival of the dead, the cauldron was opened and these spirits would descend the mountain. Then, on the night of the thirteenth, they would visit their old family temples and meet their descendants in the main hall, to be taken home to the houses of their birth. The families would later see them off again. On the seventeenth, a ceremony would be held on Mount Jizo to seal them back in beneath the lid. That Jizo and the cauldron were removed, for reasons unknown, in 1869.

The belief that ghosts dwell in the mountains is indeed very ancient. The people of the Watarase Valley have long thought that when they die their spirits rise to Akagi. The belief also developed that those who had lost their loved ones in the previous year should climb the mountain on April 8 (May 8 by the modern calendar, the day that the mountain is opened), in order to be reunited with them. This practice, which was especially important for those who had just lost a child, was known as *Akagi mairi*. In *Seta-gun Azuma-mura no Minzoku*, it is written that "climbing Mount Akagi and coming to the lake, one could see many phantoms of the dead and also people who greatly resembled the dead."

The many piles of stones on top of the mountain are closely associated with the Jizo faith and the saving of dead children. They represent *sai no kawara*, a kind of purgatory where children who have died go because they have failed in their duty to care for their elderly parents. There, a trial awaits them that seems to leap straight out of Greek legend. Some sources say that this term refers to the riverbed *(kawara)* of the river that divides this world from the next and that the children must pile up the stones in order to cross over. Most, however, explain that the children must pile up ten stones in order to be saved, but every time they reach the ninth stone, the whole pile is knocked down by blue and red devils. Then the children have to start all over again. This continues until Jizo comes along to save them. Parents, it is said, therefore pile up the stones themselves to help their children.

Interestingly, the concept of *sai no kawara* appears to be peculiar to Japan and to have appeared only in the Middle Ages as a folk tradition. There is no direct precedent for it in Buddhist scripture, though it should be noted that pilgrims in Tibet and elsewhere do pile up stones by the roadside as a form of prayer. Since a *sai no kawara* is a border area, there is also an obvious association with *sae no kami,* also known as *sai no kami,* the god of borders, (see page 177). This one is not, however, a particularly impressive *sai no kawara,* and not a patch on the one on the route up Kesamaru (see Hike 8).

Three paths lead down from the summit: to the left, one and a half kilometers to Konuma; back, two kilometers to Daido and Onuma; and two kilometers over the other side past the NHK broadcasting towers to Shinsakadaira.

The path to Shinsakadaira is quite steep and rocky at first, but soon becomes very gentle and relaxing, descending peacefully through birch woods and azalea, with views of Onuma to the right. It is fairly overgrown in places, but easy to follow. The path comes out to the road in thirty minutes, beside a yellow forestry sign at a large rest area, near the very top of the road, just after it starts descending to Onuma. Most tourist maps wrongly show this path as coming out above Shinsakadaira. (It is shown correctly as coming out below Shinsakadaira on the new Kanto Fureai no Michi map, produced by Gunma Prefecture for route numbers 20, 21, and 22, but wrongly on both the leaflet for route numbers 26, 27, and 35, and the map issued by the Akagi Tourist Association.) It is therefore necessary to turn left, not right, as Shinsakadaira lies five minutes back up the road.

Two minutes from the rest area is the Tembodaishita bus stop. Three minutes further on is the bus stop for Shinsakadaira, and, on the opposite side of the road, the unlikely Gunma Prefectural Energy Museum (Gunma Enerugi Shiryokan). This is open from April to November from nine to four, admission free. It has a rather nice tea shop and displays on hydroelectric, wind, solar, geothermal, nuclear, and other kinds of energy. Just beyond lie the cattle pastures and azaleas of Shinsakadaira itself. The azaleas are at their best around June 20. The last bus down from Shinsakadaira leaves at 16:41 in summer, one hour earlier in winter.

The path from Jizo down to Konuma is quite steep and rocky, but only takes about fifteen minutes, dropping straight down the bare mountainside. From there it is another twenty minutes or so back around to the bus stop at Daido. Konuma lies at an altitude of fourteen hundred fifty meters. It is an almost perfectly round lake that was formed by an explosive eruption from a new crater on the side of Mount Jizo. Although a road passes above, it is very peaceful compared with Onuma. The lake is surrounded by natural woods of *mizunara* oaks.

There is a legend connected with Konuma about the beautiful sixteen-year-old daughter of a wealthy man named Dogen, who lived in the village of Akabori, in the foothills of Akagi. Naturally, she had many suitors, but she refused them all. One day, although her parents tried to stop her, she suddenly set out to climb the mountain. Upon reaching this lake, she descended to the shore and placed her lips to the water. At that moment the beautiful young girl was sucked right in, never to be seen again. Three months later, however, when her parents brought an offering of pounded rice cakes for the repose of her soul, the plate on which the cakes were placed floated of its own accord across to the very center of the lake, where it spun round and round until it, too, descended to be lost in the depths.

As a sidelight on this legend, there is this quotation in *Seta-gun Azuma-mura no Minzoku* from someone living in the Kusagi area: "Since olden times, it has been said that sixteen-year-old girls shouldn't climb Akagi, because the daughter of Dogen of Akabori was sixteen when she entered Konuma and drowned."

FIRST ROUTE DOWN MOUNT AKAGI: MOUNT KUROBI ▶ HANAMIGAHARA CAMPSITE ▶ ICHINOTORII BUS STOP
WALKING TIME: 3 HOURS, 10 MINUTES

The path down to Hanamigahara starts from the junction just before the first of the two peaks of Kurobi, as described in the second section, above. This is probably the best way down the Watarase side of the mountain, with delightful paths for the first half of the walk. However, it does end with a rather long stretch along the road to the bus stop; the Hanamigahara Campsite actually states in its literature that campers ought to bring cars. The walk itself, however, is quite easy, and many people will find it rewarding even without a car waiting at the bottom. There is a very fair chance of seeing both monkeys and deer, and the rich variety of flowers, the silver birches, the larches, and the azaleas all serve to brighten the way.

Buses run about once every hour from Ichinotorii for the twenty-minute journey to the bus station at Mizunuma, a two-minute walk from Mizunuma Station on the Watarase Keikoku Tetsudo. The last bus leaves at about 19:00. At the bottom, of course, there is the Mizunuma Hot Spring Center for a timely soak in the bath.

SECOND ROUTE DOWN MOUNT AKAGI: LAKE KONUMA ▶ CHI NO IKE ▶ ARAYAMA KOGEN ▶ AKAGI HOT SPRING
WALKING TIME: 2 HOURS, 30 MINUTES

The highlights of this walk are the azaleas of Arayama Kogen and beautiful Chi no Ike, literally "Blood Pond," the least known of the three crater lakes of Akagi, and which looks rather like a lake out of Arthurian legend. The Akagi Hot Spring serves refreshments to casual visitors and also allows you to enter the bath for only four hundred yen. The water is so rich in iron that when you stand up, your whole body looks as if covered in droplets of orange juice. Legend has it that this hot spring was discovered by Toyokiirihiko, the elder son of Sujin (B.C. 97–30), the mythical tenth emperor of Japan. Sujin is also said to have been one of Shodo Shonin's ancestors. From the hot springs, you can either take a taxi to Ogo Station on the Jomo Dentetsu Line (the trains run between Nishi Kiryu and Shin Maebashi) or else walk on down along the Kanto Fureai no Michi, past the Fudo Otaki waterfall to the Chuji Hot Spring.

If you are starting this walk from the Akagi Daido bus stop, continue up the road, past the visitors' center and Kakumanbuchi Marsh, to the Torii Pass. The path up to Konuma is unmarked, but is well kept and easy to see. It leads up the mountainside to the right, just before the parking lot at the pass, heading backward toward, but above, the Akagi Daido bus stop. A thirteen-minute climb up through the woods, with views of Onuma down to the right, brings the path out onto a ridge. Turn right here. The sign indicates two hundred meters to Konuma, where you will find a large map of the route down to the Akagi Hot Spring (Akagi Onsen).

THIRD ROUTE DOWN MOUNT AKAGI: TORI' PASS ▶ RIHEIJAYA CAMPSITE ▶ ICHINOTORII BUS STOP
WALKING TIME: 2 HOURS, 20 MINUTES

There were eight routes taken up Mount Akagi by ascetics. The best known on the Watarase side leads up from the Basho monument, above Mizunuma, past two gates, Ichinotorii and Ninotorii, to the Riheijaya teahouse and the Torii Pass. The route is not recommended, as almost all of it now lies on ordinary and uninteresting roads, but it is the fastest way down.

The first three hundred meters of the path on the other side of the pass lead down concrete steps beside an old funicular railway, now virtually unused. Just near the foot of the steps, off to the right, there is a sacred rock and spring associated with the old mountain faith. There are ladles for drinking the water, labeled respectively, the water of beauty, the volcano god, wisdom, and happiness. Choose the one you need most. The souvenir shop at the pass sells containers for the water if you wish to take some home.

Then return to the foot of the railway, and take the path a short way up the steps to the right, signposted to the Riheijaya teahouse. It is said that there used to be thirteen stone Buddhas placed along the path from the pass to the teahouse, but they have long since disappeared. This is a charming, thirty-minute walk down through the woods along a well-maintained path. The trail comes out at the campsite, iris ponds, and bungalows of the holiday village that now stands where the teahouse used to be. The Riheijaya Campsite is an excellent place for families with small children and cars. It takes five minutes to walk down from the end of the path to the camp office.

From there, however, we are basically on the road all the way to Ichinotorii. It takes twenty minutes to the old stone gate at Ninotorii, and a further fifty minutes (including a brief climb) to the crossroads at Ichinotorii. The scenery has little to recommend it.

USEFUL KANJI

AKAGI DAIDO	赤城大洞
AKAGI HOT SPRING	赤城温泉
AKAGI SHRINE	赤城神社
AKAGI VISITORS' CENTER	県立赤城公園ビジターセンター
AKAGI WOODLAND PARK	赤城森林公園
ASHIO	足尾
CHI NO IKE (BLOOD POND)	血の池
DAIDO	大洞
GUNMA PREFECTURAL ENERGY MUSEUM	群馬エネルギー資料館
HANAMIGAHARA	花見ヶ原
HANAMIGAHARA KYANPUJO	花見ヶ原キャンプ場
ICHINOTORI	一ノ鳥居
JIGOKUDANI (HELL VALLEY)	地獄谷
KAKUMANBUCHI MARSH	覚満渕
KANTO FUREAI NO MICHI	関東ふれあいの道
KONUMA	小沼
KOZUKE HANAWA	上野花輪
MIZUNUMA	水沼
MOUNT AKAGI	赤城山
MOUNT JIZO	地蔵岳
MOUNT KOMAGATAKE	駒ケ岳
MOUNT KUROBI	黒桧山
NEKO IWA (CAT ROCK)	猫岩
NUMATA	沼田
ONUMA	大沼
RIHEIJAYA	利平茶屋
SHINSAKADAIRA	新坂平
"WATER OF BEAUTY"	美人の水
"WATER OF HAPPINESS"	幸福の水
"WATER OF THE SPIRITS"	御神の水
"WATER OF WISDOM"	知恵の水

PHALLIC CULTS, A LIVING BUDDHA, AND THE OLD COPPER ROAD

GODO STATION • TARO SHRINE • SEISUIJI • TOYOSATO SHRINE • HANAWA COPPER WAREHOUSE • ZEN'YUJI • SITE OF GORANDAJO CASTLE • HANAWA STATION

TOTAL WALKING TIME 3 HOURS, 35 MINUTES

MAPS 1:25,000 KOZUKE HANAWA; 1:50,000 ASHIO. A FREE KANTO FUREAI NO MICHI MAP (MARKED FOR ROUTES 28 AND 29) IS AVAILABLE FROM THE GUNMA TOURIST INFORMATION OFFICE

This walk is rather different from the others in that it sticks mainly to paved roads along the valley bottom, winding gently downhill along the banks of the Watarase. The scenery is not spectacular, though there are striking stretches in a couple of short gorges, occasional glimpses of Akagi and Kesamaru, and the views do open out toward Hanawa. Instead, this is a quiet pastoral landscape of woodland, vineyards, mulberries, and paddies, with several simple but fascinating historical remains. The most prominent among these are the Koshin stones and the phallic stones at the two shrines highlighted along this route: Taro and Toyosato. In addition, there is the fearful story of the priest of Zen'yuji, who transformed himself into a Buddha. Sections of this hike lie along the Akagane Kaido, the old Copper Road from Ashio. In Hanawa itself, there is an original copper warehouse still standing. At the finish, the route climbs up to the medieval site of Gorandajo castle, rounding off the walk with a panoramic view back up the valley and across to Kesamaru.

A large part of the walk lies along a section of the Kanto Fureai no Michi known as the Road of Nursery Rhymes. The quiet rural atmosphere of this pretty valley naturally conjures up images of goblins and fairies, but there is also a historical reason for this choice of name. Hanawa was the home of Ishihara Wasaburo, who wrote the lyrics of some of Japan's most famous children's songs.

GODO STATION ▸ TARO SHRINE ▸ SEISUIJI ▸ AZUMA SPORTS PARK
WALKING TIME: 50 MINUTES

I suggest starting this walk with a loop around to the Taro Shrine and Seisuiji before setting off toward the Kusagi Dam. One could easily, however, skip this first part if time is short.

Climb the steps opposite the station and turn left at the top. Keep left at the junction just afterward and continue past the Azuma Junior High School. Then turn left onto Route 122 at the T-junction, following the road sign to Omama. The Taro Shrine lies four minutes along the main road on the left-hand side, just past the old wooden noodle restaurant.

The Taro shrine is not much to look at, but it contains several items of interest. First, the steep road down from the shrine toward the Watarase is part of the Akagane Kaido. This "Copper Road" used to wind steeply up and down the gorge, so it is probable that travelers from Omama would have rested at this shrine at the top of the slope. There were both lodgings and a teahouse here, which I suppose must have been the origin of the restaurant.

The name of the shrine, Taro, means "man" or "eldest son." There are several Taro shrines in Gunma (including at Matsuida, Oga, and Tomioka), and the phallic stones displayed on their grounds are a striking feature of each. It is therefore suggested that Taro here is the name of a male god, a god of fertility. The phallic stones of this particular Taro shrine are located on the right at the top of the short flight of steps from the road. Here, there is a pair of Dosojin, the gods of the road, and two small phallic stones, inscribed with the characters Konsei Daimyojin. The one on the right (fifty-two centimeters high and thirty-five centimeters wide), is dated March 1819, while the one on the left is dated 1742, the same year as the stone lanterns by the gate. There also used to be a natural vagina-shaped rock here. A photograph of this from around 1965 appears in the *Seta-gun Azuma-mura no Minzoku*. Now, however, the rock has disappeared and quite possibly adorns someone's garden.

As for Konsei Daimyojin, this is a god to whom women pray if they want children or are suffering from a sexual disease. It is said that women anxious to have children would come here late at night when nobody was around and stroke the stones, praying all of the time. According to *Akagisan Fumoto no Seishin Fudoki* (Records of Sexual Faiths in the Foothills of Mount Akagi), stones like these have also recently been attracting worshipers seeking safety on the roads. This belief stems from a pun that doesn't really click in English even when it is explained: the expression *keganai* can mean either "no hair," in this case implying no pubic hair, or "no injury." The large monument at the rear of the shrine is a memorial to a locally born general.

Leaving the shrine, return along the main road past the junction up from the station. Seisuiji is about ten minutes from the shrine on the left-hand side of the road. This is a Kannon temple, said to have been founded in 1338. The Kannon statue in the main hall was carved from a whole tree, just like Shodo's Tachiki Kannon at Chuzenji. In this case, though, it is a Bato Kannon (Horse-headed Kannon), which is viewed as a guardian of livestock and also human travelers. Many horses from the neighboring village of Kurohone, decorated and hung with bells, used to take part in the festivals here on January 17 each year. Festivals were also held on March 17 every Year of the Horse. The importance given to the horse at this temple undoubtedly reflects its value to the people of this village on the Copper Road. (One of the finer statues of Bato Kannon to be seen in this area is seated alongside Amida and a Thousand-handed Kannon in the Sanbutsudo of Rinnoji, in Nikko.)

There is a virtual department store of roadside stones at the foot of the stone path up to the temple. The large one in front is a Bato Kannon, dated 1918. Next to it is a Koshin stone in the shape of a needle. Behind these, leading up the path, most of the stones are marked simply with the characters for Koshin. There are also, however, a Twenty-third Night Stone (see page 65), a Bato Kannon, with a fine carving of a horse, and a Koshin statue of Shomen Kongo (on the left at the end). Further along on the right is a row of Jizos, one of which holds the *shakujo* staff of the pilgrims.

Two long flights of stone steps lead up through the trees to the temple. The wooden building is plain but tasteful, with fine carvings of horses, a dragon, and gargoyles beneath the roof. There are also some old pagoda-style graves of priests behind the temple to the left, with tiers in shapes representing the old Chinese elements. The square blocks at the bottom represent earth; the round balls, water;

the lid-shaped ones, fire; the bowl-shaped ones, wind; and the dome-shaped ones on the top, emptiness. Taken together, these represent universal harmony, and this symbolic arrangement was the forerunner of the five-story pagoda.

Returning down the steps, cross Route 122 and go down the narrow road directly opposite, through the vegetable fields. Keep left at two consecutive T-junctions to rejoin the road just above Godo Station. This time, instead of descending the steps to the station, continue straight. The route to the Azuma Athletic Park is the same as the end of Hike 2, in reverse.

The Kanto Fureai no Michi is reached a couple of hundred meters below the athletic park. Signs point right to the Azuma Youth Training Center (Azuma Seinen Kenshu Center, 1.2 km) and straight on to the park (0.2 km). You may wish to visit the Nursery Rhyme Hall just beyond the park, described on page 86. Otherwise, it is suggested that you turn right here to commence the walk to Hanawa.

AZUMA ATHLETIC PARK ▶ TOYOSATO SHRINE
WALKING TIME: 50 MINUTES

The narrow road passes quietly between some houses and fields, through a small crossroads, and then turns right above a gateball ground (with graves, Kannons, and Jizos on the corner). There are clear views of the peaks of Akagi: Kurobi, Komagatake, and Jizo. Crossing a bridge, the road enters a forestry plantation, reaching the youth training center in a little over five minutes. This is a splendid wooden building, with various facilities. There are also benches overlooking the Watarase Valley, with a view back up toward the Kusagi Dam. Godo Station lies just below the center on the other side of the valley.

A sign indicates 3.5 kilometers to the Toyosato Shrine. The road continues for a while through the plantation, which also doubles as a mushroom farm, as evidenced by the many short logs on which the mushrooms are grown laid out beneath the trees. Then the road descends to the river to enter a narrow gorge. The railway runs directly opposite, and it is quite pretty to see the trains passing over the small waterfall. Out the other side, the walk comes to the paddies, mulberry fields, vineyards, cow sheds, pigsties, and persimmon orchards of Matsushima. There is a large map of the area at a junction which, in addition to identifying all of the farms, indicates the location of a Koshin stone, a Juni shrine, and plum blossoms. The Kanto Fureai no Michi sign reads two kilometers to the Toyosato Shrine.

The road now returns back into the trees for a little over a kilometer. There are two more Koshin stones at the eight-hundred-meter sign, where the route reemerges above a farm; there are also views of Kesamaru. The fields from here to the shrine stretch out over a suddenly very open landscape, extending toward the foothills of Akagi. Four hundred meters along on the right, there is a most unusual old stone stupa, the Marishitenzo, which was erected in 1568. Four seated buddhas are carved around the sides.

Marishiten is the Sanskrit *Marici,* a goddess of light and war. She is generally thought of as a fierce guardian of warriors and depicted mounted on a boar, elephant, tiger, dragon, or snake. According to *Seta-gun Azuma-mura no Minzoku,* however, she performs a much gentler role in this village. Actually, this is the place to pray for a cure for eye problems. First, supplicants pour water on the stupa, then bathe their eyes in the old water at the foot of the statue. This is performed every day or several times a week. Those whose afflictions are cured must write *me,* meaning "eye," once for each year of their age. This practice is probably related to one of Marishiten's great tricks in war — her ability to make herself invisible. Clearly, she has some kind of power over sight.

Only a minute further on the left, there is the Sayado Stone Five-storied Pagoda (Saiyado no Seki Goju no To), a 3.21-meter stupa erected in 1691. There is a discussion about the meaning of Sayado, the name of this district, in *Akagisan no Fumoto Seishin Fudoki.* Some suggest that it is Buddhist, Saya originally from *sai,* "to save," and *do* meaning "to cross." That would imply that Sayado is the border between life and death. It is also possible (although the effective meaning would change little), that the *sai* is the *sai* of *sai no kawara,* the limbo of dead children described earlier, and also of *sae* (or *sai*) *no kami,* the god of boundaries. This god of borders is closely related to the Dosojin and Jizo faiths. A *sayado* would then be a place for worshiping the *sae no kami* in order to obtain his protection for the village against the entry of evil and also to look after travelers.

Virtually all of the fields in this area on the left bank of the Watarase were mulberry until as recently as the mid-1950s. The appearance of rice paddies here was due to the construction of a remarkable conduit known as the Hanawa Yosui, which siphons irrigation water from the high ground on the far side of the valley right under the Watarase itself. That was completed in 1955.

The Toyosato Shrine lies just three minutes further along on the left. A Kanto Fureai no Michi stone placed in front of the shrine reads 4.9 kilometers back to the sports park and 2.2 kilometers to Hanawa Station. The Toyosato Shrine is dedicated to Okuninushi, the same god celebrated at the grand shrine in Izumo. It is thus a shrine for the god of good fortune, who protects the country, as indeed is also suggested by the name, Toyosato, "Prosperous Home." It is said that this shrine was founded in 1768.

Climbing up the short flight of steps, you first reach a sacred cedar, the Nyoin Cedar, the "Female Yin Tree." As might be expected, this is one of a pair. Its mate is a natural phallic stone that lies just behind the shrine to the right. At least, it is said to be natural, but it looks so lifelike that I somehow find that hard to believe. It has a remarkably smooth surface, standing 1.1 meters high (1.55 meters, including the base) and with a diameter of fifty centimeters. The date on the base is 1819. Again, women would pray for children at this stone. If successful, they would make offerings of *ema,* small pieces of wood with drawings of horses.

There is a story that this phallic stone was washed up by the Watarase River beside the Sayadoji, where it was discovered by people from both Shimo Sayado and Osawa. There followed a great argument about who should enshrine the stone, until eventually it was agreed to decide by seeing who could lift it. Osawa won, and it was taken there. Later, during a war, it was buried inside the border of the village. It was dug out again in the 1920s and placed in its present position.

All of these phallic stones may seem rather amusing to modern eyes, but it should be remembered that they are indirect records of many personal tragedies. Until very recently, the status of women in these villages was extremely low. It is said that newlywed women in Hanawa were not allowed to return to the home of their birth at all for the first two years after marriage. Even after that, they could visit their parents only at New Year's and the Bon Festival of the dead. Moreover, they could be divorced and have their heads shaved by their husbands if they failed to deliver a child within three years. And, of course, no medical care was available for the poor. These phallic stones stand as grim reminders of the desperate women, who came in the dark of the night when no one would see them, to clutch them and frantically pray for healthy offspring.

Behind the shrine to the left is a group of large Koshin stones and stone shrines. Six stones have the name of Sarutahiko carved on their faces, while the seventh has the characters for Koshin and also looks suspiciously phallic. The dates on five of the six Sarutahiko Koshin stones are 1740, 1745, 1784, 1785, and 1787.

TOYOSATO SHRINE ▶ INARI SHRINE ▶ HANAWA COPPER WAREHOUSE ▶ SUWA SHRINE
WALKING TIME: 40 MINUTES

The road next leads across the fields, past a number of fine old storehouses in the farmyards, each emblazoned with a family crest. The Kanto Fureai no Michi briefly branches nine minutes from the Toyosato Shrine. The sign points left to the Inari Shrine, on to Hanawa Station (1.4 km), and back eight hundred meters to Toyosato Shrine. Turning left, the Inari Shrine stands just one hundred meters across the fields. The stone gate to the shrine is flanked by two huge Koshin stones. The one on the left is dated 1783; the one on the right, 1800.

The shrine itself is an old wooden building dedicated to a god named Ugadama. The Kanto Fureai no Michi sign informs us that the *uga* of this name means "food." It then goes on to observe that since Inari is thought to be a truncation of *inenari,* meaning "plentiful rice," this is clearly a shrine at which prayers should be made for a good harvest.

Inari is, indeed, widely recognized throughout Japan as the god of the harvest. The main Inari Shrine at Fushimi, in Kyoto, dates from at least the tenth century and, according to yet another dubious legend, was founded by Kukai. Inari shrines today are common all over Japan and are easily recognized by presence of fox statues on the shrine grounds; the fox is the messenger of Inari. In addition to prayers for the harvest, a wide range of other requests are made to them. At Inari shrines in Tokyo, for example, prayers for deliverance from the pox are made at Yanaka (near Ueno), from eye disease at Ichigaya, and from possession of one's wife by fox spirits at Yushima. Inari himself appears to be an interesting composite god related to both Koshin-sama and the Dosojin.

Some authorities believe that Inari is a direct amalgam of Ugadama with Sarutahiko and Ama no Uzume, all three of whom are said to be enshrined at the main Inari Shrine, in Fushimi. Sarutahiko, in addition to being the monkey god of the Koshin faith, is also considered to be a god of fertility. In the *Kojiki,* the ancient chronicle of Japan, it is related that he married Ama no Uzume, a goddess of sexual attraction. These two together, moreover, are often identified with the Dosojin. Just as Koshin-sama later became a single god, so, too, did this earthy assembly of deities on Mount Inari.

Returning to the junction, the road quickly passes the Sankei guesthouse on the right, crossing the Watarase at the Azuma bridge and the Watarase Keikoku Tetsudo at Nakano Station. The road again passes through a narrow gorge, and then the valley opens out into a broad river plain. The house on the right, just after the road crosses the railway a second time, stands on the site where nursery-rhyme composer Ishihara Wasaburo (see pp. 86) used to live.

The Kanto Fureai no Michi continues down the high street of Hanawa, with several places to eat along the way. Just before Hanawa Station, there is a three-way Kanto Fureai no Michi sign: 1.3 kilometers back to the Inari Shrine; one hundred meters right to Hanawa Station; and four hundred meters on to the Hanawa Copper Warehouse. This is, in fact, the end of the Kanto Fureai no Michi, but it is strongly recommended that you continue to Zen'yuji and the site of Gorandajo castle, as detailed below.

First, the copper warehouse is reached surprisingly quickly. It can be recognized by the white post outside. This was one of five warehouses used to store copper carried down from Ashio to the Tone River for shipment to Asakusa. The warehouse looks no different from the many other white storehouses standing in farmyards along the route. These days it is used for keeping family possessions, although in the house of the owner, written records do remain of copper shipments made in the Edo period. There are also wooden identification tags that were placed on the loads of the pack horses. Some look amazingly new, but all are a couple of centuries old and are designated cultural treasures.

Continuing along the road from the warehouse, turn right down the narrow lane at the next junction. There is a bus stop on the corner and also a pedestrian crossing. The road bends right sharply by the railway, but turn left instead down the short, muddy path behind the gateball ground, and cross the railway at the small, level crossing. Then turn left along the road up a slight hill. The rear of the Suwa Shrine, an old wooden building, is reached in about three minutes from the railway.

The gods worshiped at the Suwa Shrine are Takeminakata and Onamuchi, the same as at the famous Suwa Shrine at Suwa, in neighboring Nagano Prefecture. Onamuchi is another name for Okuninushi, the god who is worshiped at the Toyosato Shrine. The *Kojiki,* the ancient chronicle, tells how Okuninushi pacified the earth and handed it over to Amaterasu, the sun goddess and ancestress of the Japanese imperial line. These events directly precede the descent from heaven and meeting of Sarutahiko and Ama no Uzume.

As for Takeminakata, he is traditionally thought of as the second son of Okuninushi. Whereas Okuninushi submitted to Amaterasu, however, Takeminakata did not. This clearly echoes some ancient political conflict, which some even interpret in terms of strife between Japan and the ancient kingdoms of Korea. Takeminakata was enshrined by the Suwa family of Nagano, who claimed direct descent from him.

SUWA SHRINE ▶ ZEN'YUJI ▶ SITE OF GORANDAJO CASTLE
WALKING TIME: 35 MINUTES

Go all of the way down to the bottom of the steps from the shrine, and continue by the unpaved road. Zen'yuji is reached almost immediately. The temple was founded in 806, in the Daido period, at the same time as Shodo Shonin was rebuilding the Akagi Shrine. Zen'yuji was later revived in 1338 by Chuko Shonin. There was a great fire in 1868, however, in which many treasures were lost.

One of the temple's most striking features is the great pyramid of unnamed graves by the roadside, erected in 1932. Entering the gate here, there is an unusual mirror-shaped monument in front of the temple. Known as the Basho Monument, after the famous haiku poet, it was erected in the summer of 1796. The monument commemorates a poetry meeting between Gihaku, the priest of Zen'yuji, Nikkyu, a haiku poet from Isesaki, and Soko, a visitor from Kanazawa; poems by all three appear on the back. The poem on the front was written by Basho at the Nagara River, where the scenery is supposed to resemble that of the Watarase:

Around here
All that meets my eyes
Is cool

This evening chill became the chosen theme for the verses of the three:

While talking
The shallows beckon
In the cool of evening

— *Gihaku*

Growing too cool
If we walk to the river
The moon may be out

— *Nikkyu*

The river wind
Silhouettes from behind
In the cool of evening

— *Soko*

Gihaku is also remembered as Gyokei Shonin. He entered Kaneiji in Ueno at the age of eleven. After a short spell in Nikko, Gihaku became priest of this temple in his mid-thirties. He is said to have become a Living Buddha after reaching his eightieth birthday, on March 12, 1814. It is recounted that he made his decision as follows: "Now that I have lived to the same age as the Buddha when he entered Nirvana, it is time for me to express my deepest gratitude. To repay my blessings, I shall now transform myself into Yakushi Nyorai (the Healing Buddha) and save those stricken by disease." He had a hole dug in the precincts of the temple and left these final words: "Having seen the moon and the snow, and the falling blossoms, this spring I return to the land of joy."

He gave instructions that his people should assume that he had died once they could no longer hear his bell. He then began an unceasing round of prayer in the underground hole, neither eating nor drinking. The sound of the bell is said to have continued for twenty-one days. A stone statue of Yakushi, dated March 12, was erected over this place. The statue still stands today in a small, wooden hall among the graves to the right of the temple. There are also a stupa and a Jizo statue in the temple grounds, said to have been erected by Gihaku himself.

The term "Living Buddha" may sound something of a contradiction, but the idea is based on a particular concept of life. In short, priests who undergo this kind of fast and worship unto death are thought to enter a state known as *nyujo* or *samedhi*. This is a condition of peaceful contemplation, a sort of suspended animation, that continues until the coming of the Buddha of the future, Miroku (Maitreya in Sanskrit), at the commencement of the next cosmic cycle. Even Kukai had himself buried alive at a quiet spot on Mount Koya in 835, now the Oku no In of Kongobuji, where tradition has it that he is still deep in meditation today. The mummified remains of several priests who underwent this ordeal are preserved at various temples around Japan. These days, however, the practice counts as suicide, which, thankfully, is illegal under Japanese law.

One other treasure of Zen'yuji is a scroll written by Tenkai, the priest who arranged for the building of Toshogu, when he visited in 1629. Tenkai is also said to have visited the temple in 1617, the year that he transferred Ieyasu's remains to Nikko.

Leaving Zen'yuji, keep going in the same direction, this time along the road. Turn right at the T-junction one minute later. Then go straight across the junction with the main road and continue up the narrow road on the other side. Soon the views of the valley begin to improve. The last house is passed two minutes from the main road. Take the right fork fifty meters later. The narrow, single-lane road climbs up the side of the valley, then levels out, and passes more fields. Take the left fork at the next junction. The paving gives out soon afterward. Four minutes from the fork, a narrow path leads up to the left. It is marked by a white post that reads "Gorandajo Castle Entrance." The post further indicates that the castle belonged to Matsushima Zaemon, who defied Hojo Soun and was killed in battle in 1510.

The path leads quite steeply up through the woods, but it is well maintained and easy to follow. There are a few old wooden signs to point the way where the path divides. It takes about twenty minutes to the small stone shrine just below the summit. The view of Kesamaru and the Watarase Valley is a fitting way to wind up the day, giving a fresh perspective on the walk down from Godo. It is also worth climbing the final three minutes to the very top for the view of Akagi on the other side.

SITE OF GORANDAJO CASTLE ▶ HANAWA STATION
WALKING TIME: 40 MINUTES

To return to Hanawa Station, retrace the same route down as far as the small level crossing by the gateball field. Then turn left and follow the road beside the railway.

USEFUL KANJI

ASHIO	足尾
AZUMA ATHLETIC PARK	東総合運動公園
AZUMA YOUTH TRAINING CENTER	東青年研修センター
GODO STATION	神戸駅
"GORANDAJO CASTLE ENTRANCE"	五覧田城跡入口
COPPER WAREHOUSE	銅蔵
HANAWA STATION	花輪駅
INARI SHRINE	稲荷神社
KANTO FUREAI NO MICHI	関東ふれあいの道
KONSEI DAIMYOJIN	根生大明神
KOSHIN	庚申
KOZUKE HANAWA	上野花輪
MARISHITENZO	まりしてん像
OMAMA	大間々
SAYADO FIVE-STORIED STONE PAGODA	小夜戸の石五重の塔
SARUTAHIKO	猿田彦
SUWA SHRINE	諏訪神社
SEISUIJI	清水寺
TARO SHRINE	太郎神社
TOYOSATO SHRINE	豊郷神社
ZEN'YUJI	善雄寺

HIKE 8 ▲ KESAMARU
MOUNTAIN OF MYTH AND FABLE

SORI STATION • NESHAKA (SLEEPING BUDDHA) • SAI NO KAWARA • MOUNT KESAMARU • OTAKI WATERFALL • OTSUKEBASHI BUS STOP (OR SAI NO KAWARA • OTAKI WATERFALL • OTSUKEBASHI BUS STOP)

TOTAL WALKING TIMES 7 HOURS, 30 MINUTES, VIA MOUNT KESAMARU; 4 HOURS, 50 MINUTES, BYPASSING MOUNT KESAMARU. ADD 40 MINUTES TO BOTH TIMES IF DESCENDING TO KONAKA STATION

MAPS 1:50,000 ASHIO; 1:25,000 SORI; 1:25,000 KESAMARUYAMA; 1:25,000 KOZUKE HANAWA

The full walk to the top of Mount Kesamaru and back again is close to the limit of what can be achieved in a single day. However, it is a hike with so many rewards that it should be one of the top priorities of anyone using this book. A very early start is essential if it is all to be fitted in. If you don't have your own tent, I'd suggest staying either at the Okuwatarase Log Cabins in Sori or the Izumiya Ryokan in Ashio, in which case you can catch the first train in the morning from Tsudo at 6:04. Another possibility is to take a sleeping bag and stay at the shelter just below Sai no Kawara. The shelter is only a simple hut, but it is clean. This also opens up the possibility of going on from Kesamaru and Oku Kesamaru all of the way to the Rokurinpan Pass and down to the Koshin Lodge at Mount Koshin. Be warned, though, that the trail on from Kesamaru is virtually nonexistent and should not be attempted without very thorough preparation.

The day begins with the stiff climb up a pretty valley to the statue of a Sleeping Buddha and the natural rock pillar known as Sorinto. Tradition holds that the Buddha was carved by Shodo Shonin himself, though it is almost certainly of much later origin. The carving is of high artistic merit, and is perched on top of a very precarious granite outcrop; it will surely be one of the lasting memories of any visit to this area. The Sorinto is unusual in a different way, the center of a complex web of legends that point again to an ancient phallic religion.

Next, there is Sai no Kawara and the lookout point beside it on the ridge. There are many *sai no kawara* (stone piles) in Japan, but this is one of the most impressive. From the lookout point, there are fine views of Akagi and Kesamaru. Kesamaru is a Pleistocene volcano, but it is very hard to tell exactly where its crater was. At this point, the day's main work is done, for Sai no Kawara lies at an altitude of fifteen hundred meters. For those who are running out of time, however, there is the option of descending here and taking a shortcut to the Otaki waterfall.

If you do have the time, it is smooth sailing along the ridge, with superb views on either side, on the left toward Akagi, and on the right toward Koshin, Nokogiri, and Sukai. The autumn colors, in particular, are truly spectacular. Finally, you cross over two of the four peaks and continue down the other side, along the top of another long ridge. There the views stretch out across the Kanto Plain and all of the way to Mount Fuji. The path and then the forest road come out at the ninety-six-meter Otaki waterfall, one of the little-known treasures of this region.

This is a region of abundant wildlife, including monkeys, serows, deer, bears, hares, ermine, and martens. Traces of bears are especially evident in the hemlock woods in the higher reaches of the course. In addition, as related below, the area is rich in tradition and folklore.

SORI STATION ▶ NESHAKA (SLEEPING BUDDHA) ▶ SAI NO KAWARA
WALKING TIME: 2 HOURS, 40 MINUTES

The first part of the climb lies along the Kanto Fureai no Michi, so it is generally well signposted. Turn left out of the station, cross the bridge, and turn left up the road on the far side.

It is best to go straight through the first crossroads (by the small shops and vending machines), but there are two points of interest just down the road to the left. One, a designated cultural treasure of Azuma Village, is a short stretch of the Akagane Kaido, the old Copper Road that once led from Ashio all of the way to the Tone River and, ultimately, to the warehouse at Asakusa, in Tokyo. It is a tiny lane off to the left, marked by a white post, just after a small shrine (the characters for Akagane Kaido are written on the post). The lane now leads down to a small park by the river. Just further are the tents and bungalows of the Okuwatarase Campsite. In view of the distance to Mount Kesamaru, this is one of the best places to stay for an early start up the mountain.

Going straight on at the crossroads mentioned above, however, the road immediately comes out on Route 122 to Ashio. Turn left, then right, up the narrow road five minutes later, just after Daitakuji. The Kanto Fureai no Michi signs indicate six kilometers to Neshaka, the Sleeping Buddha, and eight hundred meters back to Sori.

Daitakuji was founded in the mid-seventeenth century by Kamitsu, the priest of Kyorinji in Maebashi. Its main festival is on April 23. Entering the compound, there is a very new hutlike Koshin hall on the left, with a long row of Koshin stones and Jizos outside. Peering inside, you will see only a large drum, but there is also an old statue of Koshin-sama, hidden behind the curtain. This statue is the subject of a most peculiar legend.

The story goes as follows: When Kukai was descending from Kesamaru, he met and fought off a great white snake. As it was getting late, he took shelter for the night in a cave by a waterfall. During the night, he heard a voice calling his name and, looking outside, saw a light in the water. A small Buddha cried out for help and then suddenly was swept away. Kukai didn't know what to do. Hearing a cock crow, he realized that there must be a farmhouse nearby and decided to wait until morning. As soon as it was light, he descended to the house and organized a search. It is said that the result of that search was the Koshin-sama that stands in the Koshin hall today. Tradition has it that the statue was kept in a cave until Meiji Restoration in 1868, after which it was moved to the temple.

It is out of the question that this Koshin statue could actually date from the time of Kukai and Shodo. There are countless Kukai legends all over Japan and almost all have to be taken with a pinch of salt. The mention of the snake, though, is certainly interesting, both in view of the association of snakes with the mountain god (see page 98) and the snake legend of the Sorinto described below. The priest of Daitakuji, incidentally, is also said to be the steward of the statue of the Sleeping Buddha at the top of the valley.

Just past the junction, a house attached to Daitakuji sells *ema,* votive pictures of horses, for those intending to pray at the Sleeping Buddha. The sign outside indicates that they cost five hundred yen and are effective, as usual, for just about anything: growth of heart and mind, alleviation of disease, success in business, safety at work, prevention of disasters, happiness in the home, and road safety.

After passing a pretty wayside shrine, the road turns into a gravel track just seven minutes from the junction with Route 122. This climbs up mainly through forestry plantations, reaching the branch in the Kanto Fureai no Michi in twenty-five minutes. The signs point back to Sori, right to Neshaka, and left to Konaka. Turning right, follow this forest road for twenty more minutes to the junction at a bend where it turns up a small stream. The Kanto Fureai no Michi sign indicates 1.8 kilometers to Neshaka. The start of the mountain trail to Kesamaru is just a few minutes from here.

From this point on, the walk is truly beautiful. The path winds up through secondary woods, mainly of cedar, but actually quite varied; there are even some *sawagurumi,* walnut trees (Pterocarya rhoifolia), along the foot of a boulder-strewn valley. The climb is quite steep, though, so it takes a good forty minutes to reach the Sleeping Buddha. The end is in sight when the path reaches climbing steps cut into the side of the valley.

The Neshaka is a large carving of a reclining Buddha cut into the rock at the pinnacle of the granite outcrop, to the left of the signs. The views back down the valley from the top are invigorating. Nearby is also a natural rock pillar known as the Sorinto. The picnic tables beside the stream just behind the Neshaka are an ideal place to rest. It is also possible to walk down to the pillar from there.

Whereas one legend has it that this Buddha was carved by Shodo Shonin, another tells that it was made by Kukai. It seems more likely, however, that it was sculpted much later, during the early years of the Edo period. There is a local tradition that many skilled sculptors settled in the Sori and Hanawa area after working on the construction of Toshogu, in Nikko. It is tempting to believe that one of these sculptors may have carved the Sleeping Buddha, for it is surely the work of a master. A further tradition suggests that it was carved to bring repose to the souls of the prisoners who were sent to work in the mines of Ashio and died there. The Buddha lies with his head pointing north and gazing west, the position chosen by Gautama, the historical Buddha, when he lay down to die. The first definite record of the Sleeping Buddha comes from a travelogue written in 1782, by Takayama Hikokuro, who also described the walk up Narukami in Kiryu. Significantly, Hikokuro described the statue as a recent work. There used to be an annual festival at the Sleeping Buddha, but this was later moved to Daitakuji.

The Sorinto pillar is completely natural, eighteen meters tall, and some three meters wide. There is a story that it once stood seven kilometers away, close to the Watarase River, and was worshiped by women who would climb to the top to request favors from the gods. The Tengu of Kesamaru is said to have been so enraged to see the pillar defiled by all these women that one night he removed it, block by block, to its present position. Since he reerected the blocks in reverse order, however, the top at the bottom, and the bottom at the top, the pillar is now thinner at the base and thicker higher up. However, white snakes were buried inside to keep it standing, with the result that, however precarious it may look, not even the strongest earthquake can knock it down. (It is not actually quite true that the top is wider than the bottom, but it is at any rate a most curious structure.)

There is a further tradition that no one should approach the Sleeping Buddha and Sorinto before April 8 each year, because the white snakes will get them. On that day, the priest of Daitakuji used to climb to the Sorinto and seal the snakes back inside. In fact, Hikokuro refers to the Sorinto as the White Snake Stupa in his travelogue.

The phallic undertones of all this are unmistakable and discussed in some detail in *Akagisan Fumoto no Seishin Fudoki*. The writer makes the remarkable observation that a very comparable Sleeping Buddha and phallic pillar can be observed at the Wat Pho in Bangkok, Thailand. There, the top of the pillar is colored gold. Women who wish to bear children climb up to write their wishes. He observes that similar traditions can also be found all over Asia, from Korea and Siberia to India and Nepal. In Korea, there is a custom of hugging the phallic pillar or placing one's back to it and circling from left to right. This is said to create the perfect yin-yang balance for maximizing sexual power. It is claimed, in fact, to be more effective than even a hundred packets of herbal medicine! Korean mothers would bring their daughters to such pillars prior to their weddings in order to ensure happy marriages.

The author of *Akagisan Fumoto no Seishin Fudoki* next considers how the Tengu legend may be connected with the *shugendo,* the ascetic mountain routes which, in this area, were particularly associated with the paths opened up by Shodo Shonin. He tells us that the Sorinto pillar was a sacred place on the *shugendo*. In those days, as we know, women were strictly banned from such spots. Thus, he suggests, the old sacred object of female worship was probably taken over by the men. Tengu, with his fierce face and long red nose is obviously a male symbol; the book equates Tengu with the pillar itself. The account also notes that there is a waterfall halfway up, the Fudo no Taki (just close to the point where the forest road first crosses the stream down from the Sleeping Buddha), which elsewhere in Gunma is a recognized female symbol. The author therefore suggests that the Sleeping Buddha and the phallic pillar are jointly the male portion of a yin-yang combination. He further suggests that the *shugendo* connection is an important clue to why the pillar is known as Sorinto. He argues that the original name was probably Sorito, after the name of the village below. A *rinto,* however, is a type of five-storied pagoda; there is a famous *rinto* called Sorinto at Shodo's Rinnoji in Nikko.

Continuing up the path, the next kilometer and a half up to Sai no Kawara is equally beautiful and the gradient somewhat gentler. The path crosses in and out of the stream then briefly climbs away from it up to the left, twenty-five minutes from the Sleeping Buddha, at a small white sign to Kesamaru; it rejoins the stream three minutes later. As the path climbs higher, it enters a zone of mixed woods, with birches, azalea, *ookamenoki (Vibernum furcatum,* a kind of woodbine), alder, oak *(mizunara),* and red pine. There are quite a few steps and, forty minutes from Neshaka, an emergency shelter and toilet. The sign here reads two hundred meters to Sai no Kawara. The path now climbs away from the stream through increasingly open woods and thick bamboo grass, reaching the ridge at Sai no Kawara in just seven minutes.

Sai no Kawara is an astonishing sight, with many great piles of volcanic stones dedicated to the spirits of dead children, and also a single Jizo statue. The effect is awe-inspiring at a location so deep in the mountains, especially in mist or when the azaleas are in bloom. It is said that when Kukai first came here it was nearing sunset, and he could hear the sound of wailing children. Looking toward the place from where the sounds were coming, he saw hellish flames and a great horde of children laboring to pile up stones. As related earlier, there is a Japanese tradition that children in purgatory must pile up ten stones in order to return to this world. Every time they reach nine, however, devils knock their piles down again, so they have to start all over again. The tale goes that Kukai recited sutras for three nights to save the children. It is still thought that parents who pile stones here will be able to meet their lost children. A Sai no Kawara, as explained in Hike 6, is a border region that separates two worlds. This ridge truly seems to be just that, standing as it does halfway between the valley and the mountain.

The path to Kesamaru leads up the ridge to the right from here. Those not intending to come back this way should first walk one hundred meters to the left to the Tsutsujidaira (Azalea Plateau). In addition to the plentiful azaleas, there is a tall lookout post offering splendid views of Akagi, Kesamaru, and the mountains of Nikko. The way down from here to the Oriba entrance to the hiking course (Oriba Tozanguchi) and back to Sori or on to the Otaki waterfall is described in the next section below. As mentioned earlier, though, it is an awful waste having come this far not to go on to Kesamaru itself. The route to Kesamaru and on from there to the waterfall is described in the following two sections.

SAI NO KAWARA ▶ OTAKI WATERFALL
WALKING TIME: 1 HOUR, 35 MINUTES

The most attractive route down from Sai no Kawara is the way up via the Neshaka, but it is also possible to descend to the forest road from here. This is not especially recommended, however, because it is still a long way to the bottom and the road is very hard on the feet. If you do choose to descend to the road, continue past the lookout point at Tsutsujidaira. This path follows the ridge and generally descends quite gently. There has been quite a lot of felling in this area, so the mountainsides are completely bare in places, but the scenery is nonetheless fairly impressive, with some especially fine views of Mount Akagi at the far end of the range. The path comes out on the forest road between Sori and Konaka, at the very top of the pass just thirty minutes from Sai no Kawara, descending the final stretch down some steep steps.

Here there is a choice of routes, both downhill all the way on forest roads, and virtually the same distance. The Kanto Fureai no Michi turns left for Sori Station, 10.4 kilometers away, rejoining the path at the branch mentioned in the first section above. Turning right, the road leads 6.4 kilometers down to the entrance to the Otaki waterfall, the terminus of another stretch of the Kanto Fureai no Michi, which then descends a further 3.4 kilometers to the Otsukebashi bus stop for the infrequent bus service down to Konaka Station.

Assuming that you turn right, it takes sixty-five minutes to reach the entrance to the waterfall. There is a Kanto Fureai no Michi sign at a bend, indicating three hundred meters left down a path to the waterfall and 3.4 kilometers on down the road to the bus stop. The waterfall is well worth a visit, for it is certainly one of the better falls in the Kanto area. Like so many other places in this region, the falls are best viewed either when the azaleas (pink *yashio tsutsuji*) are in bloom or against the backdrop of the autumn tints. First, the path descends to a bridge and river beach with picnic tables, then climbs up and around the other side of the valley to a viewing point on top of an outcrop. The water plunges ninety-six meters, almost perpendicularly, in a two-stage fall. It is possible to descend a short way down toward the falls from below the lookout point. Then, it is necessary to return to the road by the same path. The route down to the bus stop is described in the final section below.

SAI NO KAWARA ▶ MOUNT KESAMARU
WALKING TIME: 2 HOURS

The next stage of the walk to Mount Kesamaru is very easy, though the bamboo grass is high in places. Close to Kesamaru, this makes the path quite hard to see. It is not so hard to follow, however, because this is a popular course. The best and easiest technique, therefore, is to take the path of least resistance through the grass. Actually, it is virtually always possible to see the way for at least a few steps in front. With a map as well, you need have little fear of getting lost, because the path runs on the very top of the ridge, with views for miles on either side. As usual, if in doubt, look for the red ribbons on the trees.

There is a second Sai no Kawara just a minute or so from the first, with many more stretches of bare andesite rocks as the route progresses. The views are stupendous, but especially fascinating for the vivid perspective they give on the hikes around Akagi and between Koshin and Sukai. This is the sort of route that really brings the maps to life, for it is all there, right in front of your eyes.

Meanwhile, the sheer peaks of Kesamaru are looming up ever closer in front of you. The simplicity of the ridge is a great relief after the climb up to Sai no Kawara but, inevitably, there is also a lurking anxiety about just how those cliffs are to be scaled.

The top of Mount Komaru is reached after a comfortable forty-five-minute stroll. This, too, is a fine lookout point. The typical trees in this area are birches, hemlock, and mountain ash *(nanakamado,* or *Sorbus commixta).* The trail then leads through deep bamboo grass toward Mae Kesamaru, the first of the mountain's four main peaks. There are plenty of ribbons to show the way, but, if in doubt, just keep heading toward the mountain. The final climb is steep, though not at all dangerous. There are many traces of wild animals on this part of the route.

The last stretch up Mae Kesamaru offers some of the most magnificent views of any of the hikes in this book. From here and onward almost all of the way to the junction with the forest road down to Otaki, there is the glorious feeling of being right out on top of the world. At the summit, a sign reads five hundred meters on to Kesamaru, the main peak, and one-and-a-half kilometers back to Komaru.

The ridge between these two peaks is very narrow, dropping steeply down, and then rising equally steeply back up again. But here, too, there is not much cause for anxiety. This connecting col is called Hattanbari, the Eight Tan Net (1 *tan* = 0.245 acres). The image appears to be that of a huge bird-trapping net strung between the peaks. The top of the main peak, Ato Kesamaru, is reached in twenty-five minutes. Here, after all of those wonderful panoramic views on the way up, you can see absolutely nothing at all because of the trees. Amusingly, there is a sign pointing *back* to Kesamaru, as if neither summit wants to take responsibility. According to the map, however, this is the real one.

As I understand it, this is where Kukai, the more famous contemporary of Shodo Shonin and the founder of the Shingon sect, is said to have hung up his cassock, his *kesa,* thus giving the mountain its name. I have come across two versions of the story about what he was doing here. Both suppose that he was trying to develop this area as another Mount Koya, the base of his Shingon sect. One account says that he was trying to build Koya on Akagi. The god of Akagi, however, resented having his mountain taken over by Buddhism. Although he allowed Kukai to find nine hundred ninety-nine valleys, he hid the one thousandth for his own purposes. Kukai came as far as Kesamaru looking for that one thousandth valley, but it wasn't here, either. Discouraged, he rolled up *(marumeta)* his cloak *(kesa)* and left it here, hence the name. It is obviously tempting to read all sorts of things into this story about the conflict between Buddhism and the older faiths.

The other version is that Kukai found one hundred valleys on Kesamaru, just like at Koya, so he decided to build a temple here. When he woke up the next morning, however, one of the valleys had disappeared. He could see only ninety-nine, because the other had been hidden by the Tengu! This second account, given in *Seta-gun Azuma-mura no Minzoku*, goes on to say that the name Kesamaru comes from a white, cloak-shaped stone that used to stand on the mountain, but that the stone can no longer be found.

There are two paths leading on from here. The one straight on leads to the third and fourth peaks (Naka Kesamaru and Oku Kesamaru), Mount Hoshi, and the Rokurinpan Pass, which is described in Hike 10. This route is shown on the map. It is five and a half kilometers long and takes about four hours to walk. It is, however, extremely little used and must not be attempted lightly. A tent is a virtual necessity in case of emergency, as is a compass. (It is assumed that anyone who has reached this far is sensible enough at least to have brought a map.) The path down to the left is the route to the Otaki waterfall described in the next section.

MOUNT KESAMARU ▶ OTAKI WATERFALL
WALKING TIME: 2 HOURS, 15 MINUTES

The path down from Kesamaru is truly delightful, much gentler than the last stretch of the way up, descending through pretty, mixed woods. The trail stays on top of the ridge virtually all of the way down, offering a panoramic view of the entire Kanto area and many of the mountains beyond. When the weather is right, there could hardly be a more refreshing place to pitch a tent and camp out for the night. The ideal off-trail hike from here is to continue to Akagi the next day.

The bamboo grass is, however, high in places. Toward the bottom, the path gets very hard to see. Keep a close eye out for the ribbons on the trees. There is a small stone shrine on the ridge about fifty-five minutes from Kesamaru. Twenty-five minutes from there is a minor peak, with a red-and-white pole on top. Take the left fork there. The path descends quite steeply and, if all goes well, you should reach the road in only about ten minutes (one hour, thirty minutes from Kesamaru), but this final part of the path is very overgrown. Even if you do lose the way, however, at this point, you can hardly miss the road, because two forest roads cut right across the ridge. Be careful, though, about the embankment shown on the map.

The entrance to the hiking course is marked by a map and a sign for Kesamaru. Here, there is a choice of turning right for the road behind Akagi down to Neri in Tone Village, for the road down to Numata, or left toward the Otaki waterfall and Konaka. Turning left, it is a relaxing forty-five-minute amble down the valley to the waterfall. An official wild-bird survey was conducted on the top half of this road four times in June and once in December 1986. The birds sighted were: gray wagtail, brown-eared bulbul, brown dipper, winter wren, Japanese robin, daurian redstart, short-tailed bush warbler, bush warbler, crowned willow warbler, blue-and-white flycatcher, willow tit, great tit, Siberian meadow bunting, Japanese grosbeak, jay, and jungle crow.

Just below the waterfall are a bridge and a junction with a Kanto Fureai no Michi sign. Turn left here. The entrance to the fall, described in Section 2 above, is just a couple of minutes up the road on the right-hand side. It is necessary to return to this junction in order to continue down the road to the bus stop.

OTAKI WATERFALL ▶ OTSUKEBASHI BUS STOP
WALKING TIME: 35 MINUTES

The scenery on the road from the falls to the bus stop is no different from that higher up, though the road becomes properly paved about halfway down. It takes about thirty-five minutes from the junction above the falls to the bus stop. The next sight on this route comes about one hundred meters before the stop, a curiously shaped cedar that has split into many separate trunks, known as the Muresugi (Clustered Cedar). This is a designated natural treasure of Azuma Village. By the bus stop is an unusual graveyard with several Kannons and no fewer than four Dosojins in addition to a variety of gravestones. There are also a couple of Koshin stones just a minute or so further down the road.

The buses are run by Azuma Village. Afternoon buses are at 13:10, 17:00, and 18:50, Monday through Saturday. The last bus on Sunday is at 13:10. If there are no buses, it is a forty-minute walk down the road to Konaka Station. Stay on the left bank of the river. The tiny station stands just behind the shop at the junction with the main road.

USEFUL KANJI

AKAGANE KAIDO	銅街道
ASHIO	足尾
ATO KESAMARU	後袈裟丸
DAITAKUJI	大澤寺
HATTANBARI	八反張
KANTO FUREAI NO MICHI	関東ふれあいの道
"KESAMARU HIKING COURSE ENTRANCE"	袈裟丸登山口
KONAKA	小中
KOZUKE HANAWA	上野花輪
MAE KESAMARU	前袈裟丸
MOUNT KESAMARU ·	袈裟丸山
MOUNT KOMARU	小丸山
NERI	根利
NESHAKA (SLEEPING BUDDHA)	寝釈迦
"ORIBA HIKING COURSE ENTRANCE"	折場登山口
OTSUKEBASHI	追付橋
OTAKI WATERFALL	大滝
SAI NO KAWARA	塞の川原
SORINTO	相輪塔
SORI STATION	沢入駅

HIKE 9 ▲ BIZENDATE
ASHIO'S INDUSTRIAL PAST

HARAMUKO STATION • GINZANDAIRA • MOUNT BIZENDATE • HONZAN SHRINE AND MINE • MATO STATION

TOTAL WALKING TIME   5 HOURS

MAPS   1:50,000 ASHIO; 1:25,000 ASHIO. A FREE KANTO FUREAI NO MICHI MAP (FOR COURSE 1) IS AVAILABLE FROM THE TOCHIGI TOURIST INFORMATION OFFICE

Ashio, as noted in the introduction, is a small town of fantastic scenic contrasts, ranging from the most devastated of industrial landscapes to unspoiled virgin forests and spectacular mountains brimming with wildlife. This course takes the walker mainly on a tour of Ashio's industrial past. Included, however, is a lovely stretch at the top of Mount Bizendate, with some of the most glorious views of any hike in this book. In addition to seeing two of the town's three main mines, one is almost certain to see deer or serows, and there is good chance of meeting groups of monkeys as well.

The course first follows the Koshin River up past Kodaki, once a settlement of ten thousand people, but today marked only by a simple stone. Reaching the park at Ginzandaira and the Ashio Hot Spring, there is a tall stupa to the memory of the many Chinese laborers who died in the mine during the Second World War. Then, turning up into the mountains proper, the course brings us to the beautiful peak of Bizendate, the mountain where copper is said to have been found by two peasants from Bizen in the year 1610. This is probably the very best vantage point for overlooking all of the walks described in this book.

Descending the other side, however, one quickly enters the bleak industrial wasteland of the Honzan mine. The sights here include the ruined houses of a veritable ghost town that is now slowly returning to forest, the oldest iron road bridge in Japan, and the site of Japan's first hydroelectric power station. Above all, however, it is the bare mountainside, still suffering from the effects of the sulfurous fumes of the copper works, that takes the breath away. It is an unusual course for a country walk, but it all adds up to a fascinating and unforgettable day.

HARAMUKO STATION ▶ GINZANDAIRA
WALKING TIME: 1 HOUR, 30 MINUTES

The first part of this hike follows ordinary roads. It is very enjoyable for all that, however, with several pretty views and interesting things to see. Go straight down the short road from the station, turn right at the T-junction, cross the bridge to your left, and turn right onto the main road up the gorge. In about six minutes you will reach a bridge over a tributary, the Koshin River. Turn left under the yellow archway. A road sign indicates five kilometers to Kajikaso, the *kokumin shukusha* lodge at Ginzandaira.

The stone monument on the corner, the Mount Koshin Monument, was set up in 1865 by a group of twenty-three devotees of the Koshin cult from Edo, together with the manager of the Ashio hostel. Actually, the stone was originally placed at a different entrance to the mountain. With the opening of the Kodaki mine in 1886, however, pilgrims all began using this road instead. The stone was finally moved here in 1950, when Mount Koshin was incorporated into the Nikko National Park. To the left of the monument is a rather fine Koshin stone, with the monkey and yin-yang motifs clearly visible.

The road leads up a narrow, pretty gorge. There is a path up to the left about fifteen minutes from the monument, just two minutes beyond the bridge, where the road crosses to the left side of the gorge for the first time. It is marked by a white forestry sign and heads up toward a small graveyard. Judging from the map, this is the way up to Mount Sujin.

The road reaches a small hydroelectric power plant and dam just a minute from here. It is not much to look at (10,000 kilowatts, 29 meters high, maximum capacity 195,000 cubic meters), but there is something to look forward to just above it, at the parking lot over the green waters of the lake. Press the button on the large, posted map to hear first details of the power plant (in Japanese, of course) and then a traditional Ashio folk song.

For the next twenty-five minutes or so, watch the surrounding hillsides closely, for there is a fair chance here and throughout this hike of seeing serows. Watch out also for places that have been leveled, with young trees and the occasional stone wall. The reason for this becomes clear when we reach a tiny park with benches, azaleas, and a simple stone monument that reads "Kodaki Village Once Stood Here." This park is all that remains of Kodaki, a village that died almost without trace when the copper mine closed. This quiet corner of the valley was once one of the three big pits of Ashio.

Kodaki in its prime was indeed a highly distinctive village of tightly packed, stepped company housing, known for the clarity of its water. At the annual Bon dance, which used to be held in the grounds of the Kodaki primary school, the dancers would sing: "Kodaki, Tsudo, Honzan, Dance! / Erect an arch in Mount Bizen!" or: "The Watarase cherry blossoms, / The green leaves of Kodaki, / The moon from Bizendate." There was also a Kodaki *oenka,* a sentimental song with the chorus: "Clear mountains, gushing water, we are Kodaki!" It is written that this was sung at the mine's sports meets.

The Kodaki mine was opened in April 1886, and produced about two-thirds the output of the Honzan mine. There had been only a single house in Kodaki before then, whose owner made clogs called *geta,* possibly for the pilgrims on their way to Mount Koshin. Initially, loads were carried to and from the mine through the mountain itself from the shaft at Honzan. In 1891, however, a horse railway was constructed up the valley. The company-run primary school opened in 1893.

The village continued to expand through the early years of the twentieth century, with the construction of more company housing and even a hospital. At one point, its population topped ten thousand. At its zenith, Kodaki had an inn, several restaurants, a couple of geisha houses, bars, and a post office. All that seems very hard to believe when one stands in that tiny, lonely park today.

Kodaki's decline was initially quite slow, the result of a long, drawn-out series of rationalizations, which culminated in the closure of the Kodaki mine in July 1954. Today, nothing of that old settlement remains. The flowers around the memorial stone are well tended, however, and there is no mistaking the nostalgia that former residents still feel for their lost village.

Another three-minutes brings the road to a small concrete pump station. This draws hot-spring water from an underground source in the mine, for use in the Ashio Hot Spring at Ginzandaira. This hot spring was developed by the Furukawa Company as a way to compensate the locality for the closure of the mine. The hot spring was opened, together with other leisure facilities, in 1971. The waters are said to be effective against rheumatism, injuries, high blood pressure, and arteriosclerosis. The water is pumped both to the Kamemura Ryokan and the Kajikaso *kokumin shukusha* hostel.

Next, there is a rusted metal bridge, now closed off, to the entrance of the Kodaki mine itself. Just opposite, there is a most unusual shrine in a cavelike cutting at the side of the road. This place, too, has the feel of ancient history, though actually it belongs to our own century.

The *kodaki* (small waterfall) is found at a bend just above the entrance to the mine. It is a little over ten minutes from here to the Ashio Hot Spring (Kamemura Ryokan). Cross the small blue footbridge to the hot spring, even if you do not intend to stay there, for this is also the entrance to the Koshin Sarutahiko Shrine. The grounds of the shrine are ordinary but not unpleasing. Here there is a huge, illustrated map of two main hiking courses on Mount Koshin, the easier of which is described in Hike 10. The Shinto god Sarutahiko no Mikoto is particularly associated with the Koshin faith, as explained in the introduction. You can orient yourself by the remains of the former Koshin Sarutahiko Shrine, shown near the bottom of the map. This is where the Kanto Fureai no Michi branches in Hike 10, just two hundred meters from the Koshin Lodge.

Returning to the bridge, it is now just three minutes to the *kokumin shukusha* hostel at Ginzandaira itself. First, the road passes the campsite, chalets, and (free) outdoor pool. There are steps up to the right, opposite the entrance to the campsite, leading to a large stupa, the Memorial Stupa to the Chinese Martyrs. Erected in 1973, it is dedicated to the one hundred ten Chinese who died here while working as forced laborers in the mines during the war. The laborers were kept in a concentration camp on the Jijigasawa River in Kodaki. Each stone in the wall represents an individual victim. Offerings are still made on the twenty-seventh of each month, with a major annual memorial event on September twenty-seventh.

Elsewhere it is written that three hundred fifty whites, two hundred fifty-seven Chinese, and fifteen hundred Koreans were brought to work as forced laborers in the mines. Local junior high school children were also mobilized, so one may reasonably suppose that they were given the safer jobs. Even so, the number of Chinese deaths seems very high. There were, not without cause, quite a lot of disturbances after the war ended in August 1945. Difficulties continued until November 1945, when one hundred U.S. soldiers were sent in, and the foreigners were finally repatriated.

The hostel itself, equipped with a single tennis court, has a hot spring bath that visitors can enter even if they are not staying overnight. The hostel also offers pottery classes every day in August and on weekends in September and October. The promotional literature says that groups of monkeys quite often come down close to the hostel.

Rather surprisingly in this copper mining area, the *ginzan* of Ginzandaira means "silver mine." It appears that prospectors found silver here while looking for copper. However, the quantity was small, and the mine quickly closed down. In 1890, people from the Kodaki mine built a Ginzandaira Yama Shrine, where the bungalows now stand, but this was later removed to make way for a tip for waste from the mine. Then, beginning in 1903, huge quantities of wood for use as fuel and props in the mine were brought across the Rokurinpan Pass from Tone in Gunma Prefecture to lumberyards at Ginzandaira. Two iron cables were used to transport the trees over the 19.7-kilometer route. The lumberyards finally closed in 1925.

Ginzandaira lies at the midpoint of the climb to Mount Koshin, so many pilgrims rested here during the late Edo period. They stopped coming after the turmoil and political complications of the Meiji Restoration. Hikers started arriving beginning in 1950, when Mount Koshin was designated a part of the Nikko National Park. The bungalows and campsite were opened in 1958. At that time, there was even a regular bus service up here from the bottom. The *kokumin shukusha* hostel followed in 1967, and finally the hot spring, in 1971.

Just opposite the hostel, signs indicate that we are once again joining the Kanto Fureai no Michi. One sign points straight up the road for Ichinotorii and Mount Koshin (see Hike 10), the other up steps to the right for the Ginzandaira Observation Point (Ginzandaira Tembodai 0.6 km) and Mount Bizendate (3.7 km). This is the path that we want.

GINZANDAIRA ▶ GINZANDAIRA OBSERVATION POINT ▶ MOUNT BIZENDATE
WALKING TIME: 1 HOUR, 30 MINUTES

The steps up through the woods lead to an unpaved road in just three minutes. Turning right, there is a three-way Kanto Fureai no Michi junction only twenty meters farther on. The signs read: left up the steps to the Ginzandaira Observation Point (0.4 km); straight on up the road to Mount Bizendate (3.5 km) and Tsudo Station (9.4 km). The observation point is not particularly spectacular, but it offers a view of the hostel and back down the valley. It is an easy climb, the first two hundred meters up a path and steps along lightly wooded slopes to the ridge, then left up a gentler gradient to the top. There is a rocky outcrop on the summit, but the observation point itself lies just beyond this outcrop, so don't turn back too early.

Returning by the same route to the road, turn left for Mount Bizendate. This is a pleasant mountain road without traffic (cars are not allowed here), rising high above the steep-sided valley. There are many deer and serows. After thirty minutes of steady climbing, the road reaches the very top of the Funaishi Pass. Here there is another junction of the Kanto Fureai no Michi, straight on down the road to Tsudo Station (7.4 km) or right along the path to Mount Bizendate (1.5 km). Despite the fact that the road is downhill all the way from here to Mato Station, it is important to resist the temptation to pass up Mount Bizendate. This, unlike the Ginzandaira Observation Point, offers some of the very best views in this book.

Remains have been found in this area dating from the Jomon period, two thousand or more years ago. In the early Meiji period, a handful of farmers grew crops like potatoes, giant radishes, and Chinese cabbages in the vicinity of this pass. It is written that they even sent their vegetables to the markets of Tokyo. They were obviously very well off, for a certain Mr. Hatakenaka had a two-story house with *tatami* in an era in which few people in Ashio could have afforded the luxury of *tatami* mats. It is further noted in *Ashio Tokorodokoro* (Ashio Kominkan, 1975) that he ordered a lot of Ebisu and Kirin beer from the wineshop in Mato.

This area used to be known for the stream which flows down from the pass to Ginzandaira. The story goes that in 1897, Furukawa Ichibei, the owner of the mine, came up here to inspect work on the cable for transporting lumber from Tone

Village to Ginzandaira. He is said to have seen a boat-shaped stone in Mr. Hatakenaka's field and declared, "Instead of a fish stream, how about calling this place Funaishi (Boat Stone)?" And so, Funaishi it became.

Mount Bizendate is an old volcano that erupted twice about one million years ago. It stands in the very center of Ashio and is the mountain whose copper made Ashio famous. It was, in fact, near here that two peasants from Bizen (present-day Okayama), named Jifu and Kura, are said to have discovered the first copper ores in 1610. They reported their find to the abbot of the Zazen'inji in Nikko and, in recognition, the mountain was renamed after their birthplace.

Turning right for the summit, the path quickly comes to a second sign pointing up to the right. This passes through pretty woodland, with some excellent views of the surrounding mountains. There are benches about fifteen minutes along the trail. Then the path bends to the left at a sign indicating one kilometer to the summit. This final kilometer is generally quite steep with many steps. At the top, however, a view of the entire region suddenly opens up in front of us. Below is the Honzan mine and Mato, while across the valley are Mount Hangetsu, the Hangetsu Pass, Mount Nantai, and just about the entire route from Kobugahara to Lake Chuzenji, across Mounts Jizo and Yakushi. Looking back, there are clear views of Mount Kesamaru and Mount Akagi, and close at hand, of Mount Koshin and Mount Sukai. Only Mount Narukami offers such a spectacular panorama for so little effort. This is the place for a long rest and lunch.

MOUNT BIZENDATE ▶ HONZAN MINE AND SHRINE ▶ MATO STATION
WALKING TIME: 2 HOURS

It takes about thirty minutes to return to the road from the summit by the same route. This time, turn right down the road to Tsudo Station. This is a refreshing, gentle descent, with some more fine views of the mountains. About ten minutes from the junction, the Kanto Fureai no Michi suddenly leaves the road to follow a narrow path to the right. This can be a little overgrown, but it is not too hard to see. It passes for about five minutes down a shallow, marshy valley, crosses a small bridge, and comes back out onto the road.

The road continues down the left bank of the stream. Although there are still no buildings, there is a growing sense of the approach of industry. The mountainsides become barer, and the naked valley begins to be dominated by a long series of debris and landslide barriers. After the great natural beauty of the mountains, it not only feels as if the road is approaching an area of appalling natural disaster, it actually is. The valley is so despoiled and desolate that it has a special grandeur all of its own.

About twenty minutes after rejoining the road, the trail comes to the first shells of old wooden houses. A minute later, we are standing in front of the Honzan mine itself, which today looks utterly decrepit. A drawing on a bulletin shows how the town looked in 1965.

The Ashio mine was under the direct administration of the shogunate in Tokyo from when it opened in 1610 until the Meiji Restoration in 1868. It was greatly expanded after 1877, when it passed into the hands of the industrialist Furukawa Ichibei. The Honzan pit became the center of the mine in the late 1880s, after the discovery here of a huge new vein of ore and the introduction of advanced technologies from the West. Many of the mine's offices were located here. It even had a thermal power station and a telephone exchange. However, the administrative center of the mine shifted to Tsudo in 1907, after the violence mentioned in the introduction. When the population of Ashio was at its peak, this valley was literally dotted with houses. Postwar rationalization and the depletion of the ores were to take their toll, however, and in February 1973 the mine was closed.

One of the most extraordinary sights in Japan can be seen along the road leading up to the left from behind this sign, just opposite the entrance to the mine: a ghost town of tumbledown houses returning to the forest. High above on the hillside, the roof of the Honzan Kozan (mine) Shrine is visible from the main road. The path winds up through the houses, at one point crossing a very rickety bridge, and comes out at the old square in front of the shrine. I was all the more impressed to see a serow feeding just near here.

This shrine was built under the direction of the Furukawa Company in 1889, using contributions gathered from the workers. It is the oldest surviving mining shrine in Ashio. The first was founded in 1611 by Jifu and Kura, the two peasants credited with discovering the copper. The Kodaki Shrine was founded in 1890, and the Tsudo Shrine in 1920. The Honzan Kozan Shrine was originally built as a small shrine next to the entrance to the mine, but was moved to its present location when the time came to rebuild it on a larger scale. The gods worshiped here are the mountain god Oyama, plus two others associated especially with mining: the male, Kanayamahiko no Mikoto, and the female, Kanayamahime no Mikoto. Great two-day festivals, with portable shrines, a lion dance, and a fancy-dress parade were held here when the mine was still flourishing, generally in April, though the dates varied a bit over the years. Up until 1941, the mine would also sponsor a variety of plays, movies, and other performances during the festival period. The festival was stopped altogether with the closure of the mine in 1973.

Returning to the junction in front of the mine, the main road immediately forks to the right. There is a sign indicating the way to Tsudo Station ahead (4.6 km) and back to Ginzandaira (5.0 km). Ten minutes later, the Kanto Fureai no Michi turns right across a bridge over the stream, just before it joins the Watarase River. This is not a bad route, but it does seem a bit strange, given that the road is now only one hundred meters short of the Furukawa bridge, the oldest iron road bridge in Japan. Those who fancy industrial history should certainly continue on to see it.

On the left, just before the bridge, is the entrance to the Ashio copper works. Despite their ruined appearance, they are still functioning at some minimal level even today, using imported ores. The bridge, which links Akakura and Honzan, was completed in December 1890. At the time, Honzan was the principal mine of Ashio. A wooden bridge had been built here previously, in 1885, but had burned down only two years later on April 8, 1887, in a great fire that spread from Matsugi. The iron bridge that replaced it is still in use today. The Furukawa bridge has an arched structure measuring 50 meters long by 4.6 meters wide. The parts were manufactured by a German company and assembled under the supervision of German engineers.

Crossing the bridge, take the road to the right on the far side of the traffic circle. This rejoins the Kanto Fureai no Michi in just a few minutes. Two minutes later, after a bridge, the road to the Hangetsu Pass (Hike 11) leads up off to the left. Ignore this and continue straight on down.

Another five minutes bring the road to a curious-looking pipe preserved in a glass case, at the foot of a tall rock on the left-hand side of the road. This is all that remains of the first hydroelectric power station in Japan. It was completed in December 1890, under the direction of an engineer from the Siemens Company of Germany, to provide a new source of power for the mines, which until then had operated on firewood and charcoal. The water was drawn from the Matsugi River (by the present Ashio Dam) and the Fukasawa River (the river followed in Hike 11 toward the Hangetsu Pass). With a head of three hundred eighteen meters, it produced an output of four hundred horsepower, which was used to drive the pumps and cages and for lighting.

Mato Station is just five minutes down the road from here, on the left. The fare to Kiryu is about one thousand yen, and the journey takes about one hour and twenty minutes. The Kanto Fureai no Michi continues along the railway line as far as Tsudo Station, which takes about twenty-five minutes to walk. This walk is not particularly remarkable, but it is quite pleasant to stroll through Ashio if you still have the surplus energy.

If you choose to continue the walk, it is worth dropping in at a couple of temples along the way. The first, about five minutes from Tsudo Station, is Hozoji, founded in nearby Watarase in 807 and moved to its present location in the nineteenth century. Shodo Shonin is said to have lived in Watarase for a while, so it is likely that he was directly connected with its founding. The temple building itself is very new. Inside, however, it has an old Buddhist statue that legend links not only with Shodo, but also with the origin of the name Ashio itself.

This legend sounds very childish at first hearing, but deeper reflection reveals a host of fascinating possibilities and even apparent connections with the Koshin faith. In essence, it is recounted that while Shodo was at Chuzenji, he would often see a mouse scampering about with ears of millet in its mouth. Surprised, for it seemed unlikely that such food could be found in these remote mountains, Shodo tied a piece of string (o) to the mouse's leg (ashi) and followed it to see where it would go. The mouse led him to a small farmstead, which he thereupon called Ashio! Looking around, Shodo recognized that this would be an ideal place for ascetic training, so he decided to make Ashio a stop on the *shugendo*.

Just as the fox, for example, is considered to be the intermediary of Inari, the mouse is known as the messenger of the Buddhist god Hashiri Daikokuten. Here in Japan, Daikokuten is popularly known as one of the Seven Gods of Good Fortune, the Shichifukujin. He is the god of the kitchen or the five grains — rice, wheat, millet, barley, and beans. Daikokuten is generally depicted as a rather pudgy, smiling old man, who wears a hood and sits or stands on a couple of bales of rice.

He typically has a sack of treasure over his shoulder and a magic hammer in his right hand.

Hozoji, as it happens, has a statue of Daikokuten that is very ambitiously claimed to have been carved by Shodo Shonin himself. In fact, it is highly unlikely that it is even half that old. The statue appropriately represents the god standing on a couple of mice. The characters for *hozo* mean "increasing treasure," but the word may originally have been written with different characters, meaning "treasure storehouse." It is easy to imagine that a god of wealth who carries a magic hammer must have seemed even more attractive once Ashio started producing copper. Ashio used to have a big Daikokuten Festival in the middle of September each year, with a grand parade through the town.

Given the utterly benign image of Daikokuten, it is surprising that this deity is actually derived from the Hindu god Mahakala, *maha* meaning "great," and *kala* meaning "time" or "blackness." "Great Blackness," or Daikoku in Japanese, is an alternative name for Shiva. Daikokuten thus started out as the god of death and destruction. Since death must precede rebirth, of course, the present association with the harvest might not really be as inappropriate as it at first appears.

Mahakala had already been converted by Buddhists into some kind of protective deity and god of fortune before his introduction to Japan. The early Japanese images of Daikokuten, however, still preserve some of his earlier, terrifying countenance. He was depicted as a fierce blue Buddha, with three faces and six arms. The front two hands clasped a sword, the central right hand, a woman, and the central left hand, a goat.

This may sound curiously familiar, remarkably like portrayals of Shomen Kongo, the Buddhist god of the Koshin faith, and also his look-alike, Kongo Doji. Indeed, Michio Iida, in his book *Koshin Shinko* (The Koshin Faith), makes a convincing case that Daikokuten and Shomen Kongo are one and the same god. The fact that Ashio, the settlement beneath Mount Koshin, should have a Daikokuten Festival suddenly seems only to be expected.

In passing, it is worth noting that Shomen Kongo has another look-alike, too. That is Kongo Yasha, one of the five Myoo, a blue, three-faced, six-armed warrior who guards the north. As explained earlier, the Myoo, like Kongo Doji, were very important to the mountain priests and esoteric Buddhism in general. As noted in

Hike 2, the Myoo, too, are thought to have had their origin in Shiva. And the north, as we saw in Hike 3, is the border that must especially be protected against the entry of disease and other kinds of disaster, the special responsibility of Shomen Kongo.

Most significantly, however, Daikokuten is traditionally the guardian of Saicho's temple on Mount Hiei overlooking Kyoto, the base of the Tendai sect of Buddhism that became so powerful in Nikko. That temple still preserves a famous three-faced statue which is thought to have been carved by Saicho himself. The statue is generally said to depict three of the Shichifukujin (the Seven Gods of Good Fortune): Daikokuten, Bishamonten, and Benten. Thinking about those three faces, however, Iida takes one final leap to make the compelling suggestion that the whole lot (Daikokuten, Shomen Kongo, Kongo Doji, and Kongo Yasha) might really all be representations of the three ancient Hindu deities of creation, continuity, and destruction. He notes in support of this idea that there is a Three-faced Shiva that combines all three of these attributes in India today. If true, it certainly adds another fascinating dimension to the Koshin faith: Shomen Kongo might be the Three-faced Shiva of Hinduism!

Continuing down the road, about one hundred meters before Tsudo Station we come to Renkeiji, which is thought to have been founded by Shodo Shonin in 767. This temple has an old stone gate, erected in 1776, which was once the entrance to a mountain shrine associated with the copper mining on Bizendate. The gate is said to be the only standing relic of the Ashio mine that dates from the Edo period. There is also a fine five-tiered stone pagoda.

USEFUL KANJI

ASHIO HOT SPRING	足尾温泉
FUNAISHI PASS	舟石峠
GINZANDAIRA	銀山平
GINZANDAIRA OBSERVATION POINT	銀山平展望台
HARAMUKO STATION	原向駅
HONZAN KOZAN	本山鉱山
HONZAN KOZAN SHRINE	本山鉱山神社

HOZOJI	宝増寺
ICHINOTORI	一ノ鳥居
KAJIKASO	カジカ荘
KANTO FUREAI NO MICHI	関東ふれあいの道
KODAKI	小滝
"KODAKI VILLAGE ONCE STOOD HERE"	小滝の里ありき
MATO STATION	間藤駅
MEMORIAL STUPA TO THE CHINESE MARTYRS	中国人殉難者慰霊塔
MOUNT BIZENDATE	備前楯山
MOUNT KOSHIN	庚申
MOUNT KOSHIN MONUMENT	庚申山碑
RENKEIJI	練慶寺
KOSHIN SARUTAHIKO SHRINE	庚申猿田彦神社
TSUDO STATION	通洞駅

RUGGED, SACRED MOUNTAINS

GINZANDAIRA • KOSHIN LODGE • MOUNT KOSHIN • MOUNT NOKOGIRI • ROKURINPAN PASS • KOSHIN LODGE • GINZANDAIRA

TOTAL WALKING TIMES 8 HOURS, 55 MINUTES (GINZANDAIRA TO MOUNT NOKOGIRI AND BACK); 5 HOURS, 35 MINUTES (GINZANDAIRA TO MOUNT KOSHIN AND BACK *OR* KOSHIN LODGE TO MOUNT NOKOGIRI AND BACK)

MAPS 1:50,000 ASHIO; 1:50,000 NANTAISAN; 1:25,000 ASHIO; 1:25,000 CHUZENJI; 1:25,000 SUKAIZAN; 1:25,000 KESAMARUYAMA

This route takes the walker far from Ashio's industrial past up into a world of high craggy mountains, spectacular views, natural forests, and abundant wildlife. The first stretch lies along the Kanto Fureai no Michi, with a gently sloping but surprisingly arduous hike up the pretty stream to the lodge beneath the cliffs of Mount Koshin. Then the trail follows the ascent up the sacred mountain itself, via a series of ladders and chains that happily have recently been renovated, thanks to the Kanto Fureai no Michi. The path on from there across the teeth of Nokogiri *(nokogiri* means "saw," and there is no mystery how this mountain came by its name) is only for the fit and the experienced. The views, however, are magnificent on both sides — toward Sukai, Nikko Shirane, and Nantai to the right, and Kesamaru, Akagi, Haruna, and Myogi to the left. From Nokogiri, one has the option of turning right along the ridge to Mount Sukai or left to the Rokurinpan Pass, where great trees for use at the Ashio mine were once transported from Tone by cable. The delightful path, down the ridge to the pass, through glorious woods of silver birch, and on from there back to the lodge, is a more than fitting reward for all the exertions across to Nokogiri.

Mount Koshin lies on the southern boundary of Nikko National Park. It is a volcano which erupted at roughly the same time as Sukai and Kesamaru. Volcanic debris, including andesite boulders and tufa conglomerates, are scattered all over the southern slopes of the mountain. The forests are natural, with oaks, birches, pines, and, at the summit, hemlocks and *aomori todomatsu* firs *(Abies mariesii).*

197

There is also a rare insect-eating plant, *koshinso (Pinguicula ramosa)*, which was first discovered here by a Tokyo University professor in 1890 and takes its name from the mountain. This pale pink flower is found only here and on Nantai and Nyoho, in Nikko. It is consequently a designated national treasure. The flower is very tiny, just five to eight millimeters wide, and blooms for only about one week each year in late June or early July. If you are lucky, you will find it in moist and shady spots among the rocks. The *koshinso* traps insects with its leaves. Tiny hairs then release a digestive fluid that liquefies the prey for absorption into the plant. As related in the introduction, this curious little flower is now the chosen symbol of the Ashio pottery that is sold in the town below. Other flowering, high-altitude plants include many azaleas such as the red *azuma shakunage (Rhododendron degronianum)* and the whitish *shiro yashio (R. quinquefolium)*.

Koshin was a center of the Koshin faith even before copper was discovered in Ashio. Tradition has it that the mountain was originally opened by Shodo Shonin, but over the past few centuries it has attracted most of its visitors on account of the flourishing of the Koshin faith during the Edo period. Descriptions of the mountain appear in the *Koshinsan Ki* (Mount Koshin Travelogue) of Mihashi Naohiko, which was written in 1819, and in one of the great works of Edo literature, Takizawa Bakin's *Nanso Satomi Hakkenden* (Satomi and the Eight Dogs), which was written in periodical installments from 1814 to 1841. In 1865 alone, more than three thousand pilgrims traveled here from Edo. Soon after, however, they stopped coming, when the Koshin faction was discredited in the political turmoil of the Meiji Restoration. Just recently, by the way, it was suggested that a secret hoard of money might have been buried here by the Tokugawa shogunate, with a current market value of one hundred trillion yen! Good luck!

GINZANDAIRA ▶ KOSHIN LODGE
WALKING TIME: 1 HOUR, 50 MINUTES)

This hike starts from the *kokumin shukusha* hostel reached at the end of Section 1 in Hike 9. It is also a feasible, but arduous walk to and from Mount Koshin in one day from Haramuko Station. Those wishing to go beyond Mount Koshin, however, to Mounts Nokogiri and Sukai, should spend a night at the Koshin Lodge.

Follow the Kanto Fureai no Michi to Ichinotorii (3.9 km). The road climbs up the side of the valley, with good views back toward the hostel. It reaches a parking lot at a bend in the road after about twenty minutes. From here the road is unpaved and vehicles are not allowed. There is another Kanto Fureai no Michi sign indicating 2.5 kilometers to Ichinotorii and 1.4 kilometers back to Ginzandaira.

The gate at Ichinotorii is reached a further twenty minutes from here. A few minutes before the gate, there is a long slide of volcanic boulders up to the right from the road. This rock slide is known as Tengu Toseki, for it is said that the stones were thrown by a long-nosed Tengu goblin. Before turning right through the gate onto the trail up the mountain, it is worth continuing an extra one hundred meters to see the Koshin Nanataki, the Seven Waterfalls of Koshin. There are picnic tables at the falls, and paths lead down both sides. However, the rather new-looking bridge at the bottom is closed off because it is unsafe.

Returning to the gate of Ichinotorii, the Kanto Fureai no Michi sign now indicates 3.6 kilometers to Mount Koshin. This is a delightful, shady path, climbing up through the woods by the side of a pretty stream. There are picnic tables in several places, and you are quite likely to come across bands of wild monkeys. At one resting place, there is a huge rock with a sign in front of it. This is the Kagami Iwa, the Mirror Rock.

The sign here tells the story of an Ashio hunter who fell to the bottom of the valley during a blizzard and was unable to climb either up or down. Just as he was about to freeze to death, an old monkey appeared in front of him. The hunter asked the monkey to save his life, promising in return his own daughter in marriage. The monkey quickly gathered its friends, and together they formed a monkey bridge for the hunter to get across. The hunter, of course, now had to keep his promise. His two elder daughters refused outright, but the youngest agreed to go with the monkey. From that day on, the hunter revisited the mountains many times in order to find his daughter, until one day he met her in front of this very rock — turned into a monkey. The father and daughter had one last tearful farewell.

Some thirty minutes later the trail comes to a rock, designated by a sign as the "Husband-and-Wife Frogs." Less obvious from below, from above the rock resembles a pair of frogs mating. The path now becomes quite steep. A further twenty minutes bring it out at the remains of the Sarutahiko Shrine. Dedicated to the Shinto god Sarutahiko, the shrine is closely associated with the Koshin faith. The present shrine is located just below Ginzandaira (see p. 187). On the right, just before the site of the old shrine, is an iron sword that was erected in 1912; on the left is a monument inscribed with the names of Shodo Shonin and Daininbo. This is a rather remarkable combination. As related in Hike 12, Daininbo was a very wild sort of man who died young after plotting against the government. Like Shodo, however, Daininbo had retreated to Mount Koshin for a period of ascetic discipline in the years before he became involved in the affairs of state.

As noted above, there is a tradition that Mount Koshin, too, was opened by Shodo Shonin, in the year 767, and that it was he who built the shrine here for Sarutahiko. This shrine was to prosper, especially in the Edo period with the popularity of Koshin societies. It once covered an area of around thirty-six hundred square feet, but was destroyed by fire in April 1946. Ceremonies are currently held at the Koshin Lodge, though even now this is officially still only a temporary arrangement.

Here, the Kanto Fureai no Michi divides. Almost all the other Kanto Fureai no Michi routes in this area are very tame and afford no real preparation for what follows. The path to the right for Mount Koshin (2.4 km) follows precipitously along a series of ladders and chains and should be treated with great caution. Hikers are warned not to attempt this course on rainy days or when the ground is slippery. The reward, however, is startling rocky scenery that fully evokes the sanctity of this ancient mountain. It rejoins the left fork seven hundred meters from the summit. For most people, the easier path will be exacting enough.

Turning left here, the sign reads just two hundred meters to the Koshin Lodge. The Kanto Fureai no Michi divides once again at the site where the old lodge used to stand. The path to the right is the way up Mount Koshin (1.4 km), the one to the left to the Rokurinpan Pass, and the observation point of Tenka Miharashi (0.8 km). The new lodge stands about fifty meters down the path to the left. It has been built beneath imposing cliffs (all the more imposing in view of the fact that we next have to go up them) and commands a memorable view from the veranda.

The first lodge was erected in 1948 and enlarged in 1952. The present one was built in 1985. It is usually unmanned, but bedding and drinking water are available. There is a charge of two thousand yen for the night. Unlike the *kokumin shukusha* hostel at Ginzandaira, there should be no difficulty staying, even in high season. Since reservations are not accepted, it might be a good idea to bring a sleeping bag if you are arriving during one of the festivals. An official from the town hall is usually in attendance at the weekends during the main hiking seasons, but the lodge itself is open every day of the year.

The most interesting (though also most crowded) time to stay at the lodge is during the spring or autumn festivals, which are held here on the third weekends of May and October. Then, you can be sure to be able to meet and talk with people who keep the old Koshin customs alive even today, plus many others who are just along for the occasion. There is a small shrine to Sarutahiko inside the lodge itself, though this is usually locked up.

Final words of warning are: try to arrive before dark and be sure to bring a flashlight, because there is no electricity. It is, however, a splendid place to stay, with beautiful woods, cliffs, starlight, and, in the rutting season, the seemingly continuous cries of the deer. If you sit quietly on the veranda, the deer will even come out into the open in front of the lodge.

KOSHIN LODGE ▶ MOUNT KOSHIN
WALKING TIME: 1 HOUR, 15 MINUTES

Starting from behind the site of the old lodge, either of the two paths can be taken, because they rejoin quite quickly. The path climbs up to a small waterfall and then follows along the base of the cliff. When you do reach the cliff, keep left. All of the many ladders, bridges, stepped logs, and chains on this route are new and firmly attached, but the mountainside is crisscrossed by numerous other highly dodgy paths. If you find yourself hanging on to a rusty wire, for example, look again, for you have certainly missed your way.

The view on the way up is quite magnificent in places. Some twenty minutes from the lodge, the path passes through a small cave, the first gate (Hatsu no Mon), leading to a ladder and chain, with a fine panorama back over the Kanto Plain. A cave on the right, just afterward, is said to have been Shodo Shonin's hermitage when he visited the mountain. There are also some old signs pointing on to Sukai, Nokogiri, and Koshin.

The path soon passes through a second cave gateway, Ichinomon, and then, at another big cave, rejoins the fork of the Kanto Fureai no Michi that has come over the rocks from the old site of the Sarutahiko Shrine. This cave is known as the Great Womb (Daitai). Passing through caves like these was another of the *shugendo* practices which has now also entered popular religion. Go left. The sign indicates that it is now only seven hundred meters to the summit. From here, the view encompasses the mountains of Kiryu, Mount Kanayama in Ota, and the plain across toward Chichibu, in Saitama Prefecture.

The path begins to level out a few minutes later, finally passing through some gentle woodland on to the summit, with further glimpses of Kesamaru off to the left. The view from the top of the mountain is almost entirely obscured by trees, but just a couple of minutes further on, there is an observation point for the most famous view of Mount Sukai, as well as of the mountains of Nikko.

MOUNT KOSHIN ▶ GINZANDAIRA
WALKING TIME: 2 HOURS, 30 MINUTES

Those who are running out of time or energy should now return to Ginzandaira by the same route. It takes about one hour and forty minutes down to Ichinotorii, a further thirty minutes to the parking lot, and twenty minutes from the parking lot to the *kokumin shukusha* hostel at Ginzandaira.

MOUNT KOSHIN ▶ MOUNT NOKOGIRI
WALKING TIME: 1 HOUR, 40 MINUTES

The path from Mount Koshin to Mount Nokogiri follows the top of a ridge that joins the main watershed connecting Kesamaru, Sukai, and on to Nikko Shirane. In fact, this whole ridge is the *nokogiri,* "the saw," with the final tooth of the saw being Mount Nokogiri itself. There are altogether ten peaks to be crossed: 1) Ontake, 2) Komagake, 3) Keiun, 4) Jizo, 5) Yakushi, 6) Hakusan, 7) Zao, 8) Kumano, 9) Ken no Yama, and 10) Nokogiri. Some guidebooks number these one to eleven, with Koshin as number one.

At first, this path seems extremely easy compared with the way up, descending quite a long way through pretty woodland and crossing the first three teeth of the saw before one is sure that one has even reached them. The ridge here is broad, and the views on both sides are excellent. The path is not hard to follow, but keep an eye out for ribbons and red-and-yellow wooden squares pinned on the trees. The bamboo grass is quite thick in places.

Jizo, the fourth peak, is reached in a little over thirty-five minutes from the viewpoint at Mount Koshin. Ten minutes from here, the first steep climb begins up Yakushi. It takes about twenty minutes from Jizo to Yakushi. At the summit of Yakushi, the path bends down to the left. From here, the cliffs of Nokogiri come clearly into view, and there is understandable (and justified) trepidation about just what the path is going to do next.

Six minutes from Yakushi, there are more superb views from the top of Hakusan, peak number six, especially back down the Matsugi Valley toward Ashio. The next peak is again reached without incident, but then the real climb begins. First, there is a rope down, and then a long rope up the other side, on a crumbling, near-vertical cliff. The path goes off to the left about three quarters of the way up the rope. That brings it to the top of Kumano, peak number eight. From there, it is a steep climb up to Ken no Yama, though with good views across to the main volcanoes of Gunma. Finally, there is one more sequence of chains, down and up.

Nokogiri is a tall, steep-sided mountain commanding a panoramic view of many of the mountains of central Japan. Most hikers coming up from the Koshin Lodge turn right here. The final hour's trek goes steeply down and then steeply up again to Mount Sukai. If this is your first time in these mountains, you should certainly then return from Sukai to Nokogiri to go back down via the Rokurinpan Pass. There are longer, optional routes, however: continuing along the ridge beyond Mount Sukai; descending to Ashio via Matsugi; or descending by the Fukazawa Valley, from the foot of the pass between Nokogiri and Sukai, to come out at the forest road in Tone. The first two options are essentially off-trail and will likely require an overnight stay (there is a lodge at the top of the Matsugi River). The third option, however, is fairly easy as far as the forest road, but then you face an extremely long walk down to the nearest bus stop.

Mount Sukai is certainly worth visiting. As mentioned, you will probably find that most people staying at the Koshin Lodge are planning to go there, leaving at the break of dawn and then returning via the Rokurinpan Pass. It is a good idea for your own safety to stick with them the whole way from Koshin to Sukai. People started climbing Sukai from the mid-Edo period as the Oku no In (remote annex) of Mount Koshin. Worshipers traveling to the Sarutahiko Shrine followed a triangular pilgrimage route around Koshin, Nokogiri, and Sukai. In 1893, a huge copper sword was placed just near the top of Sukai by a Koshin pilgrim from Tokyo,

Kibayashi Iichi. The sword still stands there today. If contemplating this route, however, be sure to keep on the move in order to allow yourself sufficient time; you should aim to arrive at Nokogiri by 9:00 a.m.

MOUNT NOKOGIRI ▶ ROKURINPAN PASS ▶ TENKA MIHARASHI VIEWPOINT ▶ KOSHIN LODGE
WALKING TIME: 2 HOURS, 40 MINUTES

The route down to the pass starts from the sign, just before the peak of Mount Nokogiri. This is a gentle path that winds up and down along the top of the ridge through extraordinarily beautiful forests. The silver birches are especially fine. There is quite a lot of bamboo grass, but generally it is not very tall, and the path is very easy to follow. The way has been clearly marked with long yellow ropes and more of those red-and-yellow squares on the trees. The pass is reached some fifty-five minutes from the top of Nokogiri. The route down to the right from here to Tone is no longer usable, and there is no proper trail on to Kesamaru. The route left to the Koshin Lodge, however, is very well maintained.

Turning left, the path now runs gently down, and sometimes up, along the side of the mountain, crossing a series of streams. I counted ten, including one that was dry. There are one or two slightly awkward parts where the path is falling away, but ropes have been provided where necessary. Certainly, no sections are as dangerous as the teeth of Nokogiri. Many of the little valleys are glorious, especially when the leaves are turning. The path occasionally rises high above these small valleys, but in all such places it is broad and safe.

About one and a half hours from the pass, the route finally reaches a Kanto Fureai no Michi sign just near the very top of the course. The direction signs indicate two hundred meters right to the Tenka Miharashi viewpoint, back to the Rokurinpan Pass, and on to the Koshin Lodge (0.5 km). Turning right here, the viewpoint at the top of a crag is reached in just four minutes. There are chains up, but these are child's play for anyone who has already come this far. The views of Kesamaru are better higher up, but this is the place for photographing the lodge and the cliffs of Mount Koshin. Looking around to the right from the lodge, there is also a clear view across to Kobugahara and Yokone. It is even possible to see Mount Tsukuba on a clear day.

Then, returning to the junction, it is a short, four-minute walk down to the lodge. It takes a further one and a half hours to walk from the lodge back down to Ginzandaira.

USEFUL KANJI

ASHIO	足尾
CHUZENJI	中禅寺
GINZANDAIRA	銀山平
"HUSBAND AND WIFE FROGS"	夫婦蛙岩
ICHINOTORII	一ノ鳥居
KAGAMI IWA (MIRROR ROCK)	鏡岩
KANTO FUREAI NO MICHI	関東ふれあいの道
KEN NO YAMA	剣の山
KOSHIN LODGE	庚申荘
KOSHIN NANATAKI (SEVEN KOSHIN WATERFALLS)	庚申七瀧
MOUNT HAKUSAN	白山
MOUNT JIZO	地蔵山
MOUNT KEIUN	渓雲山
MOUNT KESAMARU	袈裟丸山
MOUNT KOMAGAKE	駒掛山
MOUNT KOSHIN	庚申山
MOUNT KUMANO	熊野岳
MOUNT NANTAI	男体山
MOUNT NOKOGIRI	鋸山
MOUNT ONTAKE	御岳山
MOUNT SUKAI	皇海山
MOUNT YAKUSHI	薬師岳
MOUNT ZAO	蔵王岳
ROKURINPAN PASS	六林班峠
TENGU TOSEKI	天狗投石
TENKA MIHARASHI	天下見晴

HIKE 11 ▲ HANGETSU PASS
THE PACK-HORSE ROUTE TO NIKKO

MATO STATION • FUKASAWA GORGE • HANGETSU PASS • LAKE CHUZENJI • CHUZENJI • KEGON FALLS

TOTAL WALKING TIME   5 HOURS, 40 MINUTES

MAPS   1:25,000 ASHIO; 1:25,000 CHUZENJI; 1:50,000 ASHIO; 1:50,000 NANTAISAN

The walk across the Hangetsu Pass to Lake Chuzenji is a memorable hike, and strongly recommended. It follows an old pack-horse trail, now completely disused, but once a trunk route for transporting goods to and from the Ashio mines. In addition to the long climb up the Fukasawa Gorge and the fine views of Koshin, Sukai, Kesamaru, and Akagi from the top, there is also the pleasure of taking a walk back through time. This hike is now the hard way to Nikko, not so much because of the topography, but because it has not been maintained. You are not likely to meet anyone else on this route, so adequate precautions should be taken.

The newcomer to the area who comes across this old path will no doubt be astonished that it exists at all, for the route across the Asegata Pass described in the next hike is so much easier and comes out virtually at the same place on the banks of Chuzenji. Even more surprising is the date of its construction; despite its feeling of ancient history and look of utter decrepitude, the route across the Hangetsu Pass was actually opened only in December 1920. The story of the Hangetsu Pass is deeply connected with that of the pollution from the mine. Asegata was indeed the pass of choice, until the sulfurous gases emitted from the copper works killed off all the trees there, and the subsequent erosion made the valley too unsafe to use. Thus for a time the Hangetsu Pass was the only route between Ashio and Chuzenji. In addition to the route for goods to and from the mine, it became a popular trail for school excursions in the Taisho and early Showa periods.

There was once a total of five teahouses on this path, the first two quite early on, at the foot of the Fukasawa Gorge, and the third, the Kanayama Teahouse, about one hour from the entrance, just before the path crosses the river a final time and climbs steeply up the side of the valley. This teahouse served noodles, had a bath, and even allowed travelers to stay for the night. The fourth stood high up on the ridge at an altitude of fifteen hundred eleven meters, commanding a fine view of the southern flanks of Mount Hangetsu. From the fifth, the Fujimi Teahouse, it was even possible to see Mount Fuji on a fine day. The Hangetsu Pass became disused, however, after a history of just sixteen years, when the road was built across the Hosoo Pass in 1936. The Kanayama Teahouse somehow survived until 1939.

The trail is generally quite broad and frequently runs along the top of well-constructed stone walls. It is easy to imagine how it used to be when pack animals still carried goods across the mountains. Finally, the hike comes out to Lake Chuzenji, one of the most famous beauty spots of Japan. The views from the lookout point just below the summit of Mount Hangetsu are stupendous, taking in not only Nantai, Shirane, Sukai, and Kesamaru, but even the peaks of Chichibu and Mount Fuji. One of the distinctive plants to look for on Mount Hangetsu is the delicate *hashidoi,* a kind of morning glory. Then, the route descends to Chuzenji, a huge lake formed by an eruption of Nantai that blocked the river's outlet to the plains. Here, we find the Nikkosan Chuzenji temple, founded by Shodo Shonin in 784; the Tachiki Kannon, the oldest religious artifact in Nikko, carved by Shodo when he climbed Mount Nantai; and Utagahama Beach, one of the key points on the ascetic pilgrimage routes, the *shugendo.*

MATO STATION ▶ HANGETSU PASS
WALKING TIME: 4 HOURS

Turn right out of Mato Station, and follow the road up the valley. In just five minutes, you reach the remains of Japan's first hydroelectric power plant (a pipe in a glass case, see page 192). Turn right five minutes on from here, about twenty meters before the bridge over the Fukasawa River, at its confluence with the Matsugi. A sign points right to the Tokukura Kensetsu Company's Ashio Plant. There is also a wooden post with an arrow pointing straight on, not right, to Matsugi.

The road forks almost immediately. Take the right fork, which bypasses the houses. This rough road climbs gradually for about twenty minutes along the side of the Fukasawa Gorge. Turn left down to the river, where the road gives out at a fork. This river has to be forded. In the rainy season, the water comes almost up to the knees. At other times of year, it is possible to get across on the stones.

A narrow, muddy path leads up from the other side. This is a good, easy path along the wooded bank of the gorge. Stay with the river, avoiding a path up to the left soon after the ford. The banks are strewn with huge boulders between the trees, and from here on up, there are many pretty views of the river. The first of several waterfalls is reached about fifteen minutes from the ford. A further fifteen or twenty minutes bring us to a fork. Take the left fork heading backward, not the right fork forward. The path quickly turns back in the right direction after climbing a short way up away from the stream. You see a castlelike wall some five minutes from here. Cross the small tributary to the open area beneath the wall. The date on the stone lantern on the top is May 1931, just five years before the road was built across the Hosoo Pass and this route became disused.

The path continues from the opposite side of the open space beneath the old wall. The route first rises high above the gorge, then finally returns to the stream ten minutes later, at the top of the biggest waterfall on the Fukasawa. Here, you must ford the stream to avoid a river cliff on the left bank, crossing back again four or five minutes later. There has been quite a lot of felling along this stretch; but, after crossing back again, the path is again very pretty and well constructed.

After another long stretch where the trees have been felled, the path suddenly descends back down to the river at a confluence. The old route clearly just crossed the stream to the left, but that part of the trail has now fallen away. Consequently, it is necessary to ford the main stream twice in quick succession at the bend, first just below the confluence, then again just above it. The way across is marked by a red-painted stick and red marks on the trees. The path continues for about fifteen minutes up the left bank of the right-hand stream across open grassy slopes. Then, it descends to the stream once more at a very unlikely looking place, and the stream has to be forded one last time. The map does not show the stream reaching this far up the valley but, even here, the water still came almost up to my knees in the rainy season. Again, stepping stones can be used at other times of year.

The path rises directly opposite, very narrow and overgrown with bamboo grass. Then, opening up again, it begins a long zigzag ascent up through the azaleas to the ridge. It takes about ten minutes to reach the ridge, which commands some truly fine views across to Koshin and Sukai on the left, and Jizo and Yakushi to the right. The path is now broad. The climb continues for another thirty-five or forty minutes, but at a much gentler gradient.

At about the time the first significant descent begins, you can see the high concrete wall of the parking lot on Mount Hangetsu, one or two kilometers directly ahead. The smaller saddle to the left is the Hangetsu Pass, and the mountains beyond are the rim around the far side of Lake Chuzenji.

In thirty minutes, the path passes directly beneath this parking lot and here you reach the first signpost on the route. (Actually, it has fallen down, but it still functions adequately.) The sign points back toward Ashio, up to the toll road, and on to the Hangetsu Pass. It is tempting here to continue along the relatively flat path all the way to the pass, now just twenty minutes away. This temptation should be resisted, however, partly because the route is dangerous and partly because the views from the top of Mount Hangatsu are utterly magnificent, without question among the most beautiful anywhere in Japan. They come as a more than fitting reward for all of the effort put in so far.

Turning right at the sign, then, it takes only four minutes to climb up to the parking lot. The path is stepped, so although it is now little used, it is easy to follow. It comes out at the corner of the parking lot, continuing directly upward to the lookout point on Mount Hangetsu. There is no sign down to Ashio, but there is a sign pointing up that reads six hundred meters to the second lookout point. It takes a further ten minutes to climb up to the lookout point itself.

The views from here are simply stupendous. First, there is the path from Ashio leading up to the Hangetsu Pass, now capped (if you are lucky with the weather) by the cone of Mount Fuji. It looks as if the path that you have just followed leads all of the way to Fuji itself. Then there is the range leading up from Akagi: Kesamaru, Nokogiri, Sukai, and around to Nikko Shirane. There are also clear views of Senjogahara Marsh, the Ryuzu Falls, Lake Chuzenji, Kozuke Island (the site of one of Shodo Shonin's graves), the Hatcho Dejima Peninsula, Mount Nantai, as well as a view of the ridge in both directions along the south bank of the lake. The town of Ashio is not visible, but most of the valley down from the Asegata Pass is clearly in view, as is the bare, sheer face of the far side of the long Matsugi Gorge.

The top of Mount Hangetsu lies only five minutes up to the right from here (follow the sign for the first parking lot), but there are no views from there, because the summit is shrouded in trees. Instead, it is better to continue left along the unsignposted path directly beneath the lookout point. This is a good, well-constructed path, which offers many more fine views on both sides of the ridge. It descends quite steeply in places, but it is not at all hard or dangerous. The pass is reached in just fifteen minutes from the lookout point.

At the pass, a sign indicates seven hundred meters back to Mount Hangetsu and right to the Tachiki Kannon. There is no sign for the trail straight on along the ridge above the lake or for the (here almost invisible) path up from Ashio. If you are continuing along the ridge to the Asegata Pass, the path is again broad and safe, though it passes over the top of some of the most fearsome landslide slopes I have seen anywhere in this area. It takes thirty minutes to walk from the Hangetsu Pass to the Asegata Pass and, if returning to Ashio, a little over two hours from there to Mato Station.

HANGETSU PASS ▶ LAKE CHUZENJI ▶ CHUZENJI ▶ KEGON FALLS
WALKING TIME: 1 HOUR, 15 MINUTES

The path down to Chuzenji from here is not so difficult, but quite steep and narrow in places. The route winds down the forested slopes, at times presenting spectacular views of the lake and the volcanic cone of Mount Nantai. It takes about half an hour to reach the lakeside road. The path comes out just above and to the right of the distinctive Hatcho Dejima Peninsula.

Those wishing to go to the Asegata Campsite should turn left here. You reach the campsite in fifteen or twenty minutes. This is the end of Hike 12. During the summer holidays, a boat runs from there to Ojiri, the jetty just beside the Kegon Falls, and the bus stop for Nikko. It is also perfectly feasible to return to Ashio from there by the much easier course of Hike 12 in a single day.

Those heading for the falls via the temple should turn right along the lakeside road. You quickly reach a couple of fishing *minshuku* (Hangetsu Sanso and Koshu). These, too, are excellent places to stay for those who want a quiet spot by the lake away from the crowds. There are also many other *minshuku* close to the temple.

The road closely hugs the lake shore for about twenty minutes, then briefly rises away from the lake to avoid some private properties, which include the villas of the Italian and British embassies. You will also see the villas of the Belgian and French embassies, just after the temple. Half an hour from the peninsula, the road joins the main road, just before the toll gate, only two minutes from Nikkosan, the Chuzenji temple.

Chuzenji can be entered via the underpass. Admission is three hundred yen, and a free English language leaflet is available. This temple was founded by Shodo Shonin in 784. It was originally located on the other side of the lake at the foot of Mount Nantai, but was moved here in 1902. This is the home of the Tachiki Kannon mentioned on the sign at the pass above. The story goes that Shodo saw the image of Kannon, the goddess of mercy, reflected in the lake and immediately carved this statue from a standing Judas tree. The six-meter-high statue is preserved in the main hall of the temple today. It is a designated National Cultural Property and the oldest Buddhist image in Nikko. In its right hand, the statue holds a *shakujo* staff of the kind carried by the priests on the *shugendo*. As mentioned earlier the Tachiki Kannon of Chuzenji is stop number eighteen on the Bando pilgrimage route around the famous Kannons of the Kanto area.

Those who have completed Hike 5 will remember the account of the so-called Kegon Disease (see page 144). In a guide to the Bando circuit, the priest of Chuzenji instructs us on the relevance of the Tachiki Kannon with these words:

"One summer's day, I saw an old man of about seventy accompanied by a grandson who must have been of junior high school age praying fervently before the Tachiki Kannon. He looked so earnest that afterward I accosted him. He then told me this story:

" 'When I was young, I was very hard up for money and lost all hope for my future. Intending to die, I came as far as the Kegon Falls and thinking that this was the last thing that I would ever do in the world went to pray before the Tachiki Kannon. There, I heard the Tachiki Kannon say, "No, you must not die! Strive on!"

" 'On hearing Kannon's words, I gave up my thoughts of death and instead commenced working as hard as I could. I owe it to Kannon that I stand here today. Now, I always come here to worship once a year without fail. I expect that there are others like me, too.'

"It makes me truly glad that Kannon has saved such people from the disease of the Kegon Falls."

The priest then finishes with an incantation of Kannon's name.

Many other items of interest in the temple are related to Shodo Shonin. In the Hashiri Daikokuten hall, there is an image of Daikokuten, one of the Seven Gods of Good Fortune (the Shichifukujin) who fulfill people's desires. The temple brochure says that his image is placed here on account of the fulfillment of Shodo Shonin's desires when Shodo saw the reflection of Kannon in the waters from Mount Nantai. The god is said to have been enshrined here by Kukai when he visited Nikko in the year 820. Daikokuten, of course, is also the god involved in the myth about Shodo and the origin of the name of Ashio (see page 193). He is nowadays generally considered to be a god of harvests and of the kitchen. Perhaps because of this connection with fertility and creation, worshipers at Chuzenji pray to Daikokuten for confinements and safe births in addition to general good fortune.

As it happens, Chuzenji is not merely a stop on the pilgrimage course around the famous Kannons of the Kanto area, it is also a part of the Shimotsuke (Tochigi) pilgrimage route for the Shichifukujin. Chuzenji, of course, is the temple for praying to Daikokuten. Also in Nikko, Rinnoji, down by the Daiya River, is the temple for Bishamonten, the god of war. The others are: Myoshoji in Imaichi for Fukurokuju, the god of longevity and moral influence; Tokuhoinji in Utsunomiya for Jurojin, another god of longevity; Oyaji in Utsunomiya for Benzaiten, the goddess of learning and wealth; the Futarasan Shrine in Utsunomiya for Ebisu, the god of trade and fish; and Saimyoji in Haga for Hotei, the god of faith, happiness, and prosperity. A similar course exists in Joshu (Gunma), but none of those temples lie within the area covered by this book.

These Shichifukujin pilgrimage routes appear to have been fostered by Tenkai (1536–1643), the priest who brought Tokugawa Ieyasu's remains to Nikko and arranged for the building of Toshogu. The Shichifukujin faith was perceived as a means to settle the nation down again after the long period of civil war. Tenkai was himself abbot of both Chuzenji and Rinnoji. The Shichifukujin is certainly a very mixed faith, for while three of the gods have their origin in India, three come from China and one, Ebisu, is a native Japanese. Their promise of wealth and good fortune proved popular, however, and many Shichifukujin temples sprang up, especially in the capital of Edo.

Returning then to Shodo Shonin, the treasury of Chuzenji also preserves Shodo's gold-and-copper ax, which he is said to have used when climbing Mount Nantai, and the bronze head of his staff. In the ornate Godaido, we see five Myoo who appeared to Shodo in a dream at the time he opened the mountains of Nikko. The one in the center is Fudo.

Continuing, the beach opposite the temple (by the parking lot) is known as Utagahama, the Beach of Song. When Shodo founded the temple, an angel is reported to have descended from heaven to sing and dance there. As related in the introduction, Utagahama was the end point of the spring *shugendo* from Kobugahara. The priests would arrive on the second day of April each year and read *sutras* by the lakeside until April 22, thus completing their pilgrimage.

In the courtyard are more statues of Fudo Myoo, at an altar for fire purification ceremonies and a spring for ablution (Fudo no Reisen). The statue of Fudo at the Fudo spring looks just like the one at the Komori Iwa, mentioned on page 143, and is no doubt connected with it. Another spring offers Kongo water, the water of the Diamond World that ascetics drink when making their vows.

We return to earth a bit, however, with the Hoshu Jizo (Gem Jizo), which stands quite close to the spring. This Jizo dates from the early Edo period and has long been an object of worship for people seeking success in trade and money. There is also a six-hundred-year-old *kurobi* tree *(Thuja standishii,* a Japanese arborvitae).

Just beside the main gate is a fine belfry. It is said that one should strike the bell once for one's forebears, twice for longevity and prosperity, and three times or more for extra wishes. The temple is open from 8:00 to 17:00, from April to October; and 8:00 to 16:00, from November to March.

Leaving the temple by the main gate past the belfry, we enter a street packed with *minshuku,* souvenir shops, and restaurants. Just four minutes down the road on the right, there is a small, red building, Shodo Shonindo (Shodo Shonin Hall), which has a statue of the priest inside. This, too, belongs to Chuzenji.

A further eleven minutes around the lake shore bring us to the bridge above the ninety-six-meter Kegon Falls that plunge over the lip of the lake (see page 144).

Turn right here for the bus station and the falls. The buses down to Nikko are described at the end of Hike 5.

USEFUL KANJI

ASHIO	足尾
CHUZENJI	中禅寺
FIRST PARKING LOT	第一駐車場
FUKASAWA	深沢
HATCHO DEJIMA PENINSULA	八丁出島
HANGETSU PASS	半月峠
KEGON FALLS	華厳滝
LAKE CHUZENJI	中禅寺湖
MATO STATION	間藤駅
MATSUGI	松木
MOUNT NANTAI	男体山
OJIRI	大尻
SECOND LOOKOUT POINT	第二展望台
SHODO SHONIN HALL	勝道上人堂
TACHIKI KANNON	立木観音
TOKUKURA KENSETSU ASHIO PLANT	徳倉建設㈱ 足尾作業所
TOLL ROAD	有料道路

FROM INDUSTRIAL WASTELAND TO FORESTS OF DEER

MATO STATION • ASHIO DAM • ASEGATA PASS • ASEGATA CAMPSITE

TOTAL WALKING TIME 2 HOURS, 50 MINUTES

MAPS 1:50,000 ASHIO; 1:50,000 NANTAISAN; 1:25,000 ASHIO; 1:25,000 CHUZENJI

This is the easy route to Nikko, as opposed to the path across the Hangetsu Pass described in Hike 11. Its main advantage is that it provides a relatively gentle trail to Lake Chuzenji. For those who have not walked the route from Ginzandaira to Mato, however (see Hike 9), this course also gives some fascinating glimpses of Ashio's industrial past and the terrible extent of the sulfur pollution that destroyed the vegetation over a wide area of mountainside. As the trail progresses toward the pass, we gradually witness a return to unspoiled nature, with some long views back toward Mount Bizendate and up toward Mount Shazan on the left. I have now walked this route several times and never once failed to see at least a deer or a serow, and have even spotted a bear.

In addition, this is also a route with a very long history, for this was the pass that Shodo Shonin and his disciples used to travel from Utagahama on the banks of Chuzenji on their way to Ashio. At various times, Shodo Shonin himself lived in Matsugi, Mount Koshin, Akakura, and Watarase — all parts of present-day Ashio. Later, when his followers received training at Hotoji in Matsugi and Ryuzoji in Akakura, this was their pilgrimage route.

In the early twentieth century, there were two teahouses on the road to Lake Chuzenji, serving lemonade and noodles. These both closed in 1921, when the pass was no longer considered safe for use. Because of the destruction of the vegetation, there was terrible erosion and a consequent fear of flooding. The path across the Hangetsu Pass was built in 1920 to replace the traditional route to Asegata. The Asegata Pass was reopened only in 1954, when the present road and the Ashio Dam were built. The road follows virtually the same route as the old path. When in 1956 the pollution problem at the copper works was mainly resolved by the installation of a new type of smelter, the task of rehabilitation could begin.

MATO STATION ▶ ASHIO DAM
WALKING TIME: 40 MINUTES

Turning right out of Mato Station, the route first retraces the final stage of Hike 9 in reverse. In just seven minutes, as we leave the tiny shops of the main street of Mato behind us, we reach the remains of the first hydroelectric power station in Japan (see page 192). Six minutes later, there is a Kanto Fureai no Michi sign left to Ginzandaira (6.1 km) and straight on to the Ashio Dam (2.0 km). Another four minutes bring us to a traffic circle. The blue bridge across the Watarase River to the copper works is the Furukawa Bridge, the oldest iron road bridge in Japan (see page 192).

The copper works were first built here in 1884. Although they have been expanded and modernized many times since, they now look like a piece of industrial archaeology. Once the largest copper works in the Orient, they were also, as is all too obvious from the bare mountainside around, the main source of the pollution for which Ashio is so famous. The destruction came swiftly after they were built. It is recorded that all of the trees in the Matsugi Valley above the works had already been killed by the sulfurous gases as early as 1888. The farmers in the valley nonetheless somehow continued producing crops like barley, wheat, millet, and giant radish until 1900. The population of Matsugi fell from two hundred seventy people, in forty households, in 1892 to zero in 1901. The problem of sulfurous emissions was not solved until 1956, with the passing of a new law and the building of a new plant. The works are still operating at a minimal level, using imported materials.

Instead of crossing the bridge, keep straight on at the traffic circle along the right bank of the river. The view of the copper works on the opposite bank, with its still-smoldering chimney, is riveting and a popular spot for artists. The scenery from here up to the dam has all the desolate fascination of a lunar landscape. On the right side of the road, directly opposite the copper works, is Ryuzoji.

This temple is thought to have been founded by a disciple of Shodo Shonin in May 807 and revived by Ennin in 837. Ennin (794–864), posthumously known as Jikaku Daishi, was born in Shimotsuke but studied directly under Saicho at Hiei. After traveling to China from 838 to 847, it was Ennin who introduced the esoteric school of Tendai Buddhism (Taimitsu) and also the practice of *nembutsu* (the invocation of the Buddha's name) to Japan. He is also credited by some with having written one of the great travel records of all time, the *Nyuto Kyuho Junrei Koki* (T'ang Pilgrimage in Search of the Laws). Ennin returned to Shimotsuke in 848 by order of the emperor and founded the Sanbutsudo (Jinguji) at Rinnoji. He was to become the third head priest of the Tendai sect in 854. Ryuzoji was a stop on the *shugendo* for priests following the steps of Shodo Shonin right up until Meiji. Now a Tendai temple dedicated to Amida Nyorai, its head temple is Rinnoji in Nikko.

Don't neglect to see the large pyramid-shaped pile of graves in the courtyard, together with the splendid Jizo. The pyramid is dedicated to the villagers who once lived in Matsugi. Another sight is the grave of Daininbo, a priest who plotted against the Meiji government. His gravestone is marked with boldly written characters reading Homujo, literally "Phoenix Dream Castle."

Daininbo was, indeed, a wild sort of man. In his youth, he was known as something of a swashbuckling swordsman, but after killing a friend he entered Rinnoji and became a priest. Next, he retreated to a hermitage and fasted on Mount Koshin before taking over as priest of Ryuzoji. It was not long, however, before he became involved in a major plot to overthrow the Meiji government, involving prominent figures throughout Kanto and the northeast of Japan. The ringleader was Kumoi Tatsuo (1844–70), a samurai of the Yonezawa fief in Yamagata, shocked by the way those still loyal to the Tokugawa family were crushed in the Boshin Civil War that led to the Meiji Restoration. He was also opposed to the predominant position of the Choshu (Yamaguchi) and Satsuma (Kagoshima) fiefs in the new government. Daininbo first encountered Kumoi by chance at Nasu Hot Spring. They later met again at the office of the shrine on Mount Koshin to work out the details of their conspiracy. The basic plan was a series of timely assassinations of high-ranking officials. The government uncovered the plot, however, before it had time to reach fruition, and Tatsuo, Daininbo, and several of their co-conspirators were executed. Daininbo was only thirty-three years old. This was also the event that brought a rapid halt to pilgrimages from Edo to Mount Koshin.

Continuing from the temple, the dam is also an extraordinary sight. Water plunges down from its lip in a brilliant cascade of seven uneven steps, as a sort of

217

finishing touch to the harshest of industrial gardens. Like many other dams and barriers of Ashio, this one was built to contain the excessive erosion from the mountainside, denuded by pollution from the copper works and by forest fires started by miners. Not only pollutants, but also the huge quantities of silt washing down the Watarase River caused severe damage to downstream communities. It is said that the river once flowed red, and the crashing of giant boulders echoed all around the valley. Government decrees brought little improvement to the situation in the Meiji and Taisho eras. There was a long succession of pleas from the local community asking the Diet to take action. The Interior Ministry finally set up a Watarase River Silt Prevention Plan in 1927, but it was to be another ten years before any civil engineering work was actually begun. Even then, this involved only a series of small dams higher up the valley. After serious damage by a huge typhoon in 1947, pressure grew for the scale of the work to be stepped up, leading to a major expansion of projects from 1950 and the construction of the Ashio Dam. This expansion was financed partly by the money Japan was then receiving in aid from the United States. The dam took four and a half years to build, reaching completion in 1955.

The dam is 204 meters long, 39 meters high, 32.4 meters thick at the base, and just 3 meters wide at the top. Over 160,000 tons of cement were used in the construction. There is a large parking lot and viewing point by the top with a map of the dams of Ashio.

ASHIO DAM ▶ ASEGATA PASS
WALKING TIME: 1 HOUR, 55 MINUTES

The landscape just behind the dam is equally unsettling in a different way; it is a heavily silted marsh, dotted with the rusting remains of conveyers from the mine. Stay on the right bank, following the dirt track. In a little over five minutes, a road branches across to the other side. Arrows on a post point left to Matsugi and straight on to Kuzo. Go straight.

From here, the route follows the valley of the Kuzo River all of the way to the pass. There were once sixteen farming households in Kuzo, but these were bought out by the mine in 1903, leaving only the two teahouses in the valley. Then in 1914, forty-two terraced houses were built here to accommodate one hundred house-holds. There was even a Kuzo branch of the local primary school. The community was to be short-lived, however, as those buildings and the teahouses were all abandoned just seven years later when the pass was closed down. There is no trace of human settlement here today, only myriad traces of human exploitation.

Keep straight for another six minutes. Just after fording a shallow tributary, the road again forks. This time, the left fork up the river bank leads to Mount Shazan and the right fork to the Asegata Pass, though there are no signs.

Trees start reappearing from around here, at first in the form of forestry plantations. The trail rises quite high above the river, crosses it, and comes to an unmarked fork, with a concrete road to the left, an unpaved road to the right. Go right. After crossing the river one more time, about fifty-five minutes from the Ashio Dam, the trail starts winding up the mountainside, reaching a final fork in another ten minutes. The right fork leads up the Tonekurasawa River, which is named on the map, though no road is shown. This time, go left.

There are some fine views back toward Bizendate, Koshin, and Akagi as the road climbs toward the head of the valley. The mountainsides, too, are once again covered with vegetation, and there are many traces of wild animals. Despite the fact that this is a road of sorts, it seems most unlikely that many people come here. The road ends thirty minutes from that final fork, turning sharply twenty meters or so down to a stream on the left. There are two signs to Asegata, one pointing across the stream and the other up a narrow path on the left bank. There are also red marks on the trees indicating the way.

The path is astonishingly well kept and obviously used, though it is hard to imagine by whom. It starts off very easily through some fresh young woods, following up the left bank of the stream. The banks are steep, and the path briefly rises quite high above the stream. It quickly returns to the bed, however, and then climbs up the other side. The path up the right bank is marked with a sign warning you to be careful with fire. Five minutes later, the path crosses a small stream, then follows up the ridge between this and the main stream. It takes only thirty minutes to walk up to the pass from the end of the road. Just before the pass, there are again some fine views back toward Bizendate, and the delicate trees on the surrounding slopes have an almost whimsical beauty. There are signs at the top pointing left to Mount Shazan and right to Mount Hangetsu. The route to Mount Hangetsu is described on page 210.

ASEGATA PASS ▶ ASEGATA CAMPSITE
WALKING TIME: 13 MINUTES

The walk down the other side of the pass is surprisingly easy, very different from the steep descent below the Hangetsu Pass. It is a broad, uncomplicated trail down the wooded banks of the lake, with many glimpses of the water through the trees. It has a total length of a mere five hundred meters and drops just one hundred fifty meters.

The Asegata Campsite, which dates from 1958, is open only for a short season in the summer, but it lies in an idyllic spot well away from the main bustle of Nikko. The tents and bungalows are set up between the trees, and there is also a quiet beach. It is possible to take the boat from the wharf here to Ojiri at Chuzenji Hot Spring, near the Chuzenji bus station. Tickets cost about four hundred yen and can be obtained at the camp office. The boats run once every two hours, sailing to Ojiri via Chuzenji. They do not, however, stop except on request. Those wishing to take the boat must therefore buy the ticket at least thirty minutes in advance. It is very pleasant just to rest on the beach, watching the other boats and fishermen until it arrives.

The other option for those not staying at the campsite is to start straight around the lake: either left along the south bank hiking trail to Senjugahama (3 hours) and the Ryuzu Falls (4 hours, 20 minutes), or right for Ojiri, which takes about one and a half hours. The route from the foot of the Hangetsu Pass, fifteen minutes from Asegata, is described in the final section of Hike 11.

USEFUL KANJI

ASEGATA	アセガタ
ASEGATA PASS	阿世潟峠
ASHIO DAM	足尾ダム
CHUZENJI	中禅寺

GINZANDAIRA	銀山平
HOMUJO (PHOENIX DREAM CASTLE)	鳳夢城
KANTO FUREAI NO MICHI	関東ふれあいの道
KUZO	久蔵
MATO STATION	間藤駅
MATSUGI	松木
MOUNT HANGETSU	半月山
MOUNT NANTAI	男体山
MOUNT SHAZAN	社山
OJIRI	大尻
RYUZOJI	龍蔵寺
RYUZU FALLS	龍頭の滝
SENJUGAHAMA	千手ヶ浜
TONEKURASAWA	利根倉沢

SHODO'S PARADISE

FUTARASAN JINJA MAE BUS STOP • MOUNT NANTAI • SHIZU LODGE • SANBONMATSU BUS STOP (SENJOGAHARA)

TOTAL WALKING TIME 5 HOURS, 35 MINUTES

MAPS 1:50,000 NIKKO; 1:50,000 NANTAISAN; 1:25,000 NANTAISAN; 1:25,000 NIKKO HOKUBU

The ascent of Mount Nantai in 782 was the climactic event of Shodo Shonin's life, and it provides a more than suitable finale to the mountain trails of this book. At 2,484 meters, Nantai is the highest mountain in this region and is visible for many miles around. Those who have followed these courses through from the early stages will surely remember the surpassing beauty of this conical volcano as seen from the path along the ridge from Narukami to the Zama Pass. In no small way, this is the mountain that holds the region together.

Many people still climb Nantai to worship at the innermost shrine from August 1 to August 7 each year. This mass pilgrimage is supported by a number of festivities, starting with a parade of mountain priests along the lake shore on July 31. Huge crowds then gather each evening to pass through the gate at midnight and climb the mountain to greet the sunrise at the summit. Prayers are offered for the safety of the family and the fulfillment of various other wishes. Those who do not climb can worship the mountain from afar on August 2 aboard a traditional Japanese-style boat. There is also a Japanese archery tournament by the lake shore on August 4, using targets placed on pontoons in the lake. Other events include fireworks, a mass release of floating lanterns on the lake, and Shinto *kagura* dancing.

The cone of Nantai was formed in eruptions that occurred some ten thousand years ago. Structurally, Nantai is rather similar to a slag heap. Its steep slopes are extremely unstable, and the long and narrow landslide gullies down its flanks are clearly visible from a long way off. It may not encourage some to know that the path goes straight up one of these, but the route is popular and well maintained by the shrine. The Utsunomiya forestry office has been planting trees and grass and building a system of barriers up the mountainside since 1960 in order to contain the problem. These are clearly visible, for example, from Akechidaira (see Hike 5), but do not intrude too much on this course. Virtually the entire route on the mountain itself passes through beautiful virgin forest. Nantai provides a wealth of variety, from the monkey-filled forests of its lower slopes to the stunted birches and pines higher up, and finally the multicolored volcanic rocks at the rim of the crater.

Descending the other side, the route once again enters a separate world far away from the bustling tourist crowds of Nikko, winding first down a ridge and then a wooded valley beneath the magnificent peaks of Nantai and Taro. Finally, it emerges at another of Nikko's most famous beauty spots, the plain of Senjogahara.

The name Nantai means "male body." Historically, however, the mountain has been also known both as Futarasan ("two storms"), still the name of the Nantai shrine, and Kurokami, meaning "black hair." Futarasan is thought to be a Japanese rendering of the Sanskrit Potalaka, the mythical mountain paradise of Kannon on the south coast of India. That Shodo should have been questing for the paradise of Kannon should surprise no one in view of the story of his birth, his three years of ascetic discipline in the cave at Izuru, and his relation to the Tachiki Kannon at Chuzenji. The Japanese characters for Futara can also be read Niko. It is said that from this reading Kukai, in 820, derived the new name, Nikko, meaning "sunlight."

This is how the mountain is mentioned in the *Oku no Hosomichi* (Narrow Road to the Deep North), by Basho's traveling companion, Sora:

> Having lost my hair
> I came to Mount Kurokami
> On the day we donned
> Fresh summer clothes

And that is not at all a bad sentiment for finishing a series of walks like this.

FUTARASAN JINJA MAE BUS STOP ▶ MOUNT NANTAI
WALKING TIME: 2 HOURS, 15 MINUTES

This hike begins from inside the compounds of the Futarasan Shrine itself. This is the shrine that most nearly belongs to the god of Nantai who, as related in the introduction, fought a terrible war with the god of Akagi to establish which was the taller. In the first engagement, the centipedes of Akagi overwhelmed the snakes of Nantai at Senjogahara (Battlefield Plain), which also happens to be the end point of this hike. Nantai won the rematch, although one should not assume, even so, that all of the sores of that ancient conflict have now healed. On January 4 each year, in a ceremony known as Hikimeshikishinji, a symbolic arrow is still fired from this, the central Futarasan Shrine, in the direction of Mount Akagi.

When Shodo Shonin finally conquered the mountain in 782, he established a shrine at the summit, which he named Futarasan Shrine. The main Futarasan Shrine today lies not far from Toshogu, while this central shrine on the shores of Chuzenji commands the final path up the mountain. The small innermost Futarasan Shrine stands on the summit. Another shrine is down on the other side of the mountain by the Shizu Lodge. In addition, for the record, there are also Futarasan shrines at the tops of Nyoho, Akanagi, Taro, Omanago, Komanago, Zen Shirane, and Oku Shirane. All of these are climbed by pilgrims during that first week of August.

To reach the Chuzenji Futarasan from the Tobu Nikko Station, take either the bus to Chuzenji or the less frequent one to Yumoto. It is a ten-minute walk from the terminus at the Chuzenji Hot Spring to the shrine. Alternatively, the Yumoto bus stops right outside at the Futarasan Jinja Mae bus stop.

The first place to visit is the treasure house (admission ¥300, open 9:00–16:00). This contains a splendid collection of swords on the ground floor, together with a selection of stuffed animals from the nearby mountains (a deer, fox, serow, monkey, bear, and flying squirrel). On the second floor are three portable shrines built at Oyama, Tochigi Prefecture, in 1389 for use in the Futarasan Festival. Decorated in copper and silver, they were apparently renovated in Utsunomiya in 1490. Even more fascinating are the tiny seals and iron votive statuettes of horses that were excavated at the summit of Mount Nantai. These appear to date from about the time of Shodo himself. The spirit of Shodo Shonin is represented by a huge 1964 painting by Maeda Seison, depicting the moment of success: as Shodo and his eight disciples are praying for guidance on the mountain, the god appears, pointing the way to the top.

The path leads up from the gateway inside the compound of the red shrine building. The shrine requests that each visitor sign a book and pay five hundred yen to climb the mountain. In return, each is given a cloth armband, a lucky charm for protection during the ascent. Actually, it is quite a pretty souvenir. Until quite recently there was only a simple wooden gateway here. The present, more splendid affair, adorned with red lacquer and copper tiles, was erected in 1975 to celebrate the twelve-hundredth anniversary of the foundation of the shrine at the summit.

The leaflet given out by the shrine indicates that it takes three or four hours to reach the summit, but this is an extremely generous estimate. Anyone who has completed the other courses described in this book will require considerably less time. The official climbing season for this mountain is from May 5 to October 25, which seems about right, in view of the climate.

The ascent begins up a flight of old steps, raising unwarranted fears that the steps might lead all of the way to the summit. In fact, they continue for only five minutes, as far as the first stage. Just like the route at Mount Fuji, the climb is divided into ten stages, the tenth being the summit itself.

It is very tempting, though perhaps unwise, to read some deep symbolism into this figure ten, for ten is also the number of states on the path to enlightenment in the cosmology of esoteric Buddhism. The six worldly states are those realms visited by Jizo, as explained in Short Walk 1: hell, ghosts, beasts, warring spirits, men, and Devas. Above these there are four more realms: the Sravakas, Pratyekabuddhas, Bodhisattvas, and fully enlightened Buddhas — the level of Dainichi (Vairochana) — at the top.

Carmen Blacker, in her challenging book *The Catalpa Bow*, quotes a document dating from 1215 specifying the following rites for the first six stages as ascetics ascend the mountain: weighing one's karma in hell, fasting in the realm of hungry ghosts, abstention from water among the beasts, wrestling in the world of fighting spirits, repentance in the realm of men, and the dance of longevity among the Devas. No rites are recorded for the next three stages, but the final one is accompanied by baptism with water. Blacker describes how ascetics on Mount Omine in Kansai and Mount Haguro in Yamagata still go through the motions of these spiritual journeys on their own holy mountains in the month of August.

Ascending from stage one on the climb up Nantai, the pilgrim now finds himself on an ordinary mountain path, but one with many beautiful old trees. Climbing in mid-September, I was astonished by the number of monkeys. As I walked up, the forest in every direction was filled with the sound of breaking twigs and rustling leaves, as the monkeys fed on their nuts and berries. It takes about twenty minutes from here to the low, stone wall and junction with the forest road at the third stage (I didn't notice the second stage at all). There has been quite a lot of landslide-prevention work on the mountainside between the third and fourth stages, so next it is necessary to follow up a few bends on the forest road. This is really something of a blessing, as the gradient is much gentler here than on the rest of the path.

The entrance to the fourth stage is marked by a white shrine gate. The path now leads up some stone, and then earthen, steps. The mixed woods here are particularly pretty, and there are excellent views back toward Lake Chuzenji. It is quite steep, however, and iron railings have been placed most of the way up this stretch to give pilgrims something to hang on to.

The fifth stage lies some thirteen minutes from the gate. There is a shelter here for emergencies and other shelters at the seventh and eighth stages. Now, the way becomes extremely rough, climbing steeply up the boulder-strewn and unstable-looking path of a landslide slope. It is a bit of a miracle that this path exists at all, and one cannot help wondering how often it all slides away. Here you should be careful of stones dislodged by climbers in front of you.

I also failed to notice the sixth stage, but there was a standing stone on a boulder in the middle of the landslide slope that might have been it. It takes about thirty minutes to climb from stage five to stage seven and a further fifteen minutes up the landslide slope to the shrine gate, four minutes below stage eight. All of the time, the path continues steeply up this narrow funnel of debris.

At the eighth stage, beneath a huge rock, there is a small Taki no O Shrine (the main shrine is described on page 238). Soon afterward, the path levels out a little for a short while, through lovely woods of birch and pine. It soon gets steeper again, however, and the trees rapidly become sparser and more stunted. The soil is also extremely thin, giving place to red volcanic rocks and sand. There is a growing sensation that this is indeed a volcano. Just near the top, there is a wonderful array of multicolored stones. I also failed to notice stage nine.

At the top, there is a small Futarasan Shrine. The summit tends to be a bit littered, but on a fine day the views are tremendous in every direction. It is a great pleasure, of course, to trace out all of the routes you have already walked, while a challenge is presented by the many other mountains still to be climbed.

MOUNT NANTAI ▸ SHIZU LODGE

WALKING TIME: 1 HOUR, 30 MINUTES

To descend to the other side, follow the path up to the rocky, uppermost peak, and follow the signs down to the Shizu Lodge (Shizugoya). Initially, the path leads down the rim of the crater, reaching stage nine (back down toward hell again) in about ten minutes. The woods are very pretty, with the trees, naturally enough, changing in the reverse order of that of the path up, but the trail is really quite steep in places. It is another thirteen minutes to the eighth stage, after which there is a tricky patch above an old gully, before returning to the curious, contorted shapes of the pine forest. The path is fairly level between stages seven and six, then steep again from there on down. There are many fallen trees, no doubt because of the thinness of the soil, so it seems that one is always ducking under or climbing over dead trunks. There are also patches in gullies that are very slippery. For all of its difficulties, however, the path is fun to go down, and there are many impressive views of Mount Omanago opposite.

The path reaches the top of a series of landslide barriers, at stage two, and the Shizu Lodge, ten minutes later. First, there is an Oku no In, with statues of Fudo Myoo and buddhas. A sign points back toward Mount Nantai and rightish toward the Urami waterfall. The map shows an interesting route down to the right that bypasses the Iroha Road and comes out at Kiyotaki. In fact, though, I could not see any trace of the path at this sign. A few meters farther on, at the lodge, the path does appear to fork, but the right-hand fork peters out very quickly in dense undergrowth. It would be fun to try that old route. If you do, however, be sure to take good maps and a compass and allow plenty of time for getting lost.

The lodge itself is unmanned and not very inviting, but it would make sense to stay here if you are planning to climb Omanago or Taro the next day. The shrine beside the lodge is the other Futarasan Shrine mentioned earlier.

SHIZU LODGE ▶ SANBONMATSU BUS STOP
WALKING TIME: 1 HOUR, 50 MINUTES

Taking the left fork and crossing the junction of paths two minutes later, the path comes out onto a forest road in just four minutes from the lodge. A sign points left to Mount Omanago and Sanbonmatsu and back to Nantai. Two minutes later is a crossroads, where the signs point left to Sanbonmatsu, right for the Fujimi Pass (Fujimitoge), back to the Shizu Lodge, and straight on to Omanago. Turn left.

The road here is unpaved and descends at a gentle gradient through charming mixed woods. This is a very quiet valley, crowded in by towering mountains on either side. There are also splendid views down beyond the foot toward the mountains north of Chuzenji.

The road temporarily becomes surfaced some twenty-five minutes from the crossroads. Immediately afterward, there is a three-way junction: right to Mount Taro, back to Shizu Lodge, and left to Sanbonmatsu. Go left. The road heads down toward the marsh of Senjogahara, the top of which comes into sight while still more than an hour away. There is a long stretch through a vast forestry plantation. Then, leaving that behind, the road reaches another three-way junction: right for the dairy farm at Kotoku, back to Shizu, and left to Sanbonmatsu.

Kotoku is a large farm, just to the north of Senjogahara, with beautiful silver birches, hawthorns, and a pretty lake. It offers a campsite open in summer and cross-country skiing in winter. Kotoku is also the start of a hiking course that leads around the bed of the dried-up Lake Karenuma to Lakes Kirikomiko, Karikomiko, Shinnoko, and Yunoko. There, one can enjoy Yumoto Hot Spring, the one-hundred-ten-meter cataract of the Yudaki Falls, and also Yumotoji, which Shodo Shonin founded in 788 and dedicated to the Healing Buddha, Yakushi Nyorai. Unfortunately, the temple was destroyed in a typhoon, and the present building dates from only 1973, but a beautiful little golden statue of Yakushi remains. Legend has it that Shodo fought with a giant snake near there and imprisoned it in the twin lakes of Kirikomiko and Karikomiko.

The map indicates that it is possible to walk directly from this junction to Sanbonmatsu, but in fact the road has been blocked. It is therefore necessary to turn left at the roadblock two hundred meters later and then right, down the parallel road through the fields. This does have the advantage, however, of giving wonderfully clear views of Mount Nantai. There are a *minshuku* and two pensions on this road (Senjogahara Sanso, Iris Ayame Sanso, and Artistic), and also a campsite with bungalows nearby. Turn right at the next crossroads to reach the Sanbonmatsu Tea House in four minutes.

This teahouse is a very popular drive-in for visitors to Oku Nikko, so you shouldn't expect anything too traditional. The bus stop is just by the entrance to the left. Buses to Nikko Station run once or twice an hour until 20:07. It is worth remembering, however, that when the roads are congested, this journey can easily take three hours. To catch the last ordinary train to Tokyo, the last feasible bus is the one that leaves at 17:17.

On the opposite side of the road from the bus stop is a viewpoint for observing the Senjogahara Plain. There is no hiking course across the marsh from here, but there is a well-laid-out path along the roadside in both directions at the edge of the marsh. This joins up with the two ends of the 5.6-kilometer nature course farther around. The shortest route is to turn left and enter the plain from opposite the Akanuma bus stop.

The plain lies at an altitude of thirteen hundred ninety-five meters and extends for a length of about two kilometers. It used to be a lake called Akanuma (Red Pond), but after heavy silting with volcanic ash and other debris, it turned first into a marsh, then into the plain we see today. There is, however, still a short stretch of marsh in the area around the Aoki bridge (Aokibashi).

The plain's rich vegetation includes cotton grass, azaleas, reddish-purple irises, thistles up to a meter in height, and the insect-eating *mosengoke* (round-leaved sundew). There are also scattered silver birches, larches, and hawthorns. Altogether, it is estimated that there are about twenty-five hundred different species of plant at Senjogahara.

The white and pink flowers of the hawthorn trees *(zumi,* or *Malus sieboldii)* blossom from mid- to late June; the cotton grass is at its best from mid-June to early July; the azaleas can be seen in July, together with the pink flowers of the small evergreen bogberries *(tsurukokemomo)* and also the lilies — the bright orange *kuruma yuri,* the purple *koniyuri,* and the tall yellow Nikko *kisuge;* and late July to August is the time for the thistles and the delicate pink willow herbs *(yanagiran).*

In addition to the plants, the marsh is also home to many birds. Typical species include the brown thrush, various buntings and flycatchers, the long-tailed tit, brown dipper, Japanese robin, stonechat, and ducks. Senjogahara can also be a stimulating place for a walk in mid-winter when it is covered with snow.

USEFUL KANJI

CHUZENJI	中禅寺
FUJIMI PASS	富士見峠
FUTARASAN SHRINE	二荒山神社
KOTOKU	光徳
MOUNT NANTAI	男体山
MOUNT TARO	太郎山
SANBONMATSU	三本松
SENJOGAHARA LOOKOUT	戦場ケ原展望台
SHIZU LODGE	志津小屋
URAMI FALLS	裏見の滝

THE ANCIENT SITES

TOBU NIKKO STATION • SACRED BRIDGE • SHIHONRYUJI • KAIZANDO • TAKI NO O SHRINE • GYOJADO • TOBU NIKKO STATION

TOTAL WALKING TIME   1 HOUR, 35 MINUTES

MAPS   A FREE MAP, TITLED *MOHITOTSU NO NIKKO*, IS AVAILABLE AT TOBU RAILWAY STATIONS

Today, everybody knows of Nikko because of Toshogu, the magnificent seventeenth-century shrine to Ieyasu, the first Tokugawa shogun. Toshogu, Rinnoji, and the main Futarasan Shrine are always packed with visitors. The carvings and architectural structures are superb, but the colors are also somewhat garish. Combined with the commercialism of the souvenir industry, the long lines of people queuing up to clap their hands under dragons decorating the Yakushido, or admire the "sleeping cat," the excess may make one feel tempted to join forces with those famous Koshin monkeys: to see, hear, and speak nothing more.

It seems almost incredible, therefore, that there is a peaceful, deserted, and thoroughly delightful walk within literally a stone's throw of the shrine itself. Even so, the walk is replete with fascinating relics of a long and distinguished past. As one strolls the quiet, cedar-lined avenues, one feels again a sense of stepping back in time, to the days when the people who came here felt a natural awe and love for the mountains and strove to express it in offerings, prayers, and votive stones.

This walk begins at what today is the main gateway to Nikko, the Tobu Nikko Station. The view of Nantai from the main road looking toward Toshogu is quite different from any we have observed so far, for now we can see Nantai, the "Male Body" mountain, together with, and perhaps even dwarfed by, its mate, Nyoho, the "Female Peak." Nantai, of course, is the mountain that drew Shodo Shonin all the way from Izuru. Nyoho was also a part of the Nikko *shugendo*, the ascetic mountain courses, which in this area mostly followed the steps of Shodo Shonin. Gyojado has long been a place of worship and a starting point for priests ascending the mountain, and Shodo himself is thought to have used this route when he discovered Chuzenji. The *shugendo* up Nyoho, however, is nowadays associated less with Shodo than with Kukai, for two of the shrines on this course were founded by Kukai when he visited Nikko in the year 820.

In addition to these sights, this walk leads past the Sacred Bridge, where Shodo crossed the Daiya River; Shihonryuji, the first temple he established here; and also his main grave. By the time the path comes out again into the hubbub of tourist Nikko, one is tempted to walk right through, saving the more famous sights for another day.

TOBU NIKKO STATION ▶ SHINKYO (SACRED BRIDGE)
WALKING TIME: 20 MINUTES

It is possible to take a bus from the station, but it is more interesting to walk up the main road toward the shrines, glancing in at the craft shops and enjoying the towering peaks of Nantai and Nyoho up ahead. This is the view that earned the mountains their names. Although a city has now grown up at their feet, one can still imagine how impressive they must have been to Shodo Shonin as he first approached the Daiya. The Nikko Tourist Information Center lies ten minutes up the road on the left.

There are several things to see in the vicinity of the Sacred Bridge, where the road bends sharply to the left. On the right-hand side of the road is a statue and a small well called the Iwasaku Reisui. The water flows from Nantai and is said to have been discovered by Shodo and his party when they first came to the Daiya. Long used by ascetic priests to refresh themselves, it is the most delicious in all Japan according to the sign. Use the small ladle provided to see for yourself. The statue is of the priest Tenkai, the abbot of Rinnoji who brought Ieyasu's remains to Nikko and is now buried alongside Shodo on Kozuke Island in Lake Chuzenji.

On the left-hand side of the road is a statue of a more modern patron of Nikko, Itagaki Taisuke (1837–1919), one of the most prominent leaders of Meiji Japan. He is said to have saved Nikko from war during the disturbances of 1868. There is also a small red shrine halfway up the driveway to the Nikko Kanaya Hotel.

This shrine, the Hoshinogu (Star Shrine), is dedicated to Myojo Tenshi, the god who is said to have appeared to Shodo in a dream and told him about Nikko when Shodo was just seven years old. This god's other name is Iwasaku, hence the name of the well across the road. Iwasaku is also a god of mining, which seems appropriate in this area. This was the site of the Hoshi no Yado, the "Star Lodge," which, as related in the introduction, was one of the key stops on the Nikko *shugendo*. Shodo is said to have founded the shrine here in 809, in appreciation of help received. Myojo Tenshi (and therefore this shrine) was popular with the samurai during the civil wars of the fifteenth and sixteenth centuries. Then, with the building of Toshogu, the shrine came under the patronage of the Tokugawa shogunate. Various events were staged at its festivals, including *yabusame*, horseback archery. The present shrine, however, was erected only in 1980.

There are also some magnificent Koshin stones to the left and right of the shrine, with the monkey motif and the characters for Shomen Kongo, plus a statue of Fudo Myoo, minus his sword. The date on one of the Koshin stones is 1698. There is also a Koshin stone with the Koshin characters on the front, dated 1980, the newest that I have ever seen. Obviously, it was put here when the shrine was reconstructed. As it happens, however, 1980 was also a Koshin year, only the second since the suppression of the Koshin faith in the Meiji Restoration. That fact was also, no doubt, prominent in the minds of those who placed it here. It would be interesting to find out how many other Koshin stones were erected that year. The other stones were probably also brought here at the same time, as Koshin stones really belong by the wayside. Koshin years are always easy to recognize because, by sheer coincidence, they occur in precise multiples of sixty from the baseline of the Western calendar (60 A.D., 120 A.D., 180 A.D., etc.).

The bright red, lacquered wooden bridge across the Daiya is Shinkyo, the Sacred Bridge, also known as the "Snake-Sedge Bridge," marking the spot where Shodo and his party crossed the river in 766. It is said that the river was impassable when they arrived, but in response to their prayers, an old man appeared on the other side and threw two snakes across to form a bridge. When they still hesitated to cross, sedge was laid on the backs of the snakes to give them a better footing. Once they had made their way safely across, both the man and the bridge disappeared. This old man, Jinja O, is enshrined in the Jinja O Do directly opposite the Sacred Bridge, on the far side of the road. He is also worshiped as Dao Gongen, the god of snakes, and Bishamonten, the god of bridges (who is also a god of war). Before the Second World War, the use of this bridge was restricted to imperial messengers bringing offerings to Toshogu. They would come here three times each year, on April 17, June 2, and October 7. The present design of the bridge dates from 1636, although it has been restored several times since.

There is a grove of magnificent old cedars directly to the right of the Jinja O Do, the largest of which is called Taro Cedar (Taro Sugi). It is tempting once again to associate the name Taro with the old sexual symbolism (see page 161), but in this case it is quite likely that it is called Taro simply because it is the biggest, and hence the eldest, son. It is thought to be just over five hundred years old.

SACRED BRIDGE ▶ HONGU SHRINE ▶ SHIHONRYUJI
WALKING TIME: 3 MINUTES

It seems a crime to schedule only three minutes for the walking time here. Walk for three minutes and look around for twenty-seven! Continuing right, don't climb up the main flight of steps toward Rinnoji and Toshogu, but instead go up the narrower flight to the right. The name of Hongu is inscribed on a stone pillar at the foot of the steps.

Hongu is a simple red wooden shrine dedicated to Hongu Daigongen and Jigentaro Daimyojin. It was once known, however, as one of the big three shrines of Nikko, together with Taki no O and Futarasan. It was founded in 784, just two years after Shodo finally reached the summit of Nantai. Today, it has become just a branch of Futarasan. The present building was erected in 1684. There is a stone in the precincts known as the Kasakake Ishi where Shodo Shonin is once said to have rested.

Walk around the right-hand side of the shrine to enter directly into the grounds of Shihonryuji. This seemingly forgotten backwater is one of my favorite spots in Nikko. The structures are simplicity itself, but they possess a strength and dignity that is somehow lacking in the worldly flamboyance of Toshogu.

This was the first temple built by Shodo. The original temple burned down in 1177, but the Kannondo (Kannon Hall) is thought to stand on the site of the original hermitage that Shodo and his followers erected in 766. It is said that they placed a thousand-handed Kannon here. Kongo Doji was also enshrined here a little over one thousand years later, in 1874 — hence, the characters for Kongo above the doorway. The first three-storied pagoda was built on this site in 807, also during Shodo's lifetime.

Entering the grounds of the temple from Hongu, one first passes a large, flat rock known as the Shiun Ishi, the Purple Cloud Rock, with two Jizos. It is written that while Shodo Shonin was sitting and praying on this rock, which does indeed bear a striking resemblance to a purple cloud, four clouds appeared from the east. A purple cloud rose up above them and flew off in the direction of Nantai. This was taken as a sacred sign. Accordingly, Shodo founded a temple called Shiunryuji, the Rising Four Clouds Temple. This name was later changed to the very similar-sounding Shihonryuji, Four Dragons Temple, that survives today.

Next comes the pagoda, then a splendid statue of Fudo Myoo flanked by two Jizos behind a small shrine gate, and Kannondo. Continuing around farther, there is a row of tall Koshin stones, again with the monkey motifs. Then go down the steps to the left, taking the right fork about fifteen meters later, and turn right up the road.

SHIHONRYUJI ▶ KODAMADO ▶ REMAINS OF YOGEN INJI ▶ KAIZANDO AND THE GRAVE OF SHODO SHONIN
WALKING TIME: 13 MINUTES

This is a pretty lane, cobbled with large stones, leading up past a number of old houses and lodges, with large gardens. Go left at the crossroads, three minutes from the temple. On the right, there is a small red Buddhist hall, the Kodamado. This is said to have been founded by Kukai, when he visited Nikko in 820. After making various ascetic observances at Taki no O, he found two small and pretty white stones in the river. Kukai placed the smaller of these in this shrine as a symbol of the Kokuzo Buddha (Akasagarbha in Sanskrit). The other was placed in the Myokendo on the banks of Chuzenji, as a symbol of the Myoken Buddha. Kokuzo, rather like Kannon, is known for his infinite wisdom and mercy, while Myoken protects the country and the poor.

We are now on the broad road leading up to the Toshogu parking lot. Turn right up through the last parking lot, just before the road reaches the steps up to the shrine, and go through the garden. There is a suggestion that Toshogu was built as a fortress as well as a shrine, taking advantage of the natural moat provided by the Daiya River. It is not so obvious from the front, but from this angle, the shrine really does look like a castle, with high and strong stone walls. As the shrine cost an estimated 2.7 percent of the GNP of Japan in those days, it is to be expected that those who paid for it should have looked for a multiple return on their investment.

Emerging from the garden, a narrow road runs up past the side of the Toshogu office. From here, the route up to Taki no O Shrine is signposted. This walk is known as the Shisekitanshojo (The Route of Ancient Remains). Just a short way up, it quickly comes to the old stone walls of the remains of the Yogen Inji. There are a couple of stone pagodas and a seated stone Buddha inside. The inscription on the left-hand pagoda indicates that it was erected in the Kanei period (1624–44). Supplicants have piled up stones all over the Buddha's statue. This temple was erected in 1626 to commemorate one of Ieyasu's wives. It is recorded that the famous *haiku* poet, Basho, stayed here in 1689.

As the road climbs up just a few meters farther, there is a clear view up toward Mount Nyoho, with the Inari River on the right. This is a major tributary of the Daiya River that flows directly down from close to the summit of Nyoho, joining the Daiya just below the Sacred Bridge. Kaizando is reached in just two minutes from here, together with Kyoshado and the grave of Shodo Shonin.

Kaizando, a plain red building, houses a 4.5-meter Jizo, plus seated wooden statues of Shodo and his ten main disciples. Ceremonies are held here every year on the first of April to commemorate Shodo's opening of Nikko. When Shodo died in 817, at the age of eighty-three, his disciples, in accordance with his will, cremated his body on this spot. Shodo's ashes were originally buried high up in Busseki Valley, but were brought back here when Ieyasu was enshrined in Toshogu. Kaizando, which belongs to Rinnoji, also dates from that time.

Kyoshado lies just to the left of Kaizando. This is another Kannon Hall, dedicated to the goddess of mercy, and the sign outside informs us that architecturally it is an interesting early-Edo structure. More interesting, though, are the many wooden tablets piled up outside. Tradition holds that this is the place to pray for a safe birth, and each of the tablets has a child's name written on the back. These have been placed here by mothers whose prayers have been answered. Expectant women visit the hall and, after praying, each takes a tablet home. Actually I have even seen this on TV. The woman on the TV program was thrilled at having chosen a boy's name because she wanted a boy herself. If the outcome is successful (it was), she returns the borrowed tablet to the hall, as well as another one with her own child's name written on the back, giving appropriate thanks to Kannon.

Just on the left of Kyoshado, there are a couple of yin-yang stones in front of a giant cedar. The odd thing is, according to the sign, no one can remember which is the male and which is the female!

Behind Kaizando there stands the main grave of Shodo Shonin. It will be remembered that a portion of his ashes were also buried on Kozuke Island in Lake Chuzenji. There is a further tradition that some of his remains were buried close to Shobugahama Beach on Lake Chuzenji, making a total of three graves in all. Shodo's is the fine stone pagoda that stands on its own. It was erected when Kaizando was built. The other three pagodas belong to disciples.

Just beyond the graves are six small Buddhist statues in a natural cave in the rock face. One of these is Fudo Myoo. This cliff is known as Hotoke Iwa, the Buddha Rock. Apparently, there used to be a natural feature on the cliffs above that looked just like an image of the Buddha. Sadly, this was lost in an earthquake, and now only the name remains.

KAIZANDO ▶ TAKI NO O SHRINE
WALKING TIME: 15 MINUTES

The old cobbled road up to the Taki no O Shrine leads up from inside the grounds of Kaizando along a beautiful cedar-lined avenue. Leaving the temple, this road passes five more stone stupas and also statues of seated Buddhas. This road is the Taki no O Do. There are several minor sights on the way up to the shrine.

The first of these is the Kitano Shrine, a small stone shrine beneath the cliff built in 1861 as a place to pray for success in study and calligraphy. As at the famous Kitano Tenmangu in Kyoto, the god is Sugawara Michizane, otherwise known as Tenjin, the god of study. A minute further up on the right is a large rock known as the Tekake Ishi. Worshipers at the Kitano Shrine used to take chips from this stone home with them to guarantee their success.

Another two minutes bring us to the Goshinba Monument (Goshinba no Hi) dedicated to a sacred horse. Actually, this was the horse that Tokugawa Ieyasu rode in the battle of Sekigahara in 1600. It was donated to the Toshogu and dwelt there for fourteen years. Upon its death, it was buried at this spot.

For those who suspect that the tone of this walk is beginning to falter, the next stone along the way, at a junction of paths, may come as no particular surprise. Written in Kukai's *hiragana* alphabet, so that the common people could read it, this stone is known as the Daishoben Ishi. It instructs travelers not to defecate or urinate by the roadside.

We are now just two hundred meters from the Taki no O Shrine. Ignoring the path to the left for the time being, continue straight ahead. The waterfall from which the shrine presumably got its name is reached in about three minutes. This fall is known as the Shiraito Fall, *shiraito* meaning "white thread." The water does indeed appear to flow over the rocks in a stream of white threads. A stone commemorates the visit of the Taisho emperor to this waterfall in 1916. There is also a recent memorial stone to an American diplomat, John K. Emerson.

Cross the bridge and climb the steps past the stone lanterns. At the top of the steps on the right is the site of an old branch temple, the Bessho, where from the early Heian to the Tokugawa periods adherents of Kukai's esoteric Shingon Buddhism practiced their religion. It is said that this is where the famous Rice-eating Festival of the Rinnoji began. Just near here, there is also a rock known as the Yobo Ishi, the "Face the Shadows Stone." It is written that when Kukai prayed here, a beautiful female goddess appeared.

The main gate to the temple, built in 1689, stands just beyond. This gate is called the Undameshi no Torii, literally the "Try Your Luck Gate." In the spirit of one-armed bandits, the idea is to throw three stones through the hole at the top. If all three pass through, you'll be very lucky; if two pass through, you'll have slightly less luck, and so on. The Tobu Railway guide advises that it is easier to accomplish this feat from above than below.

The Taki no O Shrine was founded in 820 by Kukai. It is recorded that the characters for Nyotai Chugu, written by Kukai, survived on the wall until the suppression of Buddhism in 1871. Nyotai, of course, means "Female Body." The male body, as observed earlier, is Nantai, the two forming the pair. Chugu means "Middle Shrine." This shrine was thus conceived to be the central shrine on the route up Mount Nyoho. The grounds are very pretty, as the shrine stands beside the stream and has several ancient cedars in the courtyard. It was rebuilt quite recently after being swept away by a flood in 1966.

There are several more sights inside the compound itself. Inside a stone fence are several bundles of sedge. If used skillfully, these are supposed to be helpful for those hoping to tie the matrimonial knot. The idea is to knot the leaves using only the thumbs and little fingers of both hands. There is also a rather pleasant Inari Shrine. It is said that the Inari god used to come out and chastise the priest when he forgot to make the daily offerings. The three sacred cedars to the right (again behind a stone fence) stand where Kukai saw the waterfall god Taki no Gongen. There are said to have been three cedars here at that time, too, but the present ones are of more recent origin.

The water of the Sake no Izumi spring is thought to taste a little like sake and to be an excellent base for the rice wine. The sake brewers of Tochigi have long been coming here to pray for excellent sake in the autumn and to give thanks in the spring. Crossing the bridge, we come to a large rock called the Kodane Ishi, literally the "Seed-planting Stone." As its name suggests, this is yet another place for praying for fertility and easy birth. In front is a small, suggestive stone with a hole in the middle.

TAKI NO O SHRINE ▶ GYOJADO ▶ TAIYUINBYO MAUSOLEUM
WALKING TIME: 15 MINUTES

It is now necessary to return to the junction at the Daishoben Ishi. Turn right up the steps, following the sign to the Futarasan Shrine. The Gyojado lies just one minute from the junction at the top of the steps. The Gyoja were the ascetic priests who followed the *shugendo* across the mountains. Straw sandals, like those used by the priests, hang as offerings in front of the hall. There is also another fine stone pagoda in front of the hall. The hall commemorates the Nara period (710–794) mountain ascetic En no Gyoja. There are statues of En no Gyoja and two devils inside. The hall was founded in the Nara period but reconstructed in 1575.

The path leading up from behind the hall is the pilgrimage route, now hiking course, up Mount Nyoho. This is a long course that requires a very early start if it is to be completed in one day. From here to the top, there is a difference in altitude of seventeen hundred meters. There is a box for filing your name if you intend to climb the mountain.

The path then continues down another beautiful cedar-lined valley. There are quite a lot of steps, but all downhill. Just after the path turns into a road above the mausoleum, there is a large, seated Jizo on the right. Erected in the 1670s, it is known as the Kuen Jizo. It is also associated with the Shodo legend, for it is supposed to represent a Jizo that appeared to Shodo and gave him encouragement on his way up Nantai.

It is another couple of minutes from there to the mausoleum, with the main Futarasan Shrine on the left. Here, we reenter tourist Nikko. The splendid mausoleum of the third Tokugawa shogun and the main Futarasan Shrine are well worth seeing, but perhaps on another day.

TAIYUINBYO MAUSOLEUM ▶ TOBU NIKKO STATION
WALKING TIME: 30 MINUTES

There are various ways back to the station from here, and it doesn't really matter which you take. The most direct is to continue straight down the hill. Alternatively, you can turn right at Ennin's Futatsudo to reach the bus stop at the bottom in only about four minutes. Buses to the left go to Nikko Station; those to the right go to Kiyotaki and Lake Chuzenji. For the infrequent service to Ashio, see page 146. Turning right at the bus stop, it is only a five-hundred-meter walk to the Nikko Museum.

USEFUL KANJI

FUTARASAN SHRINE	二荒山神社
GOSHINBA NO HI	御神馬の碑
GYOJADO	行者堂
HONGU SHRINE	本宮神社
HOSHINOGU	星の宮
IWASAKU REISUI	巌烈霊水

KAIZANDO	開山堂
KITANO SHRINE	北野神社
KODAMADO	小玉堂
KODANE ISHI	子種石
KYOSHADO	香車堂
SAKE NO IZUMI	酒の泉
SHIHONRYUJI	四本龍寺
SHINKYO (SACRED BRIDGE)	神橋
SHIRAITO FALLS	白糸の滝
SHISEKITANSHOJO	史跡探勝路
SHIUN ISHI	紫雲石
TAIYUINBYO MAUSOLEUM	大猷院廟
TAKI NO O SHRINE	滝の尾
YOGEN INJI	養源院跡

OTHER PLACES OF INTEREST ALONG THE WATARASE KEIKOKU TETSUDO

Rail access for many of the hikes in this book is provided by the beautiful single-track Watarase Keikoku Tetsudo (Watarase Gorge Railway) that runs from Kiryu through Azuma to Ashio. The scenery is a delight, and many tourists now visit the area simply to ride on these trains. If you are going up the line, from Kiryu into the hills (which happens to be down, in the railway's way of thinking), it is best to sit on the right-hand side of the train as far as Sori, then move to the left side for the remainder of the route.

Ashio actually holds a rather special place in the railway history of Japan, for it was here in 1893 that Japan's first electric railway was put into operation. It ran for only a short distance within Ashio itself, from Tsudo to the Shibukawa Bridge in Matsubara. Three years later, Furukawa Ichibei spearheaded a project to build a railway that would connect Omama and Nikko, but nothing came of it at that time.

The present line was opened for steam trains in 1911, replacing the old horse-drawn line. At first, it was directly managed by Furukawa Ichibei, but in 1918 it was bought by the state for 1.6 million yen. Diesel trains were introduced in 1957, and the last steam train was run in 1970.

The railway was known as the Ashio Line until 1989. It generated big losses under Japan National Railways, however, and in 1980 the National Diet proposed to close it down by 1985. There was a big local citizens' movement to prevent the closure, and in 1986 the Minister of Transport visited Ashio to review the situation. In March 1989, the line became independent, one of what are known in Japan as "third-sector companies." This basically means that it is private but still receives government subsidies, and that its finances are regulated by local bureaucrats.

The old carriages were entirely replaced to give the railway a fresh image. The new ones each have different exteriors, and there is also a variety of interior designs, ranging from the fairly luxurious to the very functional. It is a bit of a toss-up which you will get to ride in, as most trains have only a single carriage.

The line is 44.1 kilometers long, and it takes about one hour and twenty minutes to cover the entire distance from Kiryu to Mato, the final station for passengers (though the railway also has a freight terminus at Ashio Honzan, inside the copper works). The following is a rainy-day list of other places of interest along this line that are not described elsewhere in this book:

TEXTILE MUSEUM YUKARI   This fine museum has displays of old wooden looms, spinning wheels, spools, shredding machines, silk cocoons, shuttles, sizing reels, twist testers, warping machines, smoothing machines, and player-pianos, several of which are unique to Kiryu. There is also a special exhibition room, a handloom and dyeing workshop, a fully operational factory (closed on Sundays), and a well-stocked gift shop selling local silk products.

The museum is a fifteen-minute walk from Kiryu Station. Cross the square outside the north side of the station and turn right into the broad shopping street. Turn left at the junction with the main street five minutes later (with Daiichi Kangyo Bank on the corner), then right at the Honcho 4-chome junction. This road leads directly to the museum, after several more junctions. The tower of the Catholic church opposite the museum is visible from a long way down the road. The museum is open from 10:00 to 17:00; closed Mondays. Admission is ￥600. Address: 4-2-24 Higashi, Kiryu City. Tel: 0277-45-3111.

KIRYU FESTIVAL   The Kiryu Festival, although not well known outside Gunma, is one of the brightest and most cheerful festivals in Kanto. In addition to its countless stalls, decorations, and giant floats, it is noted for the *yagibushi* dance, said to have been invented by carters on the road between Kiryu and Ashikaga in the Meiji period. The dance is performed quite differently depending upon age group, with the old parading gracefully down the street while the young turn it into a virtual disco number. The festival is held over three days on August 5th, 6th and 7th each year. It is also worth visiting the neighboring city of Ashikaga on the first Saturday of August for the annual fireworks display on the banks of the Watarase.

UNDOKOEN
This station features a public sports complex with such facilities as tennis courts and a large open-air pool.

ODAIRA STALACTITE GROTTO   A small grotto, with a total length of only ninety-three meters, but containing many fascinating geological features. In addition to the staple stalactites, stalagmites, pillars, and flowstones, there are also curved helictites and heligmites, rimstones, and extensive curtains and also grid-iron boxwork patterns on the ceiling, which cannot be seen anywhere else in Japan.

The Akagi Kanko company runs a bus between the grotto, at Shonyudomae stop, and Akagi Station on the Tobu and Jomo Dentetsu lines. Departing about once every ninety minutes, the bus stops en route at Omama Station on the Watarase Keikoku Tetsudo. The journey from Omama Station takes about twelve minutes. The grotto is open every day of the year, from 9:00 to 17:00 between April and September and 10:00 to 16:00 between October and March. Admission is three hundred yen.

OMAMA HISTORY AND FOLK MUSEUM (CONODONTOKAN) A fine and varied collection, covering the history, natural history, geology, and folkcrafts of the region. Exhibits include: a 3-D film introducing the history and main sights of the area; Omama's natural environment, including several stuffed animals and the fossils of the conodont (a tiny sea creature less than one millimeter long, from which the museum takes its name); Jomon and Heian pottery; samurai armor; old maps; a corner on the Akagane Kaido, the old Copper Road from Ashio to the Tone River; a reconstruction of an old living room, with furnishings from the Meiji and Taisho periods; a wooden well; and many agricultural implements. The exhibits are so down-to-earth and varied that it would be hard to find a better introduction to traditional life in turn-of-the-century Japan.

The museum is just a five-minute walk from Omama Station. Go straight out of the station across a couple of minor junctions to the main road (Route 122). Turn right, and the museum is just a short way down the road on the left. It is open from 9:00 to 17:00 (last admissions 16:30), and is closed Mondays, days following national holidays, and from December 27 to January 4. Visitors are requested not to take photographs or eat inside the museum. Admission is one hundred yen.

MIZUNUMA STATION HOT SPRING CENTER (MIZUNUMA-EKI ONSEN SENTA) This hot spring center is run directly by the Watarase Keikoku Tetsudo and can be entered directly from the platform of Mizunuma Station. It is obviously an ideal place for washing and relaxing after coming down from the mountains. The hot spring water is piped from a spring in Kurohone on the slopes of Akagi. A two-hour ticket costs just three hundred yen. In addition to the indoor bath, there is an open-air bath on the balcony, with a view down the Watarase Valley. The center also has a souvenir shop and a restaurant that serves simple meals. It is open from 10:00 to 21:00. It is closed on the twenty-fifth of each month except when that happens to be a Sunday or holiday, in which case it closes the following day. Tel: 0277-96-2500.

ASHIO COPPER MINE (ASHIO DOZAN KANKO)   This is a must for anyone visiting the Ashio area. For many, it will be their only opportunity to go down into a real mine and see, in complete comfort, how awful conditions really were. The Ashio Dozan Kanko was opened in 1980. A small train takes visitors down into the mine, where there is a walking course around some of the passageways. The experience is enhanced by many life-size models of miners doing their various jobs. These are arranged in historical order, to give an idea of how the work changed over the years. Quite sophisticated explanations are written in English. The route winds around for about seven hundred meters out of a total twelve hundred thirty-four kilometers. Afterward, there is a small museum, with miniature models showing how coins were minted here in the Edo period, and a large group of souvenir shops and restaurants.

The mine is a five-minute walk from Tsudo Station, and admission for adults is 620 yen. Tel: 0288-93-3240. There is also a large open-air public skating rink right next to the mine.

USEFUL KANJI

ASHIO COPPER MINE	足尾銅山観光
CONODONTOKAN	コンドント館
(OMAMA HISTORY AND FOLK MUSEUM)	
DAIICHI KANGYO BANK	第一勧業銀行
HONCHO 4-CHOME	本町四丁目
KAWAUCHI	川内

245

KIRYU FESTIVAL	桐生祭
KIRYU NATURE SANCTUARY	桐生自然観察の森
ODAIRA STALACTITE GROTTO	小平鍾乳洞
MIZUNUMA STATION HOT SPRING CENTER	水沼温泉センター
SHONYUDOMAE	鍾乳洞前
TEXTILE MUSEUM YUKARI	森秀織物参考館
UNDOKOEN	運動公園
WATARASE KEIKOKU TETSUDO	わたらせ渓谷鉄道

INDEX

SHUGENDO RETREATS

TEMPLES

The "weathermark" identifies this book as a production of Weatherhill, Inc., publishers of fine books on Asia and the Pacific. Editorial supervision: Anna Idol. Typography, book and cover design: Liz Trovato. Production supervision: Bill Rose. Composition: Trufont Typographers, Hicksville, N.Y. Color separations: ISCOA, Arlington, Virginia. Printing and binding: R.R. Donnelley, Reynosa, Mexico. The typeface used is Frutiger 47 light condensed.